IMPRESSIONISM

Reflections of Beauty

DEBRA N. MANCOFF, PH.D.

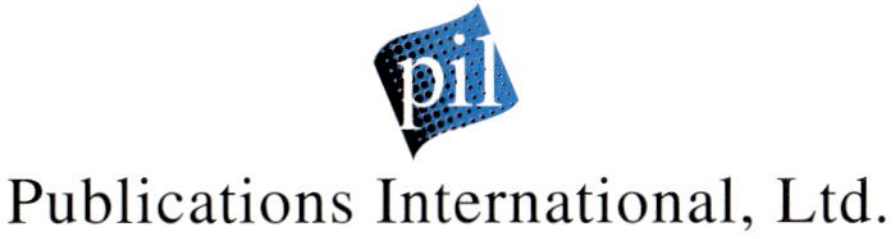

Publications International, Ltd.

Contents

Louis Weber, CEO
Publications International, Ltd.
7373 North Cicero Avenue
Lincolnwood, Illinois 60712

Manufactured in China.

8 7 6 5 4 3 2 1

ISBN: 0-7853-8300-X

Library of Congress Control Number: 2003100962

From Anonymity to Independence

The idea, the first idea, was to take away the partition separating the studio from everyday life.... It was necessary to make the painter leave his sky-lighted cell, his cloister where he was in contact with the sky alone, and to bring him out among men, into the world....

Edmond Duranty, "The New Painting," 1876

In the last quarter of the 19th century, a small circle of aspiring artists undertook a bold experiment. Struggling for recognition in an art world bound by long-standing traditions and outdated conventions, they decided to exhibit their works in an independent exhibition, free from sponsorship and affiliations. Taking responsibility for the financing, organization, and promotion of an exhibition was not an easy task, and it seemed insurmountable in Paris, where the arts were controlled by an official academy with government sanction. Determined to succeed—and have their art judged for its own merits—the artists first exhibited as the Société Anonyme des artistes, peintres, sculpteurs, graveurs, etc., in 1874. It was a small and diverse group, which included Claude Monet (1840–1926), Pierre-Auguste Renoir (1841–1919), Hilaire-Germain-Edgar Degas (1834–1917), Berthe Morisot (1841–95), Paul Cézanne (1839–1906), and Camille Pissarro (1830–1903).

Over the span of 12 years (1874–86) they mounted eight exhibitions, and although they quickly became known as the Impressionists, they never adopted an official name. Their styles remained distinctive and diverse, but they shared common goals in their rejection of traditional academic ideals and their support of a modernist vision based on the experience of visual sensations and a personal point of view. From more than a century's perspective, it is difficult to comprehend why their endeavor—as well as their art—met with resistance and ridicule. But, as the critic Théodore Duret observed in his essay "Les Peintres Impressionistes" (1878), if the Impressionists' paintings were different—if they did not follow the directive and style of previous painters—they would be perceived as bad. And so the Impressionists encountered many obstacles

Claude Monet, Impression Sunrise *(1872). In his evocative title, Monet acknowledged that his painting captured the visual experiences of a time and place rather than the topographical details of a locale. While the participants of the debut exhibition were variously known as independent, intransigent, and radical, the term* Impressionist *came to designate the work of a diverse circle of artists who shared a desire for artistic independence and an allegiance to modern expression.*

Musée Marmatton, Paris. Oil on canvas (18⅞×24¾ inches).

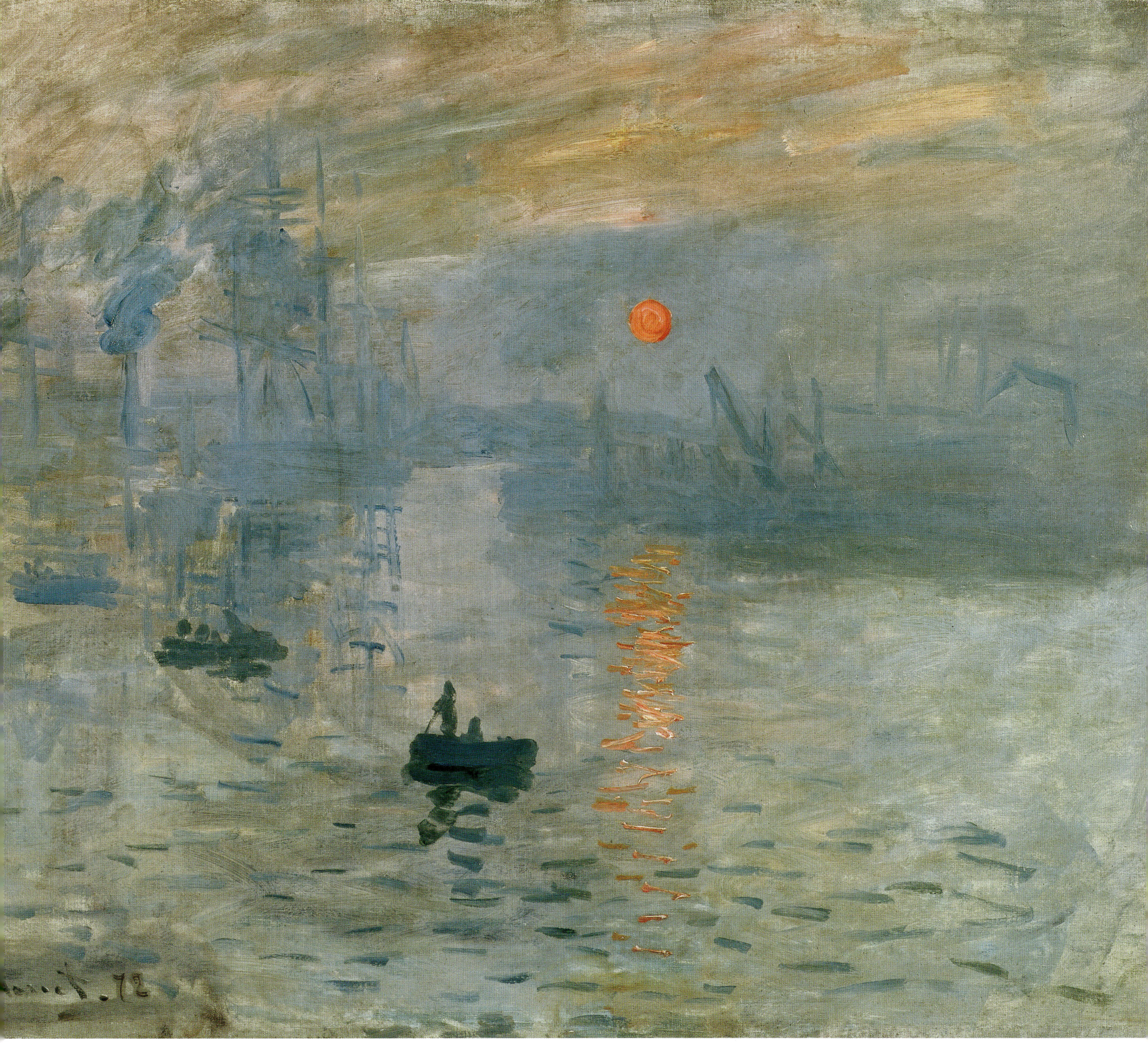

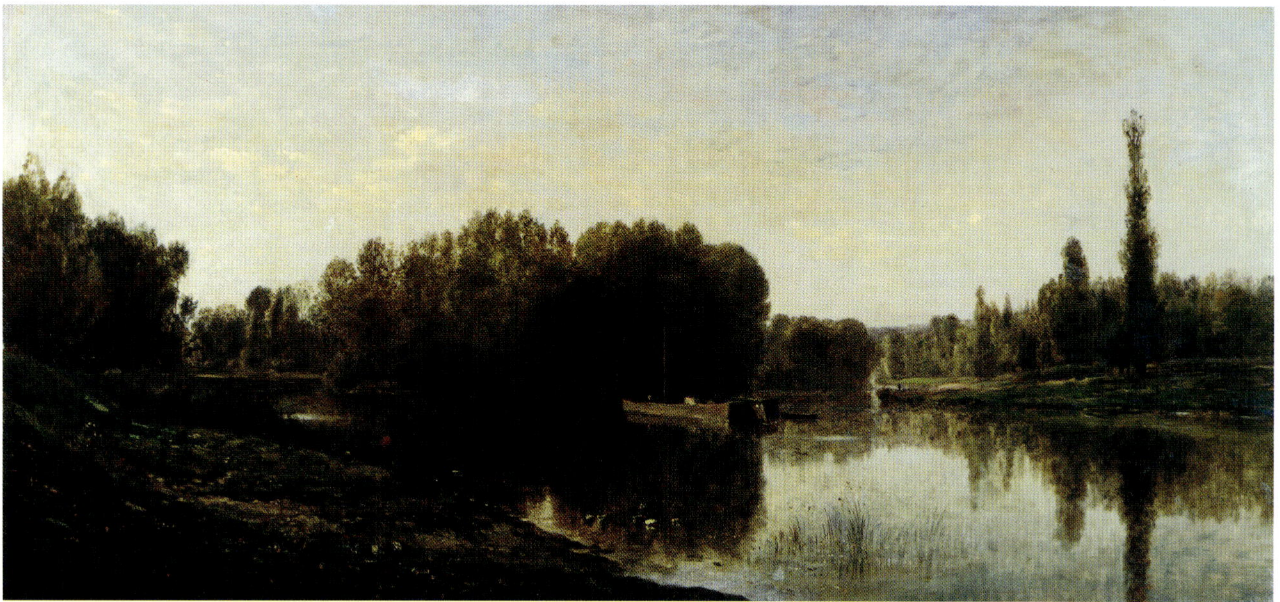

CHARLES-FRANÇOIS DAUBIGNY, The Banks of the Oise *(1859). Daubigny's naturalistic approach to landscape involved painting in the open air. Prior to the early 1840s, artists composed their landscapes in the studio from sketches and from memory. Advances in lightweight easels and portable art materials allowed an artist to work outdoors and record the effects of light, shadow, and atmosphere from direct observation.*

MUSÉE DES BEAUX-ARTS, BORDEAUX, FRANCE. OIL ON CANVAS (35⅜×71⅝ INCHES).

because they dared to defy convention for something undefined and new.

The origin of the popular name is often attributed to a satirical review of the first exhibition, written by the critic Louis Leroy for the humor journal *Le Charivari* and published shortly after the opening. Leroy presented his comments as a dialogue between a conservative academic painter and his fawning companion. As they stroll through the galleries, the painter makes acid comments, disparaging the works for their lack of smooth finish, modulated color, and fine brushwork associated with conventional technique. They pause in front of Monet's painting *Impression Sunrise.* Confounded by the evocative color and brushwork in a scene of early morning light cutting through the dawn mist over a harbor, the academic painter consults his catalogue and declares, "*Impression*... I was just saying to myself, if I'm impressed, there must be an impression in there."

But the word *impression* had already been established in the vocabulary of art criticism as a hallmark of modernity, and it signified the collection of the sensations experienced in the moment of observation. Leroy may have used the word *impression* to ridicule the lack of technical expertise and finish he perceived in the landscape paintings on display, but Jules Castagnary, writing for the journal *Le Siècle,* showed a deeper comprehension of the word as well as genuine respect for the aims of artists who participated in the exhibition. He stated, "If we must characterize them with one explanatory word, we would have to coin a new term: *impressionists.*"

It is worth noting that the core circle of artists never agreed upon a name. When they planned their first exhibition, Degas suggested they call themselves La Capucine (Nasturtium) after the Boulevard des Capucines, the location of the borrowed studio that served as their gallery. But Renoir argued that any name would restrict them. The group refrained from adopting a label, calling themselves a Group of Independent Artists—or sometimes nothing at all—in their promotional advertising and in their exhibition catalogues, and so the critics dubbed them with a variety of names: independents, intransigents, even radicals. By 1877, at the third exhibition, Georges Riviere declared, "They have finally put the word Impressionist over the entrance door." Riviere served as a spokesman for the group, writing and editing *L'Impressionniste*, a short-lived journal meant to explain and promote the Impressionist's endeavor. His statement was symbolic; there was no official name above any door. But the public now recognized the name *Impressionist* as a new force in contemporary art, dedicated to individuality, innovation, and above all, artistic independence.

GUSTAVE COURBET, The Edge of the Sea at Palavas *(1854). Courbet refused to idealize his subjects or his aesthetic. He painted a blunt image of modern life in a frank and rough style that came to be known as realism. He rose to public attention during the brief democratic rule of the Second Republic (1848–51), when the restrictive Salon policies were relaxed. He maintained an independent identity as an artist as the art world returned to more conservative standards during the Second Empire (1851–71).*

MUSÉE FABRE, MONTPELLIER, FRANCE. OIL ON CANVAS (10⅜×18⅛ INCHES).

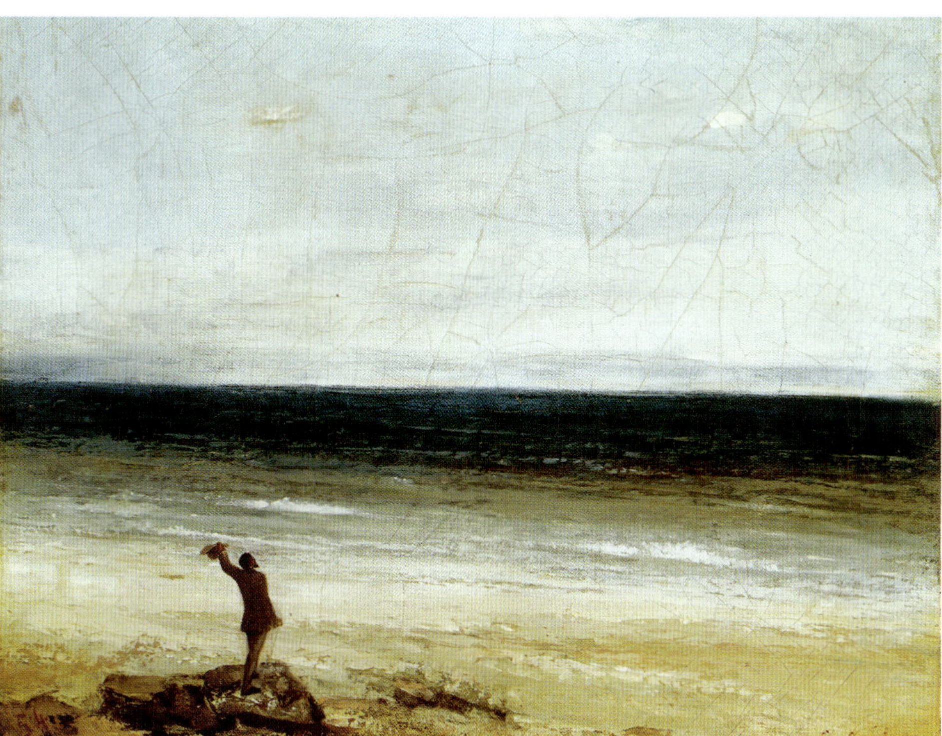

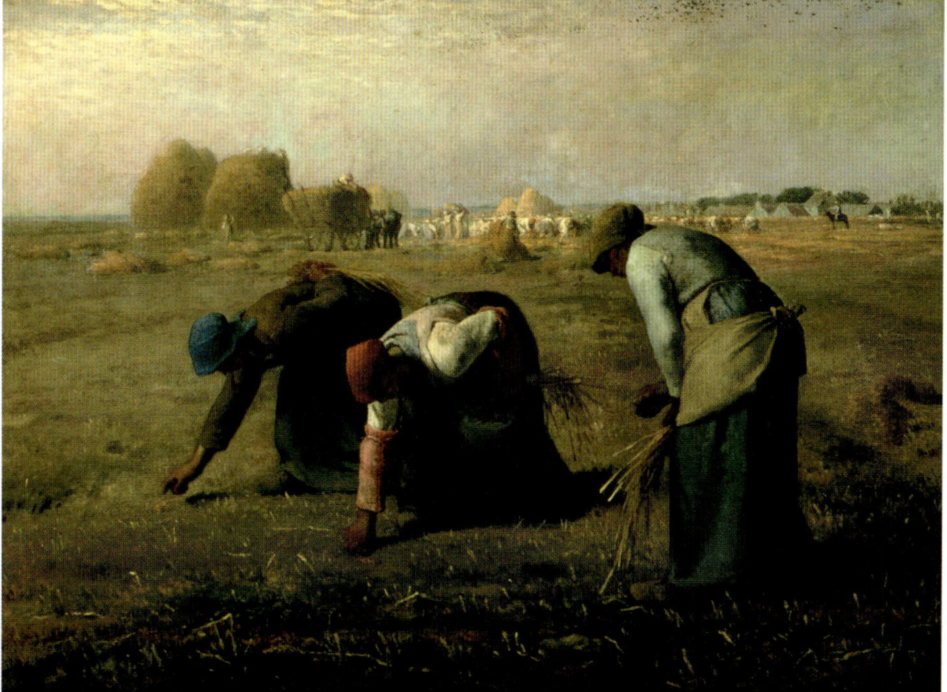

JEAN-FRANÇOIS MILLET, The Gleaners *(1857). The village of Barbizon, on the edge of the Forest of Fontainbleau on the outskirts of Paris, attracted a community of outdoors painters in the 1840s and 1850s. Although Millet settled there in 1849, he rarely painted pure landscape. His approach to the subject of agricultural labor was both naturalistic and romantic, balancing the monumental forms of his farm workers with the stunning effects of natural light in the rural landscape.*

MUSÉE D'ORSAY, PARIS. OIL ON CANVAS (32⅞×43¾ INCHES).

In the middle of the 19th century, Paris reigned as the capital of the European art world, but its standards and practices were based on centuries-old traditions rather than current interests and demands. In the 17th century, under the regime of Louis XIV, the French government founded a state-sponsored academy for artists. Intended to train painters and sculptors to serve the monarch and the nation, L'Académie Royale de Peinture et Sculpture controlled the education of artists and the production of art. The curriculum featured years of disciplined study, under the tutelage of a member of the academy, to develop a correct style based on the examples of classical antique sculpture and the masterworks of artists of the Renaissance. Students stayed within an assigned atelier (master's studio), learning to first draw, and then to paint, the idealized human form.

From Anonymity to Independence

They were taught to compose paintings according to the established rules of composition and narrative content. Even subject matter reflected the hierarchy: Grand scenes of history, mythology, and religion marked an artist's highest aspiration while genre, subjects taken from everyday life, was of low regard. As students advanced, they remained closely associated with their professors, who served as their mentors in a series of competitions that would promote the artist's reputation and eventually lead to membership in the academy. Women were barred from the system.

As early as 1673, to demonstrate the superiority of academic training and elevate the standards of French taste, the academy initiated an official Salon. At first, the privilege of exhibiting in the Salon was restricted to members of the academy, but in the course of the 18th century, as the exhibition became a notable event attended by the public and reviewed by critics, other artists lobbied for acceptance. The Salon remained restricted until 1791, when it became possible for nonmembers and foreign artists to participate by submitting their works to a committee for consideration. This jury, appointed by the government, controlled the course of an artist's career; it was difficult to build a reputation without the jury's approval. In the early 19th century, the Salon was small, but as the decades passed, it kept growing in size until the mid-century when annual Salons regularly displayed as many as 2,000 works crowded into a suite of rooms in the Louvre. To accommodate the vast array, paintings were hung edge to edge on the wall, rising in rows from waist height to the ceiling. With so many paintings on display, it was difficult for an artist to attract the public's attention, and prime placement in the center of the wall was generally reserved for members of the academy and their favorite pupils. If a work was small or "skied" (hung in the top tier near the ceiling), it went unnoticed.

As well as the capital of the art world, mid-century Paris was a modern city. Industry and transport systems had brought new wealth and an increas-

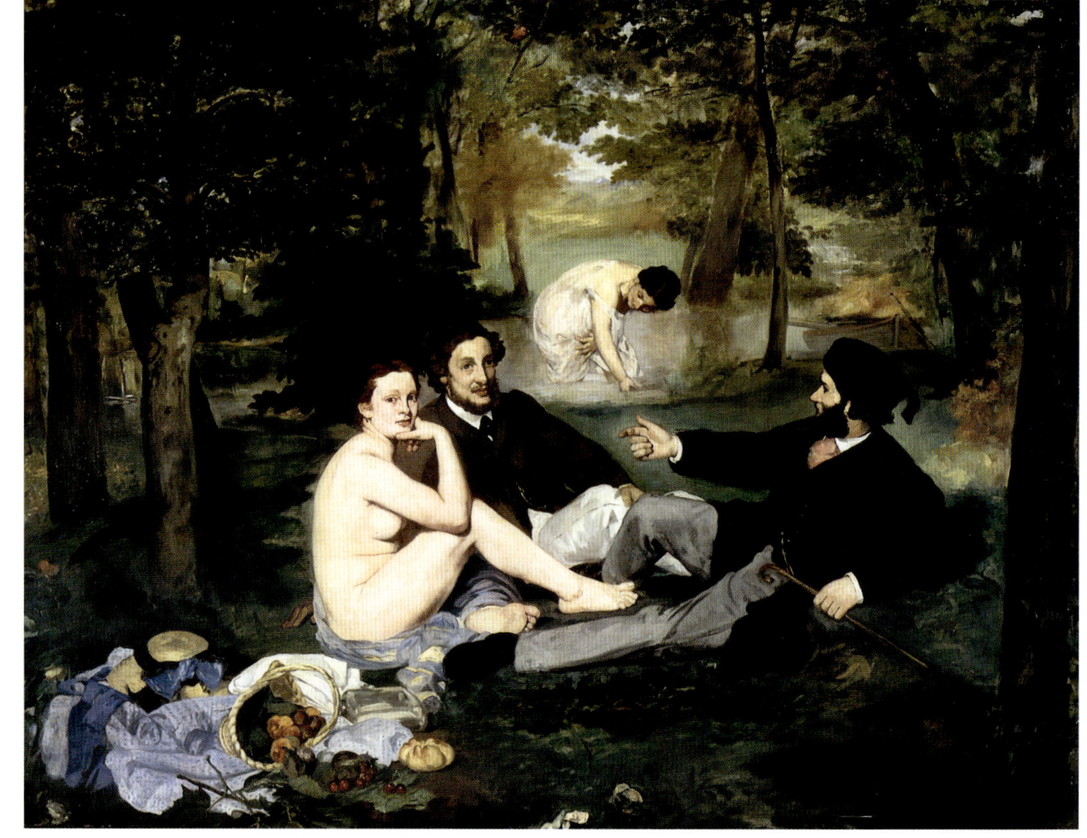

Edouard Manet, Le Déjeuner sur l'Herbe *(1863). Shown at the Salon des Refusés, Manet's painting of two contemporary men having a picnic in the Tuileries Garden with two disrobed women was ridiculed by the critics. His work—intended to provide a modern counterpart to the pastorals painted by the Venetian masters—was thoroughly misunderstood. His dark palette and rough brushwork prompted critics to call the work unfinished, and the direct gaze of the woman seated in the front transgressed the conventions for painting the nude.*

Musée d'Orsay, Paris. Oil on canvas (81⅞×104⅛ inches).

ingly diverse population. The middle class gained power and affluence, establishing a new audience for culture and entertainment. In the 1850s an urban plan developed by Baron Georges Eugène Haussmann under the auspices of the emperor swept away the narrow confines of the old city to make room for broad avenues, public parks, and multistory apartment buildings. In an essay "The Painter of Modern Life" (1863), the poet Charles Baudelaire observed that, in every era, a spirit of the times—or modernity—was evident in the work of artists, and he regarded the spirit of this modernity as the ephemeral—even the fugitive—aspects of human experience that change with the times. Baudelaire urged a new generation of artists to heighten their awareness of this essential spirit by becoming passionate observers of contemporary society.

While Baudelaire associated the urban with the modern, landscape artists working in the countryside had already defined new challenges for their art. The change was prompted, in part, by two simple inventions in the early 1840s: premixed pigments that could be purchased in tin tubes and lightweight collapsible easels. Prior to this time, artists painted landscapes in their studios, working from sketches made on the spot or from memory. The portable art materials allowed an artist to work outdoors, observing the temporal effects of light and atmosphere. A small group of artists, who had gathered in the picturesque village of Barbizon on the edge of the Forest of Fontainbleau, pioneered the practice of *plein air* (outdoors) painting. As seen in Charles-François Daubigny's *The Banks of the Oise* (1859), the plein air painter achieved a fresh effect based on direct observation that could not be matched in the confines of a studio.

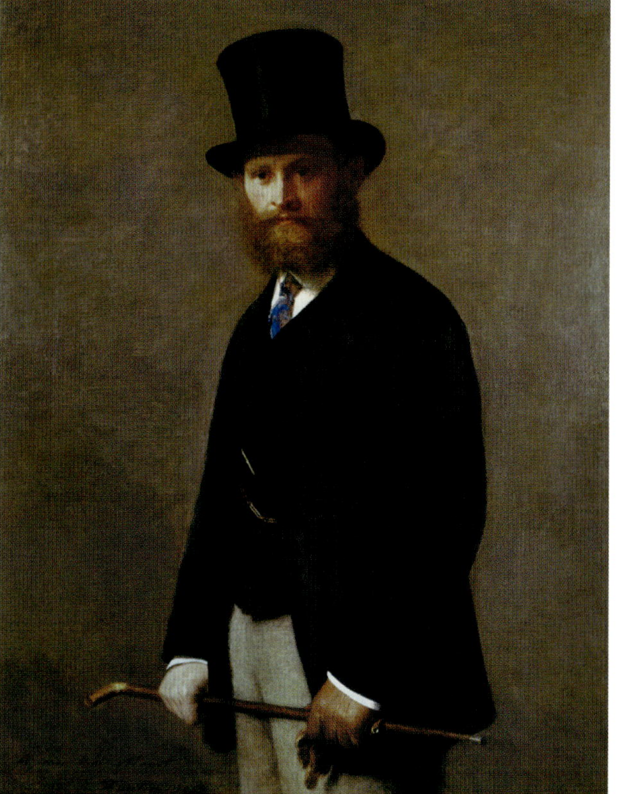

HENRI FANTIN-LATOUR, Portrait of Edouard Manet *(1867). Fantin-Latour conceived his portrait of Manet to present him as a respectable man of his times. Impeccably dressed and with a reserved demeanor, this depiction of Manet countered the wide-spread perception of him as a renegade that had been promoted in the conservative art press. In fact, Manet never regarded himself as a revolutionary—it was his choice to pose as a bourgeois gentleman—but he insisted that his art reflect the image and interests of his own society.*

THE ART INSTITUTE OF CHICAGO. OIL ON CANVAS (46¼×35½ INCHES).

At the same time, the artist Gustave Courbet applied the idea of direct observation to his subject selection. Working in a dark palette and a rough style that opposed the standard convention of Salon finish, Courbet rejected the established artist's repertoire drawn from history and mythology. He preferred subjects that recorded his own experience: the working people of his native village Ornans and scenes of his life as an artist. Courbet became an outspoken advocate of "realism," a modern approach that was frank in style and unsentimental in expression. Throughout the 1850s, the direct approach—whether in style or subject—appealed to a widening circle of artists. As seen in *The Gleaners* (1857), Jean-François Millet struck a balance between romanticism and naturalism in his depictions of dignified agricultural laborers in a natural setting. Eugène Boudin adopted the plein air practice to modern seascapes, setting up his easel in the sand alongside the tourists at popular resorts. Each of these artists offered an alternative to the Salon standard and, in their own way, expressed the fugitive essence of modernity.

In modern Paris, the annual Salon was a popular event. New wealth brought by new industry had widened the audience for art. The most affluent members of the middle class were now able to purchase contemporary art, an investment expected to rise in value. But even if a city-dweller's budget was too small to build an art collection, a visit to the exhibition held each May in the Louvre was regarded as a pleasant and sophisticated diversion. Popular journals featured art reviews written in a lively and accessible style. The Parisian art public was well informed and highly opinionated, and the Salon played a critical role in an artist's professional advancement as the premier venue for critical reception and wide recognition.

Each year the number of works submitted to the Salon rose; each year more works were rejected. Artists complained of unfair selection practices. Not all jury members were artists; they were appointed by the government, and politics, as well as favoritism, tainted their decisions. Furthermore, the jury continued to base their choices exclusively on academic conventions. Innovative artists and those trained outside the academy were summarily dismissed. Required to review thousands of submissions in the course of a

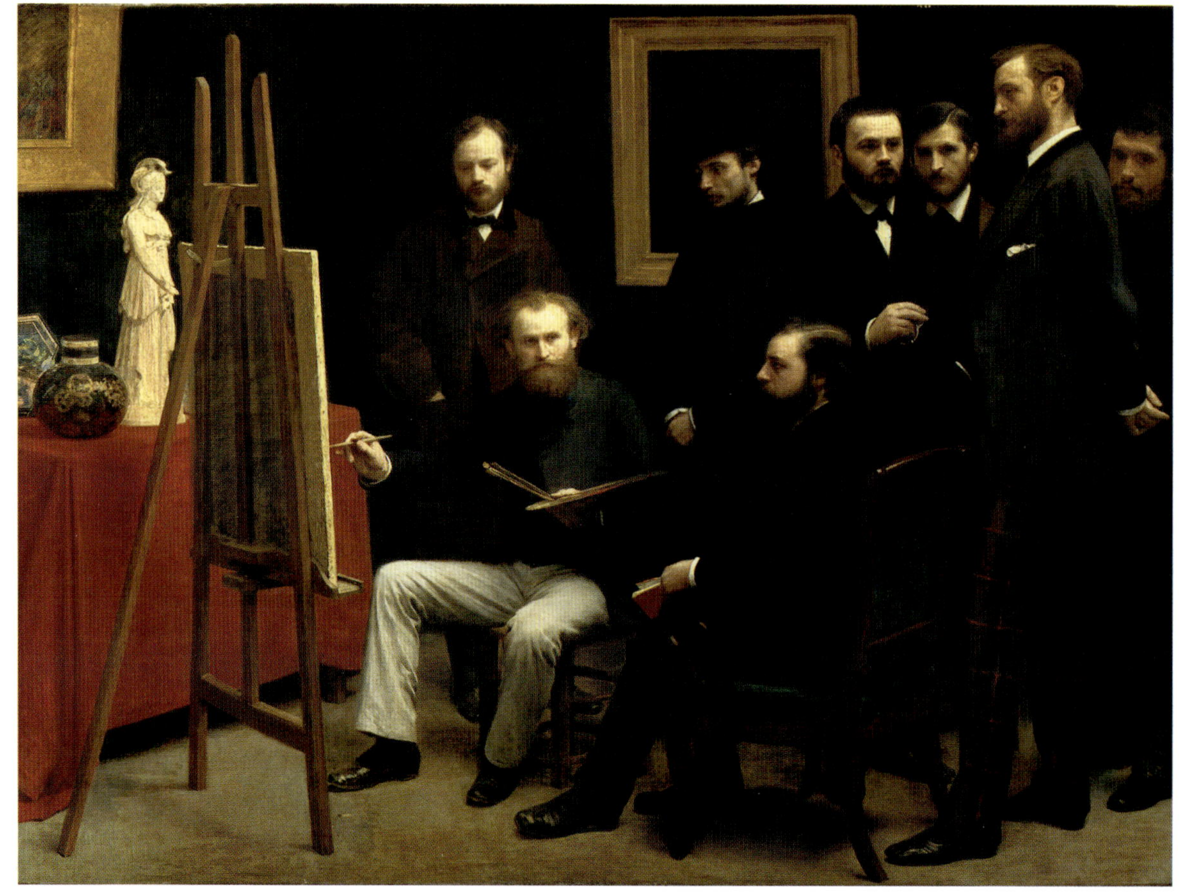

Henri Fantin-Latour, A Studio in Batignolles Quarter *(1870). In this group portrait, Fantin-Latour honored Manet's influence on a new generation of artists. Manet, seated at his easel, is painting a portrait of the artist and critic Zacharie Astruc. The tall figure standing behind Astruc's chair is Bazille; Monet can be seen at the far right behind him. Renoir stands in the center, and the critic Émile Zola is to his immediate left.*

Musée d'Orsay, Paris. Oil on canvas (80⅜×107⅝ inches).

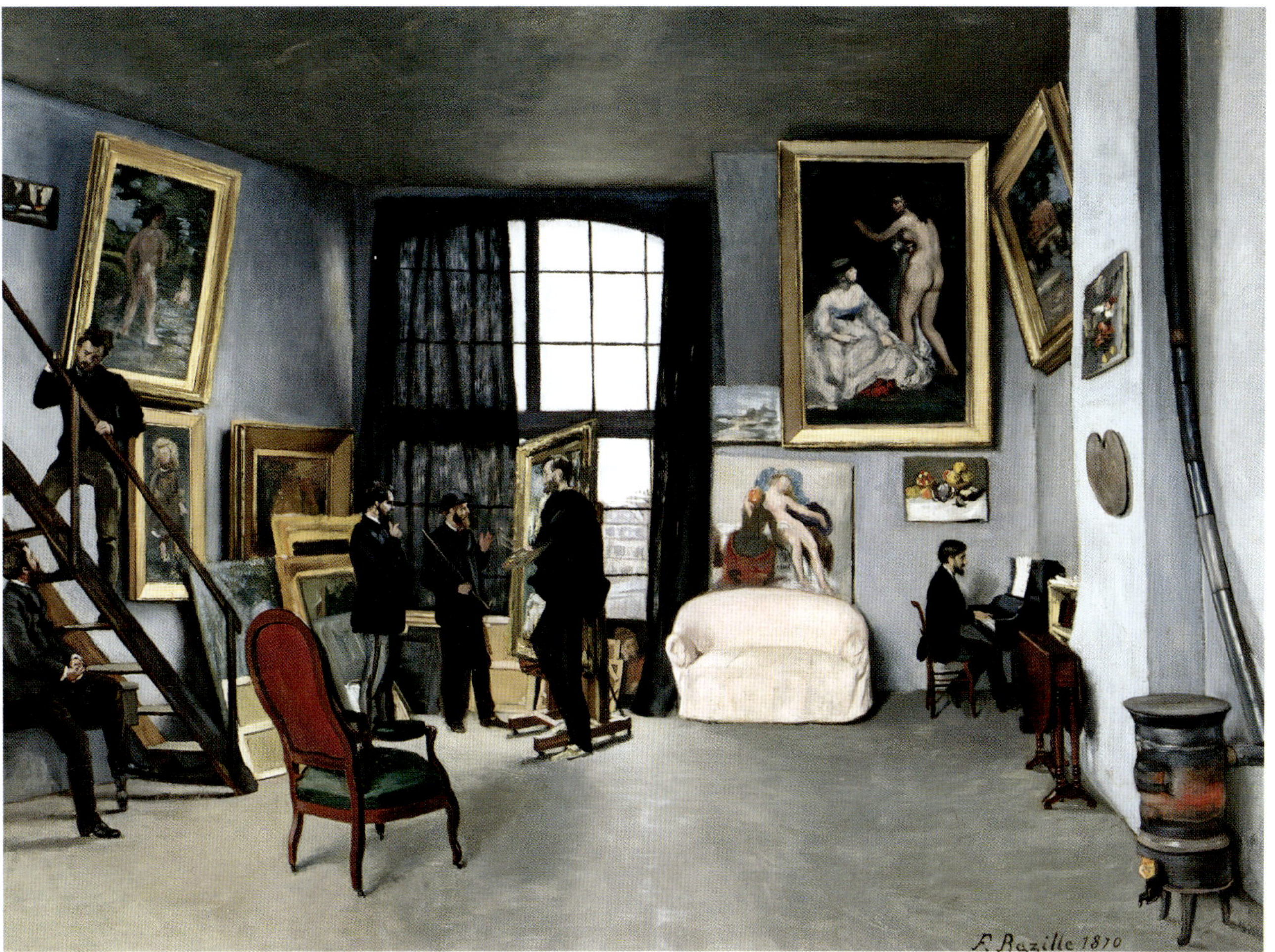

Frédéric Bazille, The Studio on the rue de la Condamine *(1870). Bazille depicted a gathering of like-minded friends in the studio he shared with Renoir. At the left, seated on a table, Renoir looks up to talk to Zola, who is on the stairs. In the center, Bazille shows Manet one of his recent works, while Monet stands behind him. Bazille's close friend Edmond Maitre plays the piano at the right. Each of these men appeared in Fantin-Latour's formal group portrait, but Bazille's approach is more intimate and natural.*

Musée d'Orsay, Paris. Oil on canvas (38⅝×50⅝ inches).

month, jury members rarely gave unknown works more than passing consideration, and this was regarded as a form of censorship that screened out new artists with progressive ideas.

In 1863 more than 5,000 works were submitted to the jury; nearly 4,000 were rejected. In response to the artists' outspoken accusations of unfair treatment, as well as to validate the decision of the jury, the government gave the artists an opportunity to exhibit their rejected submissions in a Salon des Refusés. Many of the artists refused to participate, believing that the context of rejection would prejudice public judgment. But more than 1,000 artists agreed to risk condemnation and notoriety to have their works displayed for public review. The Salon des Refusés was regarded as more of a spectacle than a serious exhibition. The critic Maxime du Camp used harsh words to describe it, and his words were indicative of the public's brutality toward the Salon des Refusés artists. Du Camp even went so far as to thank the Salon jury for rejecting these artists' works and for attempting to shield the public from such awful art.

Edouard Manet (1832–83) was among the artists represented in the Salon des Refusés. As a student in the atelier of Thomas Couture, he had been resistant to his professor's advice to idealize his modernist vision, but even without Couture's sponsorship, he debuted in the Salon of 1861 to favorable critical notice. But in the Salon des Refusés his painting *Le Déjeuner sur l'Herbe*

(1863) drew a savage response from the critics. In his desire to join the traditional past with the present, Manet created what he regarded as a contemporary counterpart to Giorgione's *Fete Champetre* (c. 1510), a painting he had copied in the Louvre as a student. But unlike the classicized setting and idealized figures in the Venetian master's allegory, Manet's work was rooted in reality, presenting identifiable models, a familiar location, and a bold and naturalistic nude who frankly returned the viewer's gaze. Rather than bridging the past and the present, Manet brought the modernist point of view into direct conflict with conventional standards, and his intentions were misunderstood.

Sensing a kindred spirit, Baudelaire wrote an essay in Manet's defense. Also, the art critic Émile Zola, known for his honest portrayal of contemporary society, visited Manet in his studio and, in a lengthy article, explained that Manet followed his own creative direction. Zola challenged viewers to judge the painter's work by new rather than conventional standards. Manet's resistance to the critical onslaught attracted the attention of younger artists, who sought to meet with him in the Café Guerbois, a bar near his studio in the rue de Batignolles that he was known to frequent. Three of the artists, Claude Monet, Pierre-Auguste Renoir, and Frédéric Bazille, had met in 1861 in the atelier of the academic painter Charles Gleyre, who was known for a grand, historic manner and for setting his works in classical and prehistoric times. Bored with the conventional curriculum of the studio, Monet, already an accomplished plein air painter, convinced his fellow students to work with him outdoors. Paul Cézanne and Camille Pissarro, both veterans of the Salon de Refusés and advocates of painting outdoors, also joined in the conversation. As a group, they exchanged ideas and debated issues. Manet wel-

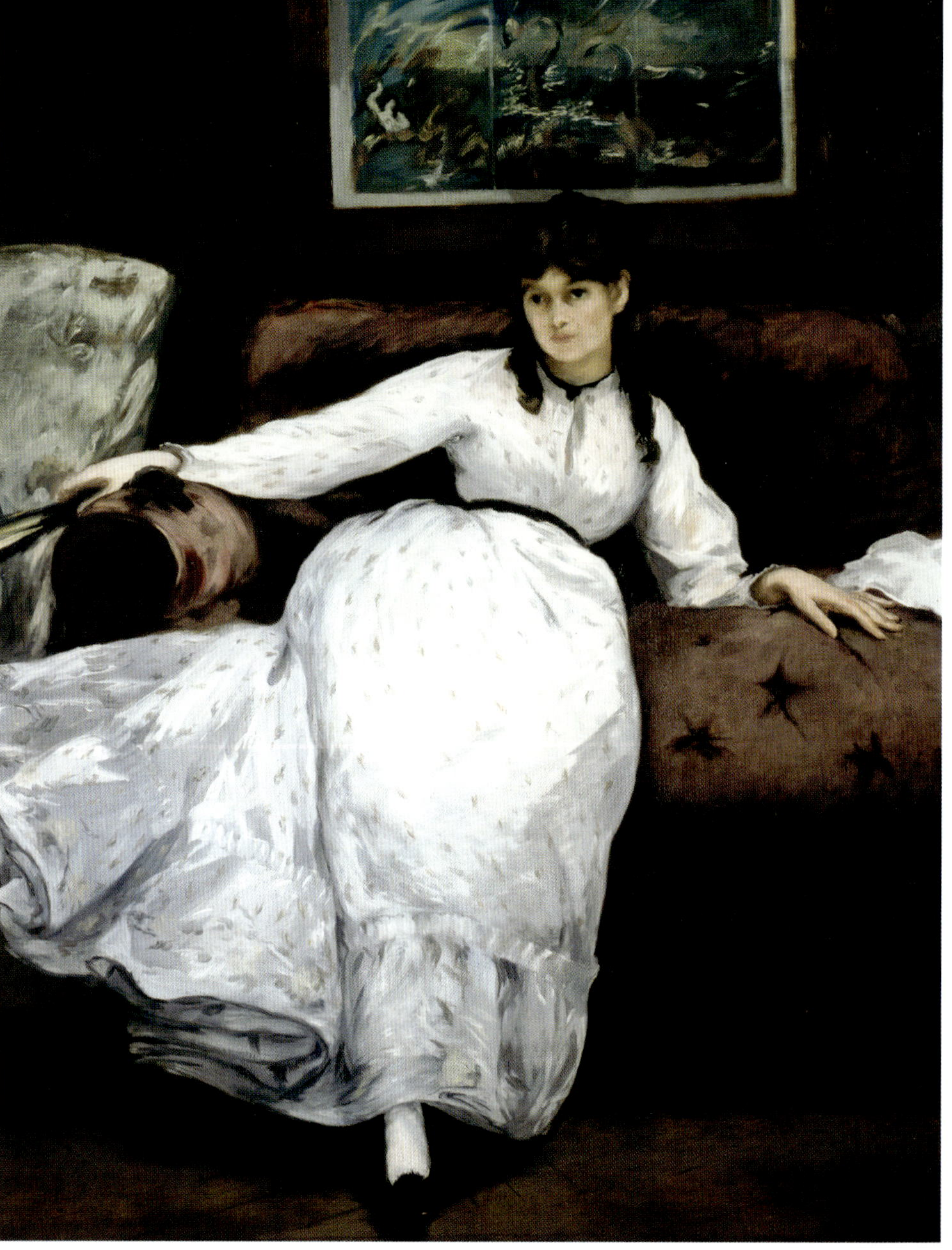

EDOUARD MANET, La Repose (Portrait of Berthe Morisot) *(1870). Morisot was introduced by Manet into the circle of artists who would become the Impressionists. She was briefly Manet's student, and she married his brother Eugène. Unlike many of her colleagues, her works were regularly seen at the Salon, but she took part in all the Impressionist exhibitions except the fourth in 1879.*

RHODE ISLAND SCHOOL OF DESIGN, PROVIDENCE. OIL ON CANVAS (57⅞×43¾ INCHES).

comed the opinions and the support of this informal circle, and he introduced his friends to other aspiring painters: Hilaire-Germain-Edgar Degas, a traditionally trained painter whom Manet had encountered as the younger man was copying a work by Velazquez in the Louvre, and Berthe Morisot, a talented pupil of the pastoral painter Camille Corot. Degas and Morisot had experienced more success than the others with the Salon jury, but all of the artists agreed that modern painters faced academic prejudices. The solution was simple but bold: To have their works judged fairly and on their own merits, they would have to mount their own exhibition.

The group remained a loose circle, each painter having a distinctive style and an individual identity. However, each, in their own way, represented a modernist point of view that motivated them to build upon recent innovations—the fresh plein air landscapes of the Barbizon School painters, the frank realism of Gustave Courbet, the direct naturalism of Manet—through their own experiments. As seen in *Hoarfrost* (1873), Pissarro stripped the rural subject of sentimental romanticism and concentrated on the expressive atmospheric effects through color. Degas worked with a strong sense of line and a bold composition, influenced in part by the new medium of photography and the rising popularity of imported Japanese prints. By cutting off figures, flattening his perspective, and canting the organizational axes of his composition, Degas overturned the strict rules of academic pictorial construction. The figures in Degas's pastel *Visit to a Museum*

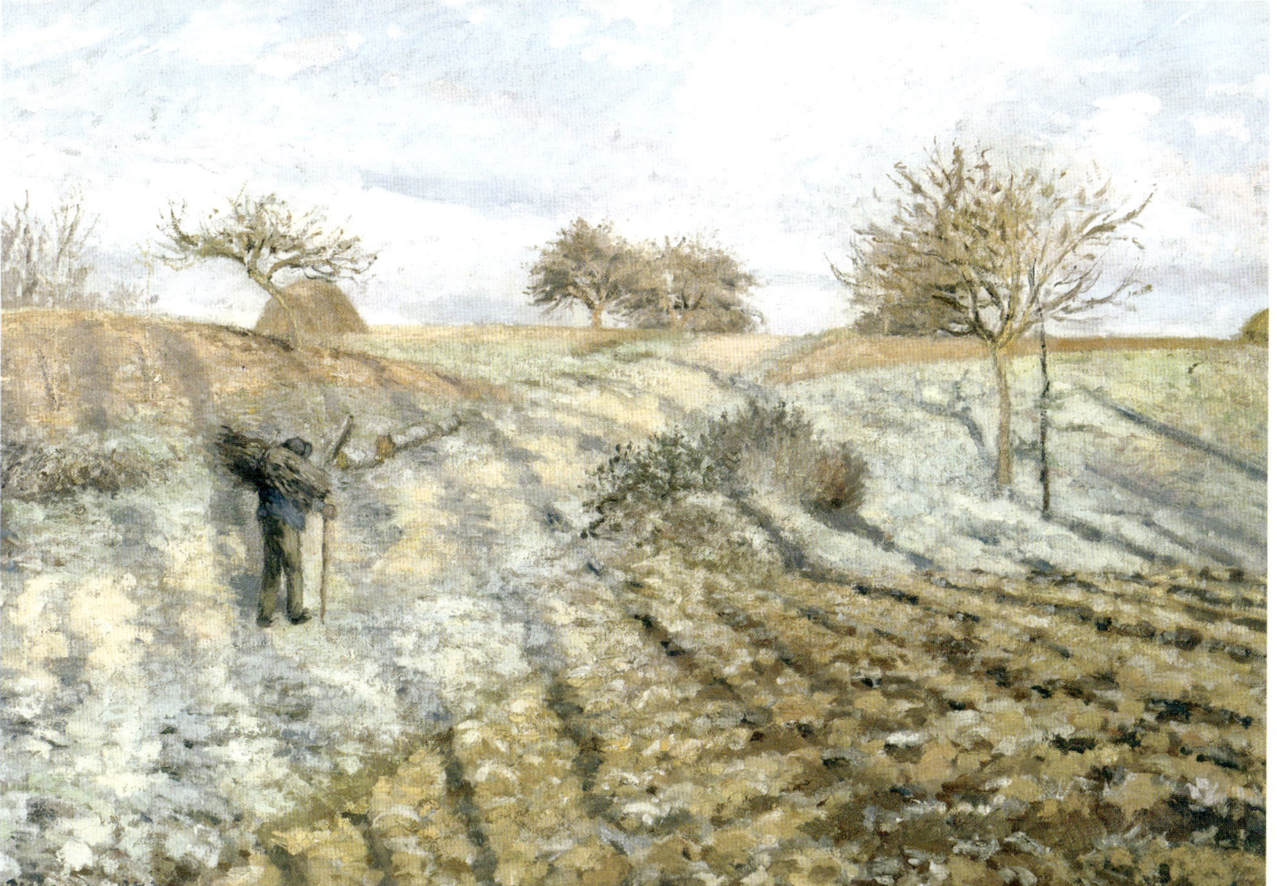

CAMILLE PISSARRO, Hoarfrost *(1873). Pissarro became a dedicated plein air painter early in his career, focusing on rural settings and temporal effects.* Hoarfrost *illustrates the fresh spontaneity achieved by painting from direct observation. He modulated the tone of his color to convey specific atmosphere, as seen in the bright blues of the warming sky in contrast to the muted hues of the brittle frost on the frozen ground.*

MUSÉE D'ORSAY, PARIS. OIL ON CANVAS (25⅝×36⅛ INCHES).

From Anonymity to Independence

(c. 1879–80) seem to be caught by a momentary glance; the sense of immediacy in the setting and their postures suggest they will soon move on. Renoir set his paintings in beer gardens, public parks, and at the opera, capturing the spirit and sophistication of urban entertainment, while Morisot often portrayed the middle-class domestic interior, offering a glimpse of a contemporary woman's life. Monet employed his painterly technique—pure color, dabbed in deft and confident strokes directly on his canvas to transpose his observations from eye to hand—to express the sensations of a purely visual experience, such as the light sparkling on the water in his *Impression Sunrise* (1872). Each individual approach confirmed Baudelaire's recognition that modernity must be expressed through the ephemeral and fugitive aspects of human experience.

Bazille's letters to his family reveal that in both 1867 and 1869 the group actively discussed plans for an exhibition. Although he did not name the potential participants, it is likely the project included the group of artists gathered around Manet. To mount an exhibition, they would have to pool their resources, rent a space, and take full responsibility for the organization, installation, and promotion of the event. This was a difficult and financially challenging undertaking, but without creating their own alternative venue their careers would continue to depend upon the standards of the academy, the limitations of the Salon, and the whims of the jury.

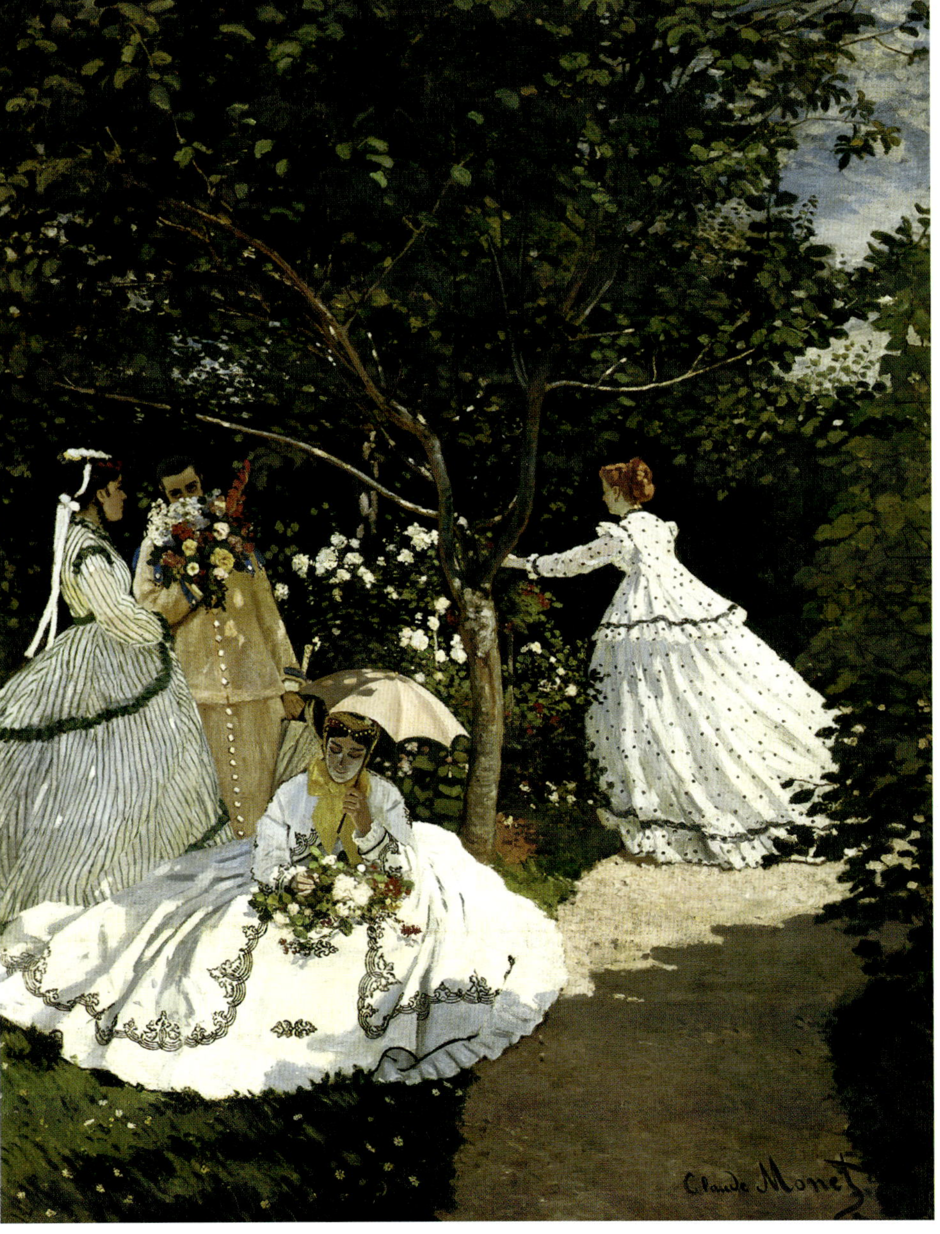

Claude Monet, Women at the Garden at Ville d'Avray *(1866–67). In contrast to Manet's* Le Dejeuner sur l'Herbe, *Monet's* Women at the Garden at Ville d'Avray *is free from any reference to older art traditions. The four women are fashionably dressed. They exist in the present, and their random positions suggest fleeting movement rather than allegorical ideas. Monet's wife posed for three of the four figures. The painting offers neither story nor allegory but records Monet's observation of light and motion in an outdoor setting under a summer sun, and when Monet submitted it to the Salon, it was rejected.*

Musée d'Orsay, Paris. Oil on canvas (100¾×81⅞ inches).

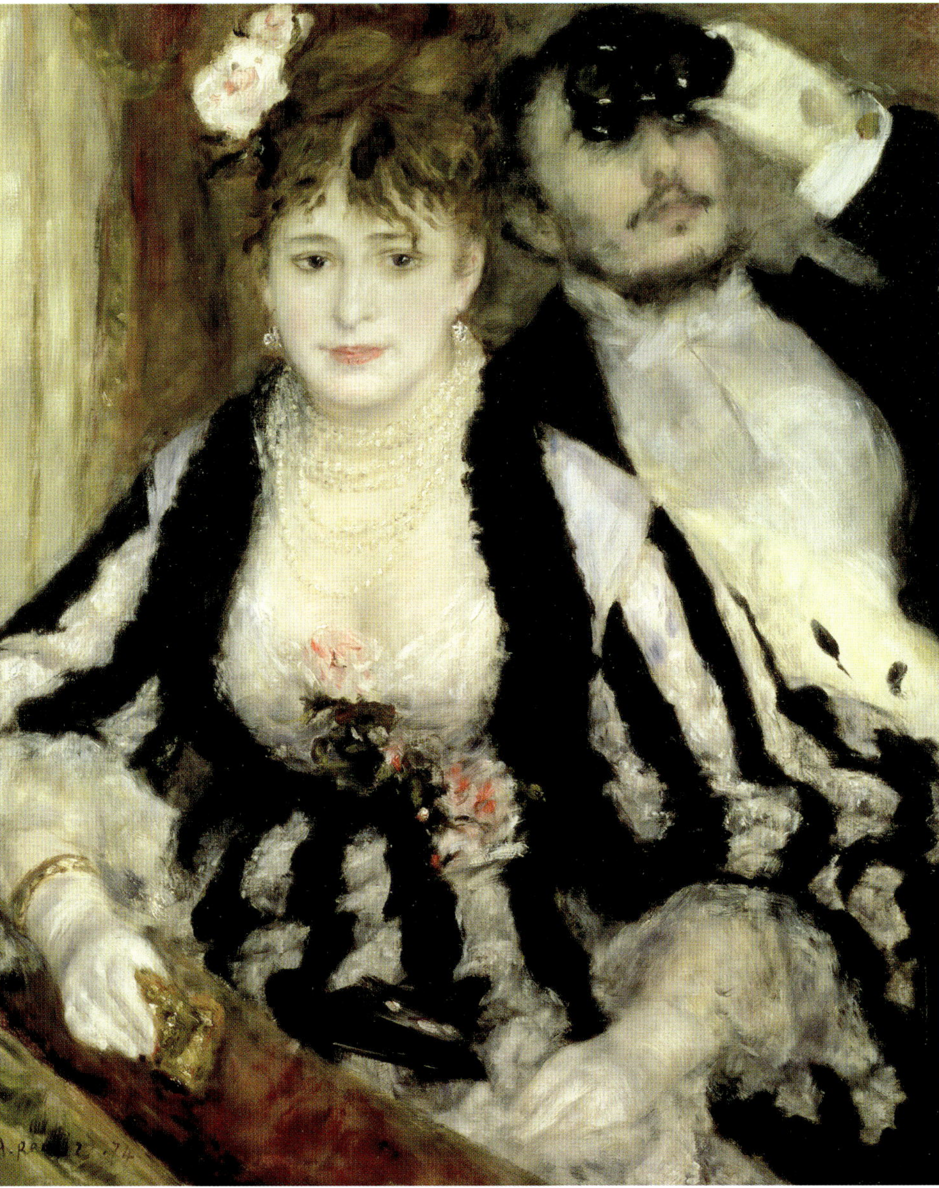

Pierre-Auguste Renoir, La Loge *(1874). Pursuing the modern-life subject, artists such as Renoir and Degas portrayed the night life of Paris. Here Renoir presents a fashionable couple at the opera. The woman's accessories—fresh flowers pinned to her dress, a painted fan, and gold opera glasses—as well as the man looking through his glasses at an audience member in a balcony above reveals Renoir's sharp eye for contemporary detail.*

Courtauld Institute Gallery, London. Oil on canvas (31½×25 inches).

The outbreak of the Franco-Prussian War in 1870 shattered any immediate plans. In September, Prussian forces invaded Paris. Manet shut his studio; Renoir, Degas, and Bazille enlisted. Both Monet and Pissarro sought refuge in London, where they met the art dealer Paul Durand-Ruel, who would play a crucial role in the promotion of their ideas and the sale of their works. To avoid conscription, Cézanne fled to L'Estaque. That November, Bazille was killed in battle. In January 1871, a Prussian victory was declared, and France was forced to cede most of the regions of Alsace and Lorraine to Germany as well as submit to other humiliating concessions. An armistice was declared in February, but civil disorder ravaged the capital, and Emperor Napoleon III was deposed. For a few months the Commune, a radical alliance of Marxists, socialists, and anarchists, controlled Paris. The Commune held power until May, when the moderates mounted a military campaign against them, seized power, and established the centrist Third Republic. Thousands were killed in the civil uprisings, and even more political prisoners were executed. Private property and public parks lay in ruins, but by the end of the year calm had been secured and the city began to rebuild.

In 1872, after a year's suspension, the Salon reopened. Renoir and Morisot succeeded in having their works accepted, but Degas, Monet, and Pissarro declined to submit. That June, Cézanne, Manet, Pissarro, and Renoir signed a petition to the government, demanding another Salon des Refusés. The following May, Morisot and Manet exhibited in the Salon. Renoir's rejected work was well received at the Salon des Refusés, but Monet and Pissarro again refused to put their works before the jury. Late in December 1873, the circle of artists applied for a charter to found the Société Anonyme. For a modest fee, each member was entitled to submit two works of their own choosing, which would be included—without any judgment of a selection committee—in an exhibition to be held in April

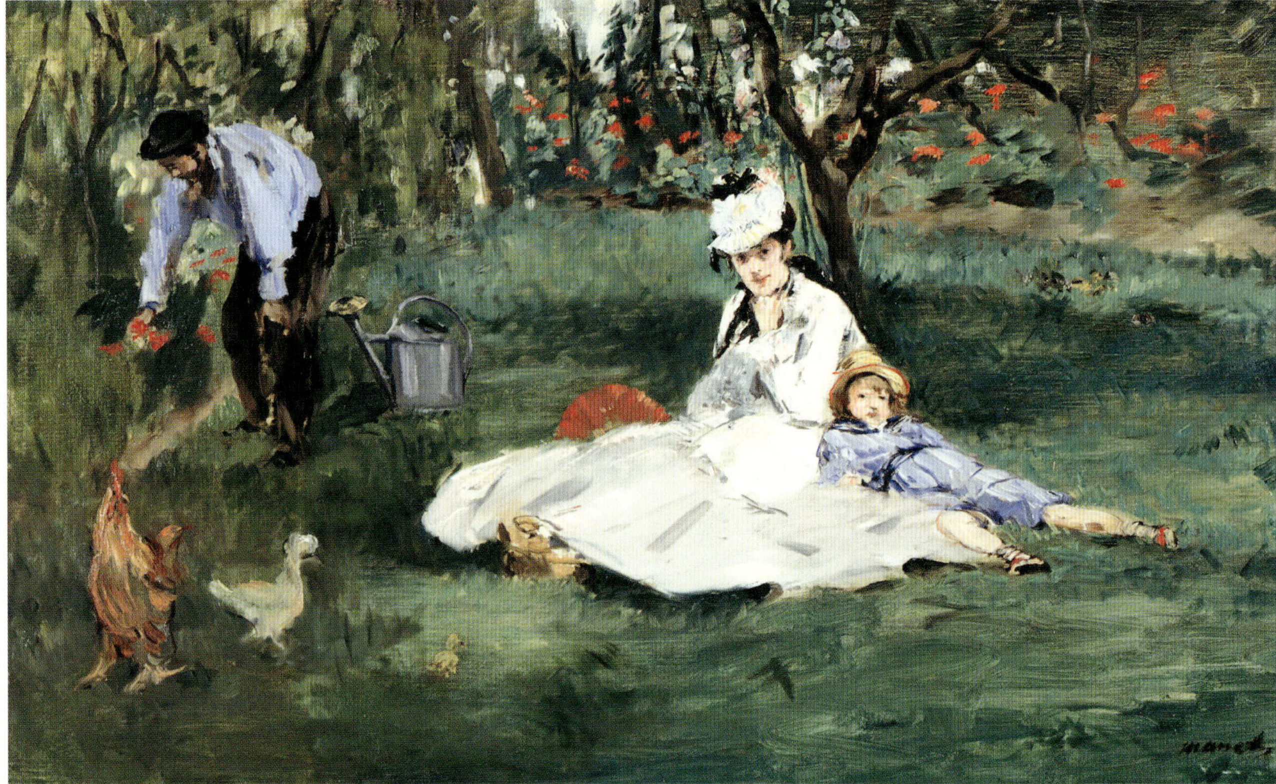

EDOUARD MANET, The Monet Family in their Garden at Argenteuil *(1874). Although Manet never accepted the invitation to exhibit with the Impressionists, he remained sympathetic to their desire to provide an alternative venue for contemporary art. He was also increasingly influenced by aspects of their stylistic innovations. In painting outdoors, as in this portrait of Monet and his family in their garden, Manet used a lighter, fresher palette and broken brush strokes that suggest a natural—rather than a composed—impression.*

THE METROPOLITAN MUSEUM OF ART, NEW YORK. OIL ON CANVAS (24×39¼ INCHES).

1874. The members were allowed to set their own purchase price for their works and agreed to pay 10 percent of that price to the corporation on all sales. If a profit resulted from the exhibition, each member would be entitled to an equal share. There were 16 signatories, including Cézanne, Monet, Renoir, Morisot, Degas, and Pissarro. Manet chose not to participate.

The exhibition of the Société Anonyme provided an unprecedented alternative to the Salon. The founding members generously invited other artists to join the endeavor, and when the doors opened on April 15, 1874, 30 artists were represented. The exhibition was held in the photography studio of Nadar (Felix Tournachon) on the fashionable Boulevard des Capucines. The modernist setting was matched by an extraordinary installation: Works were arranged in two rows on the red walls of Nadar's studio. Most were presented in simple frames. Paintings, drawings, and prints were hung together, and each work of art occupied a commodious space on the wall. Nothing was crowded or obscured. Although there were traditional works in the diverse exhibition, the modern point of view—varying according to individual interpretation—prevailed. The critical response ranged from enthusiastic support to distaste, satire, and ridicule. Sales were modest, but the exhibition fulfilled its initial objective. By creating their own venue for contemporary art, the artists presented a genuine alternative to the politics of the academy and the dominance of the Salon.

Seven exhibitions followed in a little more than the span of a decade. Over the years, the participants changed. Gustave Caillebotte (1848–94), a friend of Monet's since 1873, participated in the second exhibition in 1876. A strong supporter of the group, he missed only the sixth (1881) and final (1886) exhibitions. Caillebotte's background as an engineer and architect was evident in his sleek urban views. Each year, drawing upon family wealth, he purchased a selection of works from the exhibition. In 1877, at the third exhibition, Cézanne appeared with the Impressionists for the last time; he soon left Paris to work in solitude in Aix-en-Provence. The fourth exhibition (1879) saw the Impressionist debut of Mary Cassatt (1845–1926). Degas had noticed her work at the 1874 Salon and invited her to join with his fellow independents. She enjoyed the distinction of being the only American to exhibit with the Impressionists. In the same year, Paul Gauguin (1848–1903) joined the circle. In 1880 both Renoir and Monet refrained from submitting works to the fifth exhibition, exhibiting instead at the Salon. The sixth exhibition (1881) marked the absence of so many of the core members that Caillebotte confessed to Pissarro—the only stalwart to exhibit all eight times—that he feared the experiment was at its end. But the seventh exhibition of 1882 was large and impressive, marking the return—as well as the final appearance—of Monet and Renoir. The eighth and final exhibition was held in 1886, and rather than striking a valedictory note, it featured startlingly new innovations, most notably in the work of the young painter Georges Seurat (1859–91). Epic in scale, his *Sunday Afternoon on the Island of the Grande-Jatte* (1884–86) was based on a scientific rather than a sensory premise. By placing dots of pure pigment in close

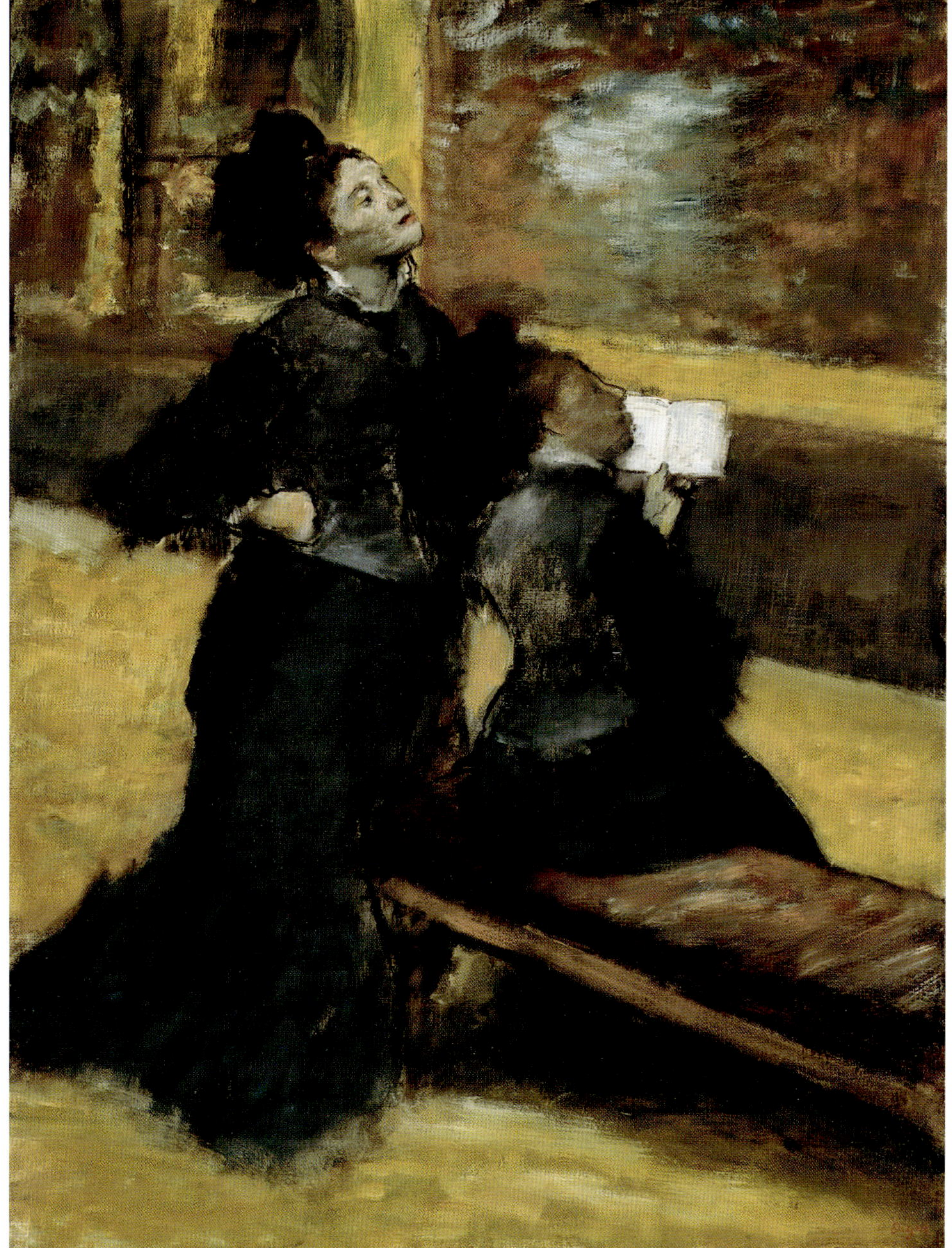

HILAIRE-GERMAIN-EDGAR DEGAS (French, 1834–1917), Visit to a Museum *(c. 1879–80). Degas's bold compositional arrangements gave his work an immediacy that suggests the observations of a passing glance. In this pastel of two women in a gallery at the Louvre, the floor meets the wall at a raking angle, the bench is cut off at the right, and the standing woman's skirt trails out of the image at the left. It is as if these women—Mary Cassatt and her sister—will soon rise and move on to another gallery.*

MUSEUM OF FINE ARTS, BOSTON. OIL ON CANVAS (36⅛×26¾ INCHES).

and calculated proximity, Seurat developed a theoretical approach to color and light, requiring the viewer's eye, rather than the painter's hand, to regulate the tonal luminosity. Even after the final exhibition closed, the Impressionist experiment continued: They influenced a new generation of artists that included Vincent van Gogh (1853–90) and Henri de Toulouse-Lautrec (1864–1901).

In 1876 the writer Edmond Duranty wrote an extensive review of the second Impressionist exhibition. He published the essay as a 38-page pamphlet entitled "The New Painting: Concerning the Group of Artists Exhibiting at the Durand-Ruel Galleries." Long a defender of the realist tendency in art and the naturalist movement in literature, Duranty had made his reputation in Paris as the editor of the short-lived journal *Realisme* (six issues 1856–57). His critical stance was uncompromisingly modern, and in his review he applauded the independent artists for creating an artistic expression that captured the temper of the times. Although he stated his willingness to champion individual works, he acknowledged that his interest was sparked by the underlying motivation behind the exhibition far more than its contents. Questioning the place of the new artists in a world that had seen many stylistic discoveries and innovations, Duranty inquired, "What, then, do these painters contribute? A new method of color, of drawing, and a gamut of original points of view." But these were small details, diminished by the transformation of the realm of art that was in evidence at the exhibition. More than a matter of color, drawing, or even an original point of view, the Impressionists succeeded in freeing the artist from isolating conventions and traditions, for according to Duranty, the first step was "to make the painter leave his sky-lighted cell, his cloister . . . , and to bring him out among men, into the world . . . ."

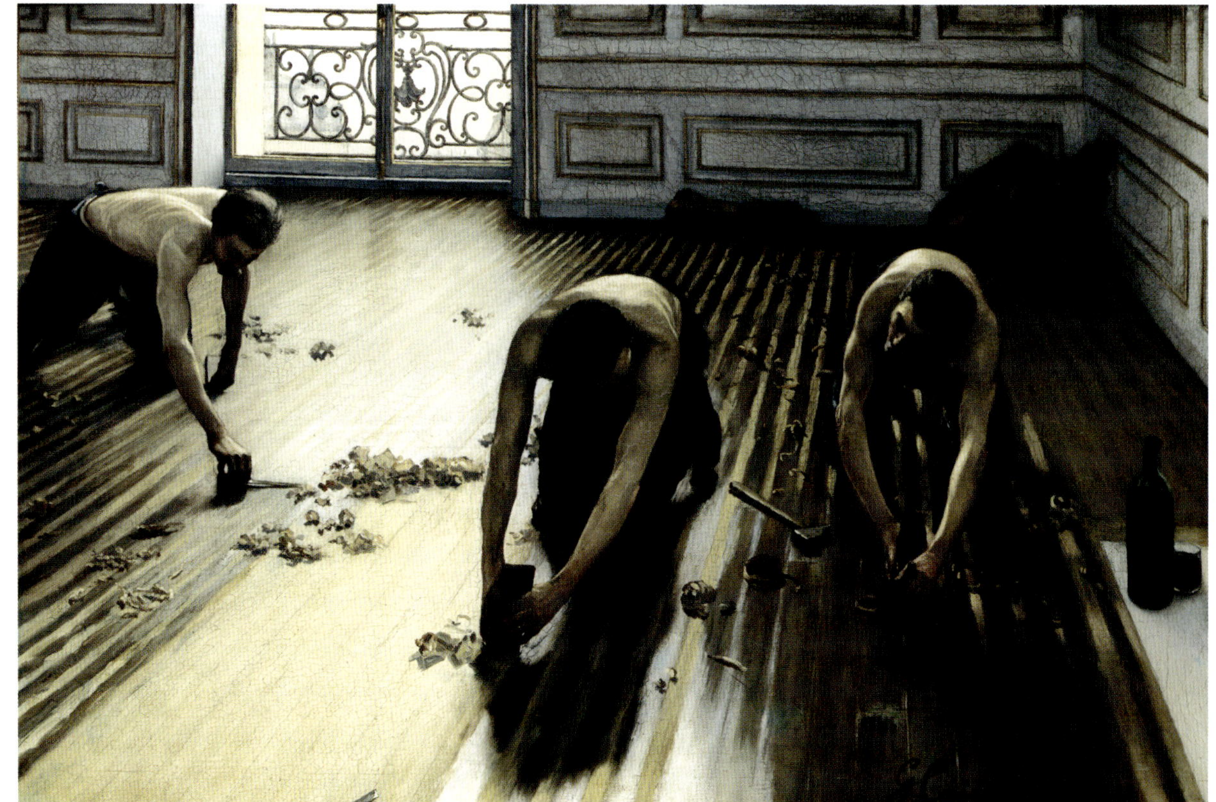

GUSTAVE CAILLEBOTTE, The Floor Scrapers *(1875). Caillebotte joined the Impressionist circle for the second exhibition and participated in four subsequent exhibitions. His vision was adamantly modern, choosing subjects that preserved glimpses of Parisian life: interiors, views over the rooftops from balconies, strollers on the bridges and avenues, and even workmen finishing a fine wood floor in a new apartment.*

MUSÉE D'ORSAY, PARIS. OIL ON CANVAS (39⅜×57¼ INCHES).

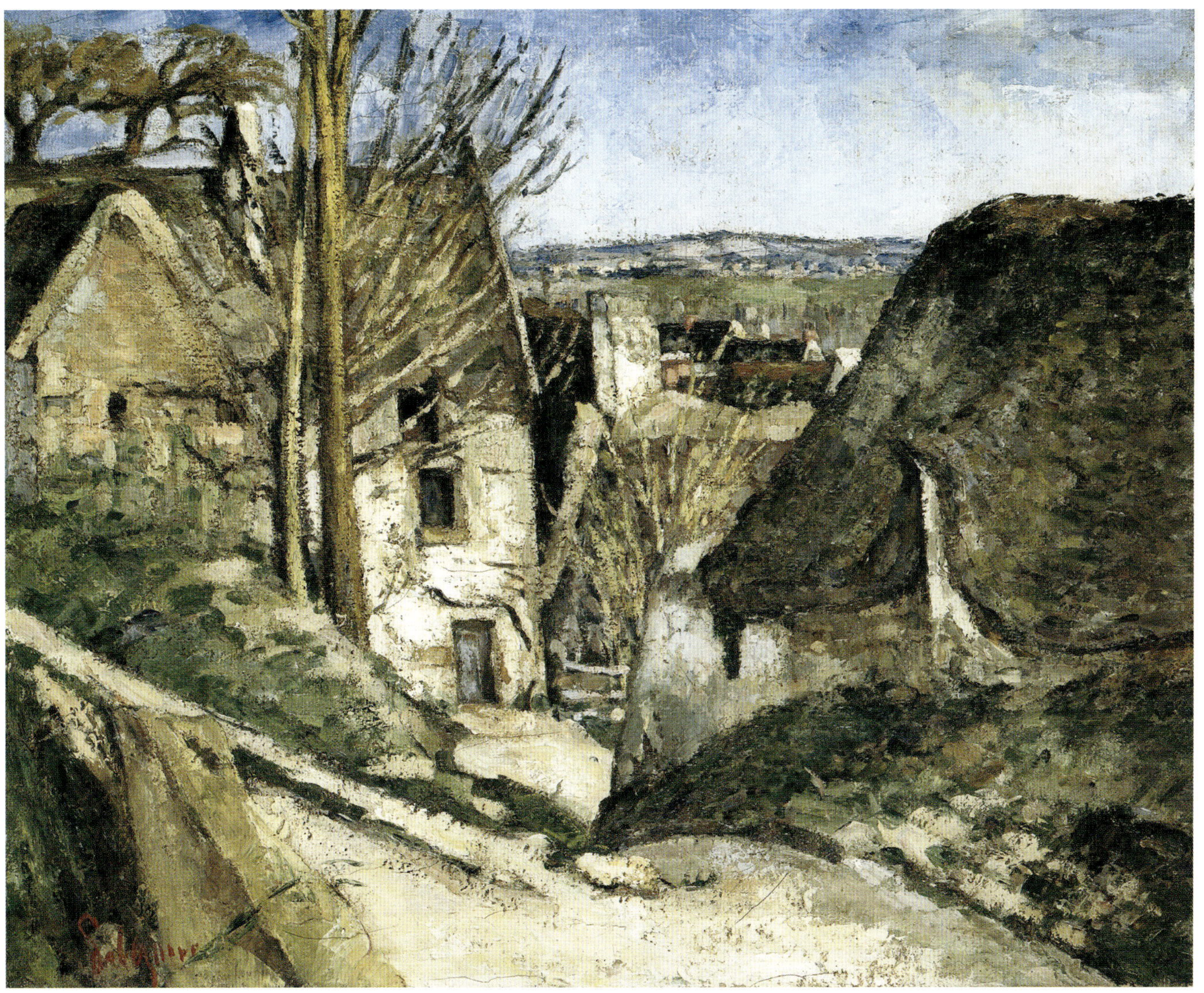

PAUL CÉZANNE, The House of the Hanged Man *(1873). Among the original circle, Cézanne held a firm conviction that artists should never be subjected to the whims of a jury. Like Pissarro, he had had little success with the official exhibition and presented his work at the Salon des Refusés. His strong structural approach to painting differed from the plein air spontaneity associated with the work of Monet and Renoir, and he participated in only the first and third Impressionist exhibitions.*

MUSÉE D'ORSAY, PARIS. OIL ON CANVAS (21¾×26 INCHES).

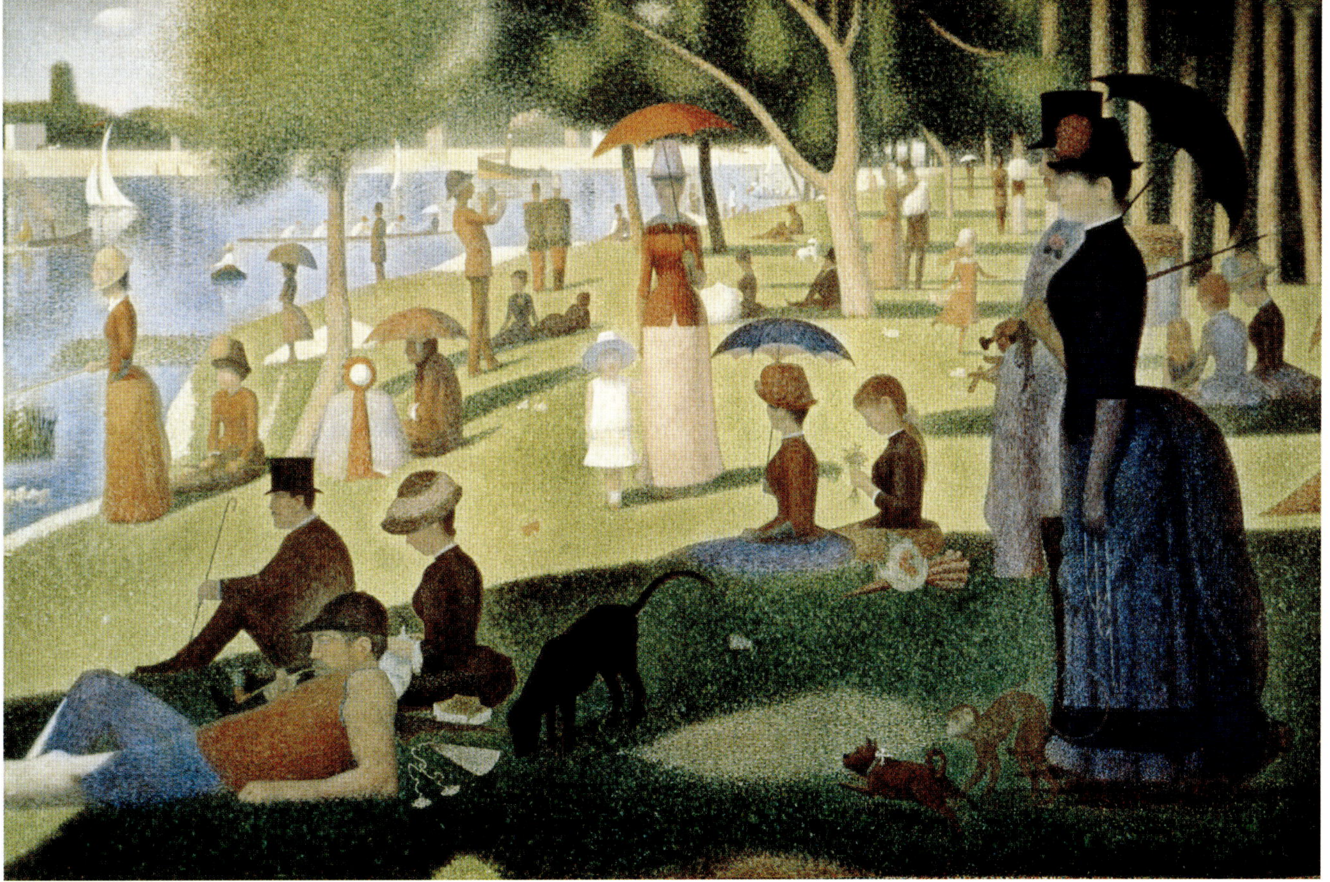

GEORGES SEURAT, Sunday Afternoon on the Island of the Grande-Jatte *(1884–86). Seurat's painting of a leisurely summer afternoon in a public park frequented by the Parisian bourgeois populace employed a theory based on current optical research. This research proposed dabs of color placed in close proximity on the canvas would resonate in a luminous blend on the viewer's retina. This painting, shown at the final Impressionist exhibition, pioneered a more structured formal approach to art that came to be called Neo-Impressionism.*

THE ART INSTITUTE OF CHICAGO. OIL ON CANVAS (81×120⅜ INCHES).

Painters of Modern Life

Those painters who love the times they live in from the depths of their hearts and minds as artists perceive everyday realities in a different way. Above all, they try to penetrate the exact meaning of things. Not content with ridiculous trompe-l'oeil, they interpret their era as men who feel it living within themselves, who are possessed by it and happy to be. . . . Their works are alive, because they have taken them from life and painted them with all the love they have for modern subjects.

ÉMILE ZOLA, "THE ACTUALISTS," *L'ÉVÉNEMENT,* 1868

In 1845 poet and essayist Charles-Pierre Baudelaire reviewed the Salon, the annual government-sponsored exhibition of contemporary art. After considering the usual display of historic tableaux, grand portraits, high-minded mythological narratives, and sentimental anecdotes, Baudelaire concluded that something essential was missing from the exhibition. He decided he wanted to find a painter who could capture the feel of the times. He was searching for someone to exemplify the people of his day. And, in his desire to see an artist paint the spirit of the times, Baudelaire was asking artists to confront the changes that defined life for his—and their—generation.

In the past decades, industry and improved transportation had altered France—as well as other European countries; the countries had become urban rather than agricultural economies. Cities were becoming more populous and more diverse with a newly empowered middle class and a rising working class. Through the course of the 1850s, the fabric of the city also changed. Under the direction of urban planner Baron Georges-Eugène Haussmann, the narrow, twisted streets with their ramshackle buildings were swept away to make room for broad, straight avenues lined with modern, multistory apartment buildings, department stores, cafés, and theaters. Parks and gardens, once attached to royal residences, were now open for public use. Paris had become a

CLAUDE MONET, Women at the Garden at Ville d'Avray *(1866–67). Monet believed that the freshness of plein air painting could not be matched in the studio. Despite the huge size of this canvas, he worked outdoors on this image of four women. Camille (his wife) posed for three of the four figures, but it was the natural light and evocation of summer pleasures—rather than accurate portraits and fashionable details—that concerned Monet. Rejected by the official Salon, this painting won praise from art critic Émile Zola for its modern spirit.*

MUSÉE D'ORSAY, PARIS. OIL ON CANVAS ($100\frac{3}{4} \times 81\frac{7}{8}$ INCHES).

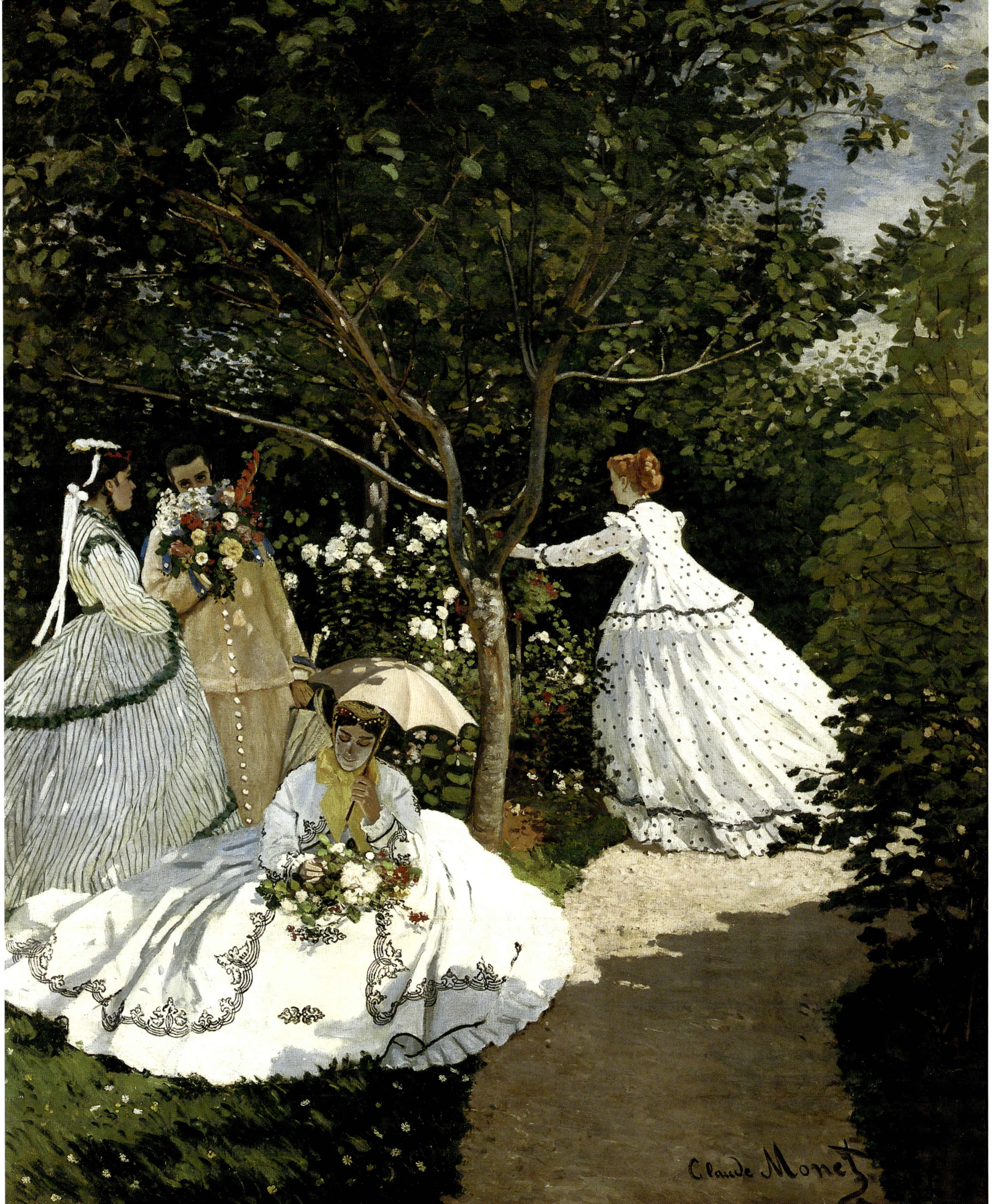
Claude Monet

modern city, and Baudelaire repeated his call to artists in the essay "The Painter of Modern Life" (1863) to shift their attentions from the obsolete—that realm of history and mythology that constricted the painter's repertoire—to the modern.

Advances in technology gave artists new means to capture their rapidly changing world. Photography allowed the artist to fix an image through light on paper with the speed of a shutter. New art materials—pigments in tin tubes and light, portable easels—freed artists from the confines of their studios. In the early 1840s, a small circle of landscape artists led by Théodore Rousseau and Charles-François Daubigny gathered in the village of Barbizon, outside Paris on the edge of the Forest of Fontainebleau, to paint plein air (outdoors). They tried to capture the natural effects of light and atmosphere from direct observation rather than by working indoors from memory. In "The Painter of Modern Life," Baudelaire linked this directness of response to the spirit of the times, or modernity. He thought *modernity* encompassed the ephemeral and fugitive aspects of human experience. Artists applied this idea to their subjects; for instance, Gustave Courbet's depictions of working people celebrated the inherent dignity of everyday life. And, more than any other artist in his time, Edouard Manet was determined to position the modern life subject in the painter's repertoire. As seen in his *Music in the Tuileries Garden* (1862), Manet painted his contemporaries in fashionable dress and placed them in the Paris of his day. This painting shows his emulation of the rough, realist handling pioneered by Courbet and the evanescent light effects seen in the Barbizon painters' plein air landscapes. Conservative critics castigated Manet for his work, which by conventional standards seemed slapdash, unfinished, and of passing interest. However, his bold work was championed for its daring, modern energy by Baudelaire and the art critic Émile Zola.

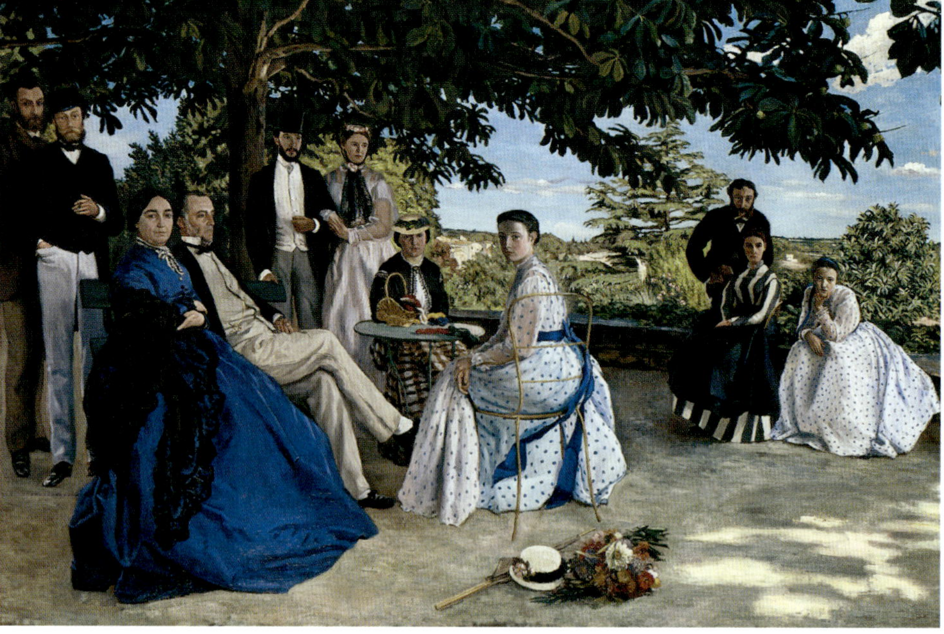

FRÉDÉRIC BAZILLE, The Artist's Family on a Terrace near Montpellier *(1867). Bazille's admiration for Edouard Manet's pioneering formulations for modern-life painting is evident in this painting of his family on a terrace outside their home in Montpellier. Clear color, simple massing of forms, and attention to the natural action of light recalls the spontaneous freshness of Manet's* Music in the Tuileries Garden.

MUSÉE D'ORSAY, PARIS. OIL ON CANVAS (59⅞×89⅜ INCHES).

A young circle of artists gathered in admiration around Manet. They included Claude Monet, Pierre-Auguste Renoir, and Frédéric Bazille, all three of whom had met in the early 1860s as students in the atelier, or studio, of the academic painter Charles Gleyre. A native of the coastal town Le Havre, Monet had already experimented with painting seascapes outdoors under the encouragement of the marine painter Eugene Boudin. Bazille followed Manet's example and posed his family in the open air on a terrace in his home in Montpellier.

With Camille Pissarro and Paul Cézanne, both dedicated plein air painters, Manet debated issues and shared ideas at the Café Guerbois near Manet's studio in the rue de Batignolles. As aspiring artists they shared the frustrating experience of having to submit their works to the jury that made the selection for the annual Salon. They were frustrated because they thought the jury's standards were arcane and antithetical to the modernist spirit of their painting. While they each had some success getting into the Salon, just as often their works were rejected or, as in the case of Manet's paintings, met with hostile criticism. Despite this, it should be noted that a few open-minded critics recognized the new and exciting direction of their work. Writing a review for the journal *L'Événement* in 1868, Zola regarded Monet's *Women at the Garden at Ville d'Avray* (1866–67)—a sun-drenched depiction of four fashionably dressed women that had been rejected by the official Salon—as exemplary of "an exact and candid eye." In the work of Monet and his colleagues, Zola took note of "painters who love the times they live in from the depths of their hearts and minds" and dubbed them Les Actualistes (of the moment).

Realizing that the Salon jury's official standards conflicted with and restrained their artistic ambitions, the small circle of painters considered holding their own exhibition. They envisioned a small, intimate venue where critics and collectors could assess their works apart from the Salon jury's restrictive judgment. They formulated a plan first in 1867 and then again in 1869, but organizational and financial difficulties proved impossible to surmount. In 1870 the outbreak of the Franco-Prussian War temporarily dispersed the group. Monet and Pissarro sought refuge far from the conflict in London, where they met Paul Durand-Ruel, a sympathetic art dealer from Paris. Renoir and Bazille served in the military; Bazille was killed in action. In 1873, as Paris began to recover from the ravages of war and civil disorder, the circle reconvened, now joined by Hilaire-Germain-Edgar Degas and Berthe Morisot, to formulate their plans to hold an exhibition the following spring.

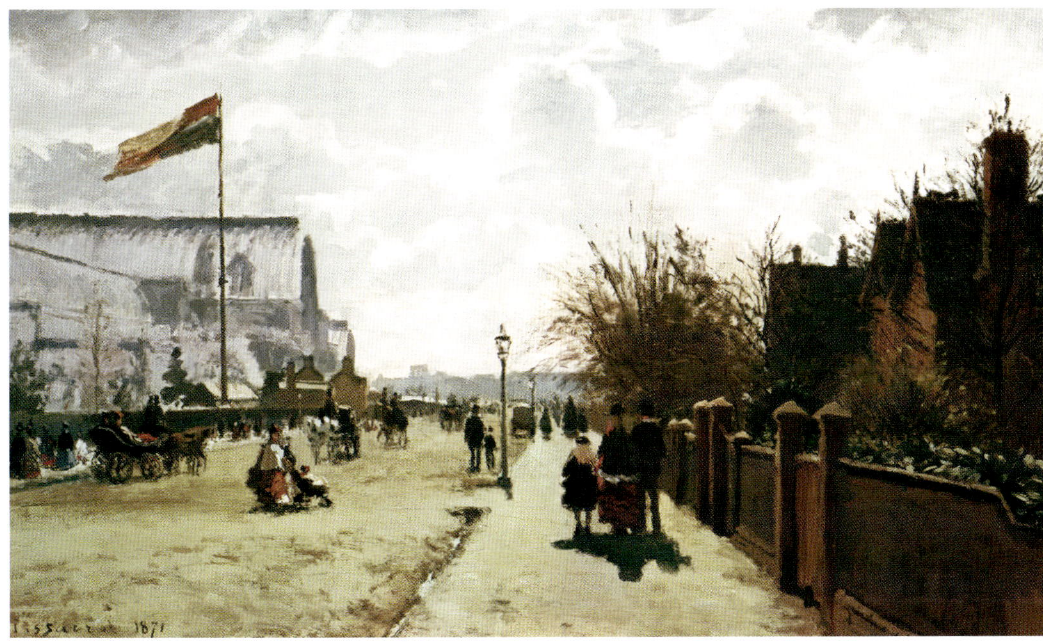

CAMILLE PISSARRO, The Crystal Palace *(1871). During the Franco-Prussian War and the subsequent uprising of the Paris Commune, Monet and Pissarro took refuge in London. Pissarro painted more than a dozen pictures during his residence, focusing on the modern-life scenes that the civil disturbance at home would have made impossible. Here he painted the famous exhibition building—all made of glass—in translucent shades of gray that emphasize the tonal subtlety of the low-lying clouds in the sky.*

THE ART INSTITUTE OF CHICAGO. OIL ON CANVAS (18⅝×28⅞ INCHES).

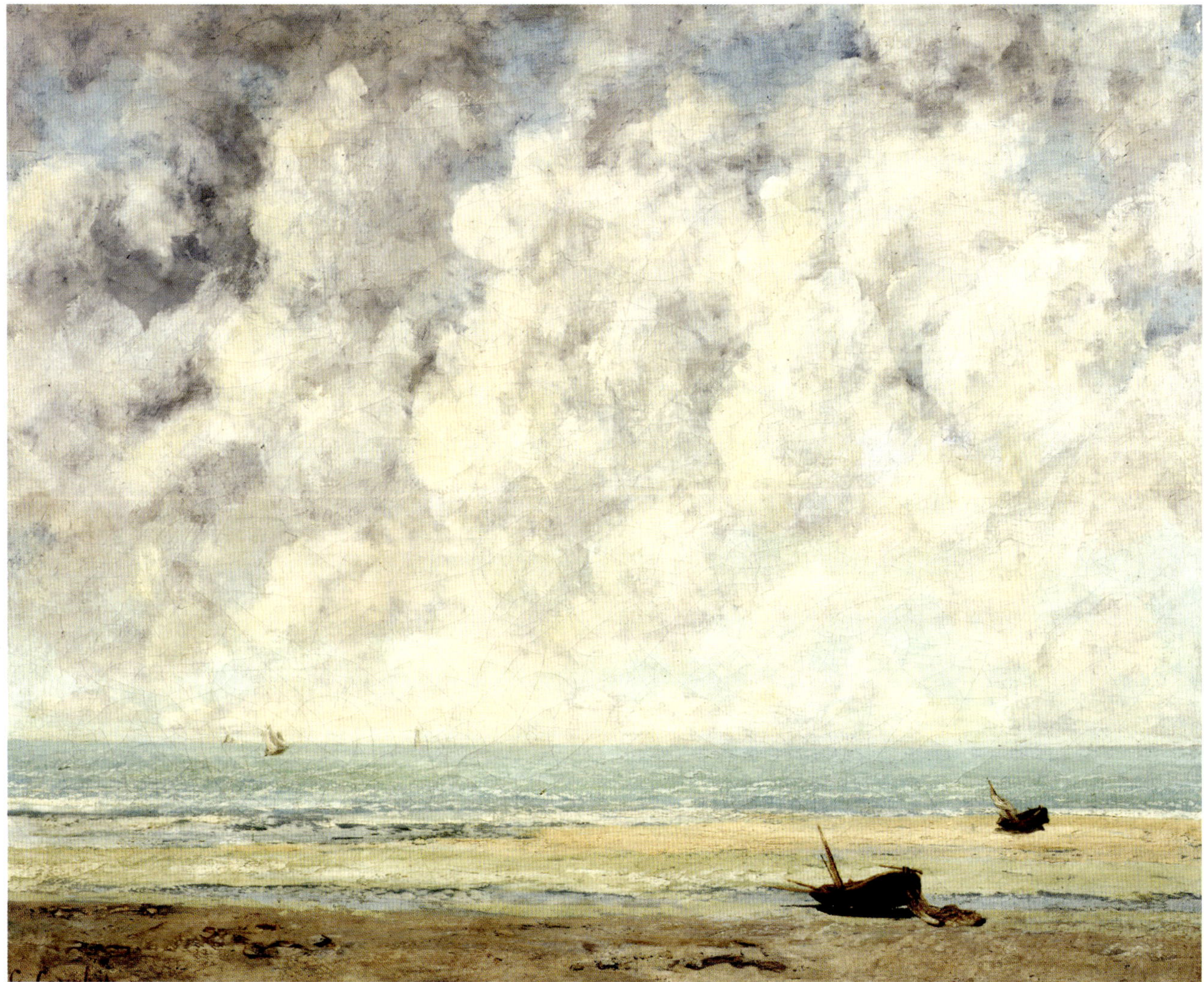

GUSTAVE COURBET, The Calm Sea *(1869). This view of calm waters seen from the coastline at Trouville demonstrates the fresh color quality and careful observation associated with plein air painting. With his easel set up on the shore, Courbet was able to record the light and the moving clouds over the serene sea. The result is a work that evokes atmospheric sensation rather than detailed observation.*

THE METROPOLITAN MUSEUM OF ART, NEW YORK. OIL ON CANVAS (23½×28¾ INCHES).

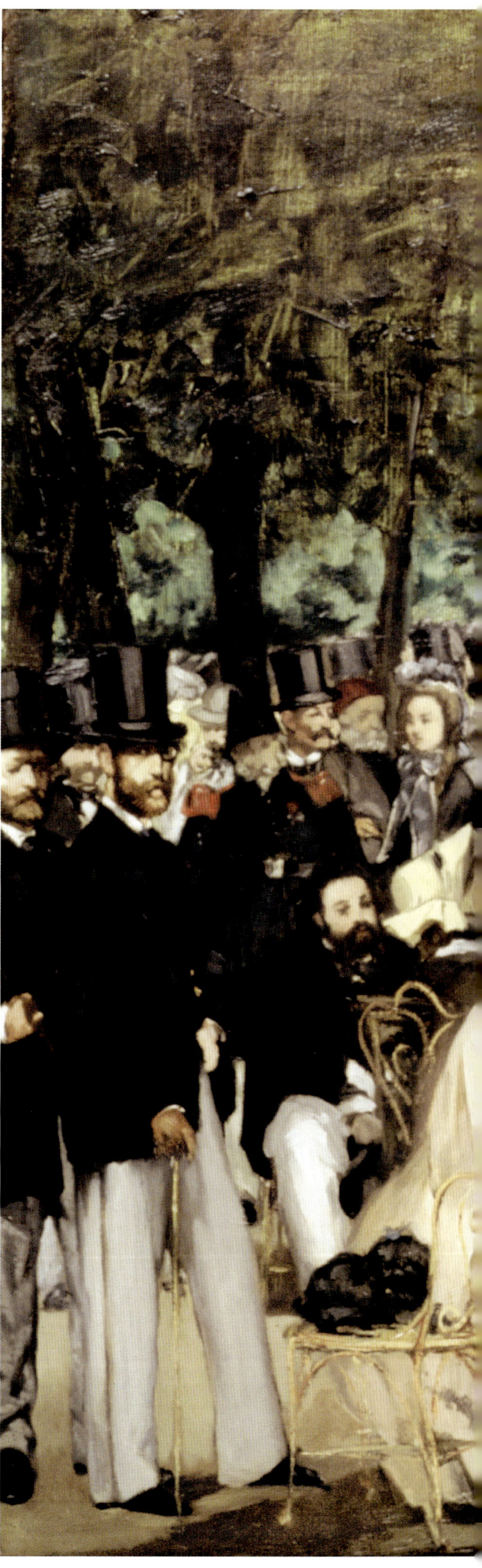

EDOUARD MANET, Music in the Tuileries Garden *(1862). Manet's chosen subject was the middle-class population of Paris. This painting of a fashionable crowd gathered in a public park to listen to a concert contains many portraits, including one of poet Charles-Pierre Baudelaire and several members of Manet's family. The loose brush stroke and quickly executed masses of color suggest the spontaneous energy of the moment.*

THE NATIONAL GALLERY, LONDON. OIL ON CANVAS (30×46½ INCHES).

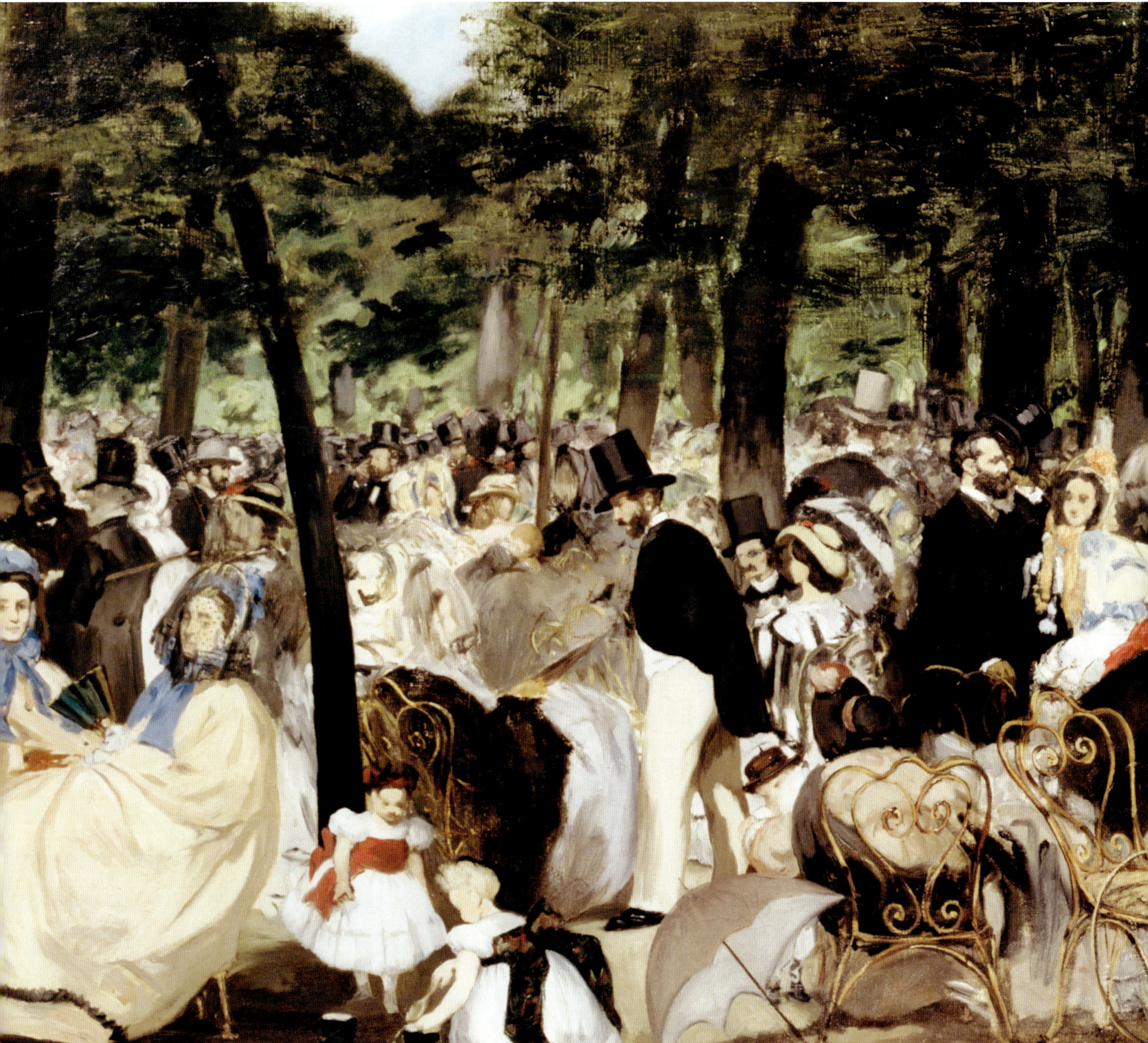

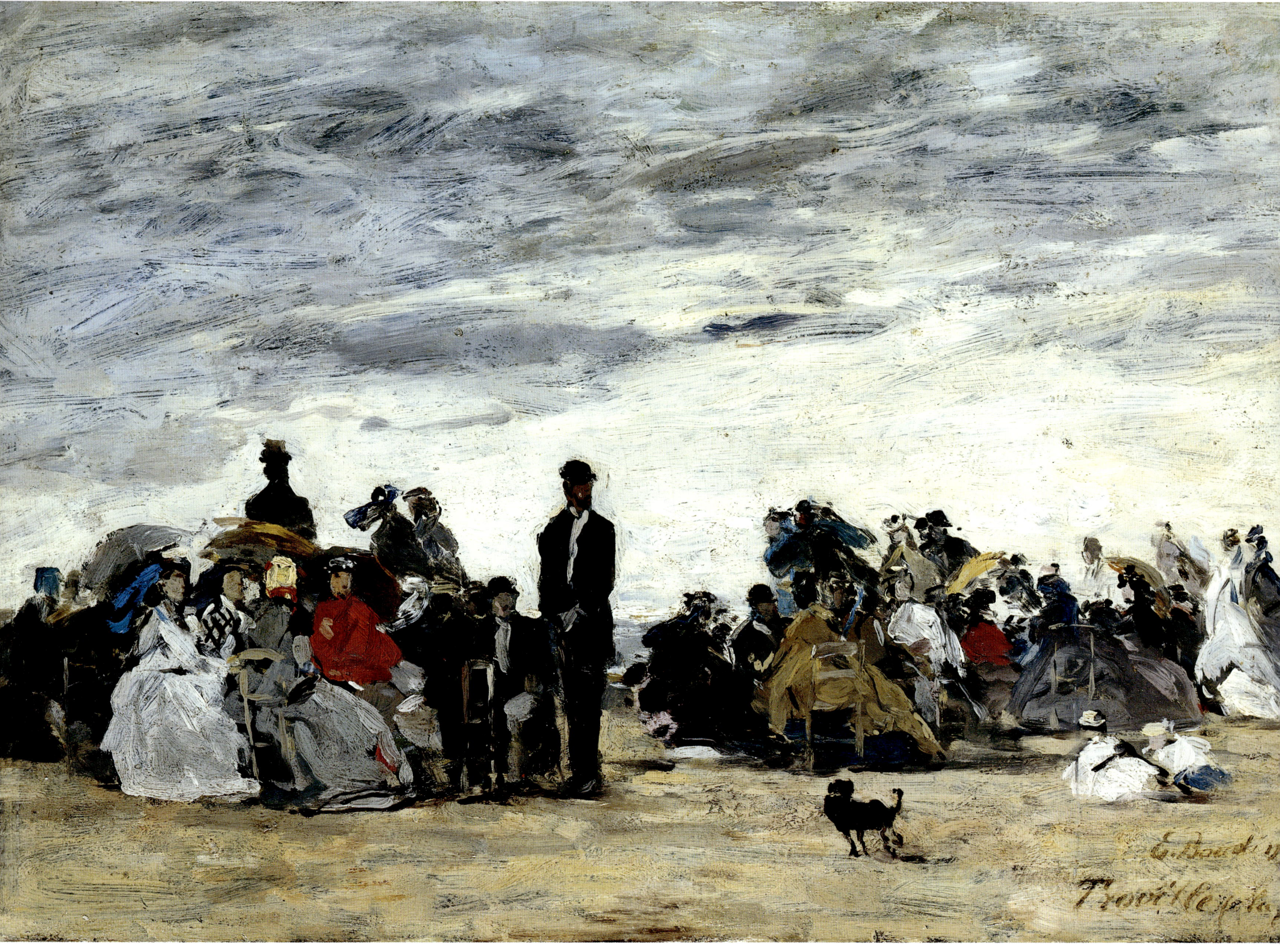

EUGÈNE BOUDIN, La Plage de Trouville *(1865). Boudin seemed to enjoy painting fashionable beach resorts crowded with tourists on seaside vacations. He had a sharp eye for detail and color, allying himself with the new modernists who painted subjects of contemporary life. He portrayed the scene as he saw it, disdaining narrative and anecdote and presenting the figures as part of the setting.*

MUSÉE D'ORSAY, PARIS. OIL ON CANVAS (10⅜×16 INCHES).

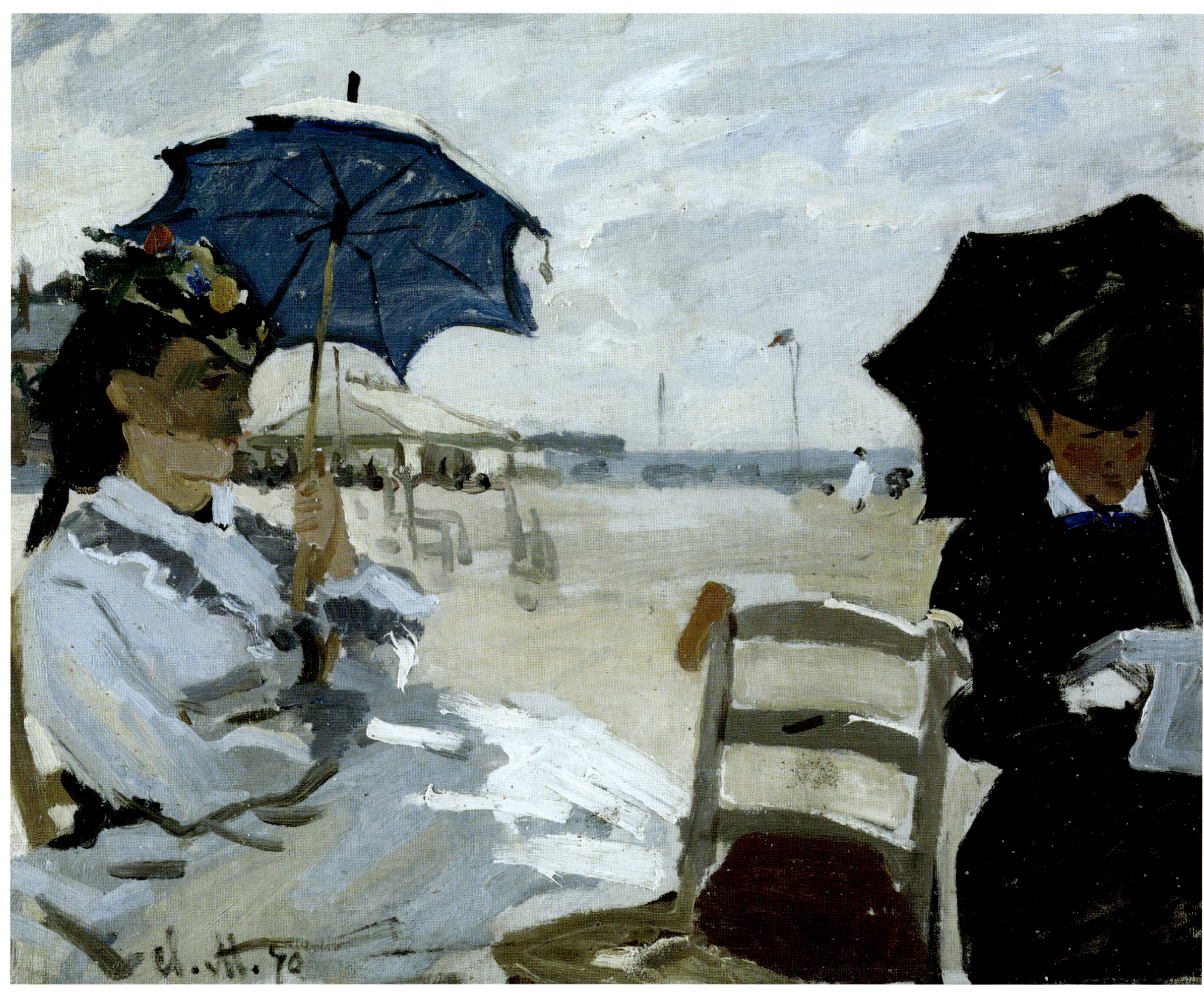

Claude Monet, The Beach at Trouville *(1870). Boudin's early influence on Monet had a long and enduring effect. Light on sand and water always fascinated Boudin, and Monet traveled to a number of the sites that sparked Boudin's interest. Here there is an echo of Boudin's own scenes on the beach at Trouville, with the simple shapes of elegant seaside tourists.*

The National Gallery, London. Oil on canvas (14¾×18 inches).

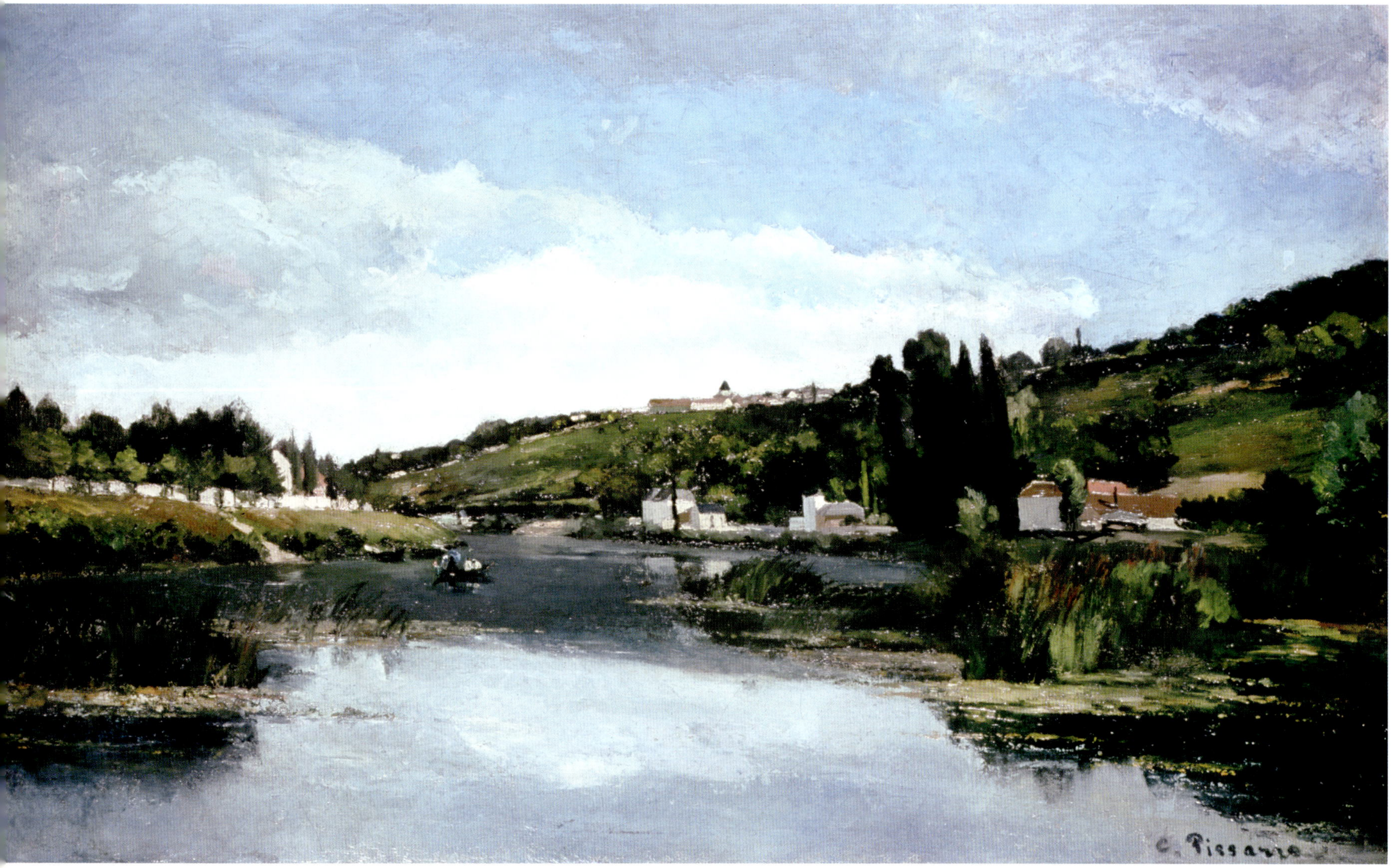

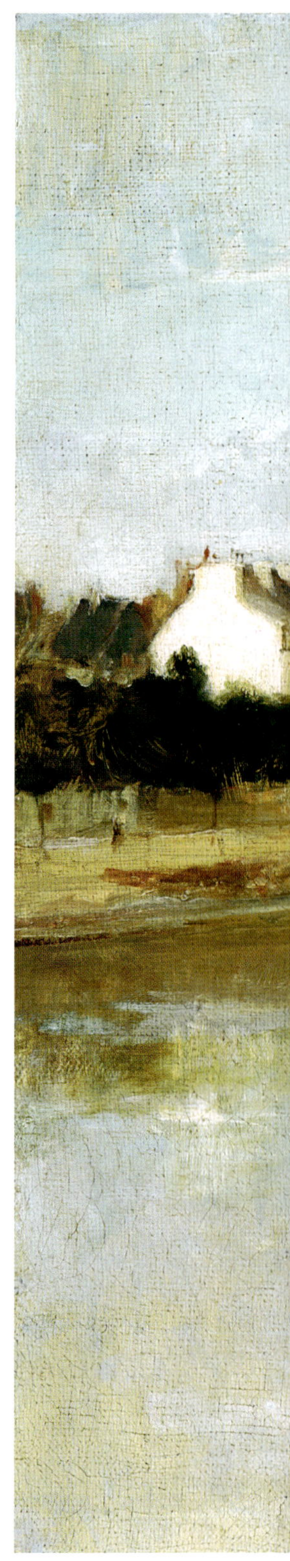

CAMILLE PISSARRO, Chennevières on the Banks of the Marne *(c. 1864–65). Pissarro was deeply influenced by the landscapes painted by the artists of the Barbizon School. As pioneering advocates of plein air painting, they took their easels outdoors to capture every subtle variance of natural light and color. This serene vista—with a broad, low sky and calm, reflecting waters—recalls the rivers and canals painted by Barbizon School artist Charles-François Daubigny.*

NATIONAL GALLERY OF SCOTLAND, EDINBURGH. OIL ON CANVAS (36×57¼ INCHES).

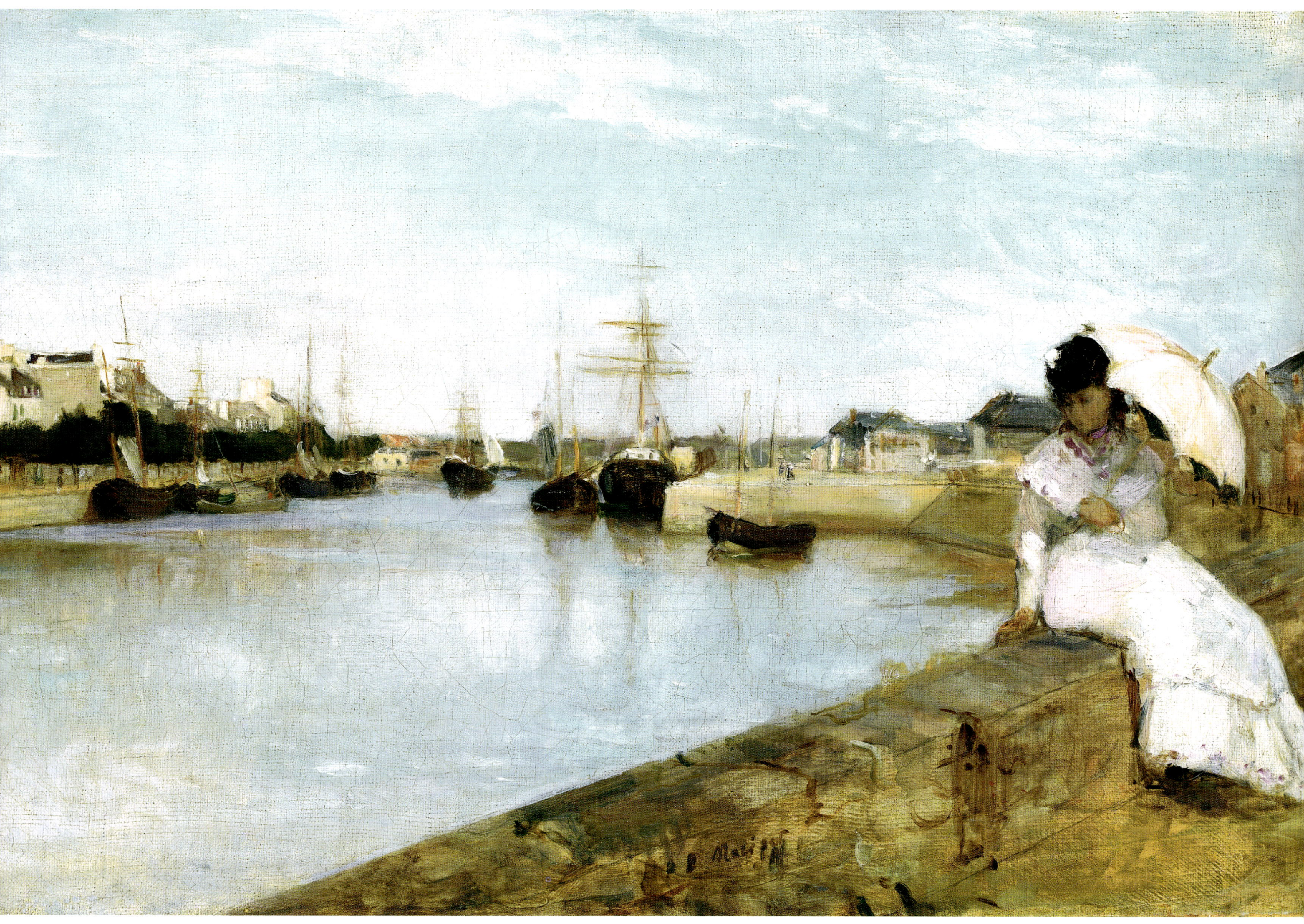

Berthe Morisot, The Harbor at Lorient *(1869). Morisot began to study drawing at the age of 16. For a brief time, her teacher was the Barbizon painter Jean-Baptiste-Camille Corot. He encouraged her to work outdoors and paint landscapes, and even though she developed her own style, his influence was evident. While on vacation in Brittany, she painted coastline scenes, and the fresh tonality and shimmering brush stroke indicate her continuing allegiance to plein air painting.*

National Gallery of Art, Washington, D.C. Oil on canvas (17⅛×28¾ inches).

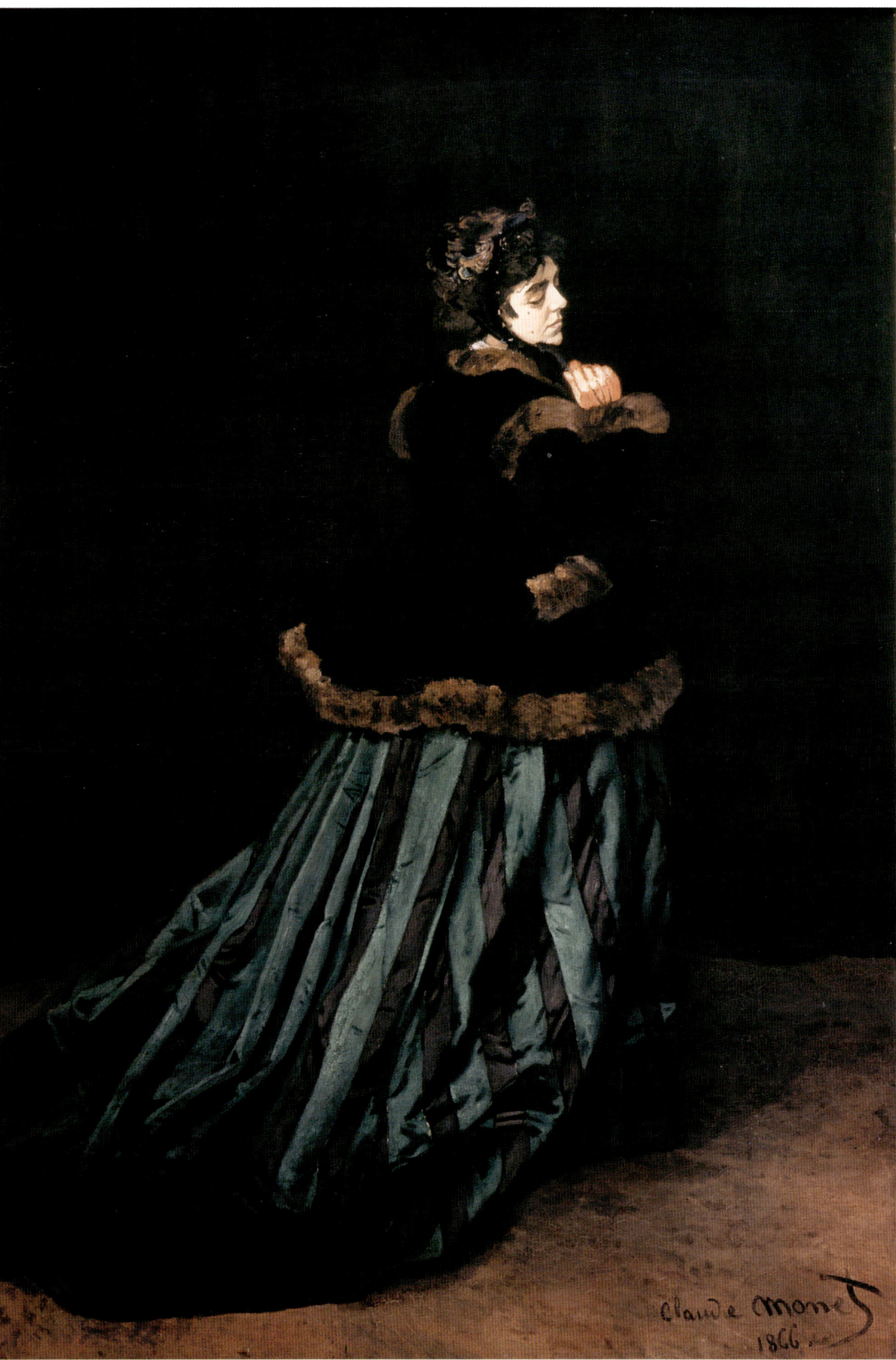

CLAUDE MONET, Camille (The Woman in the Green Dress) *(1866). Monet painted this portrait of his wife Camille Doncieux for the 1866 Salon. It was accepted and highly praised—especially by the famous art critic Émile Zola—and the dark neutral setting that highlights Camille's fair complexion and emerald green gown reveals Monet's command of a traditional approach.*

KUNSTHALLE, BREMEN, GERMANY. OIL ON CANVAS (91×59½ INCHES).

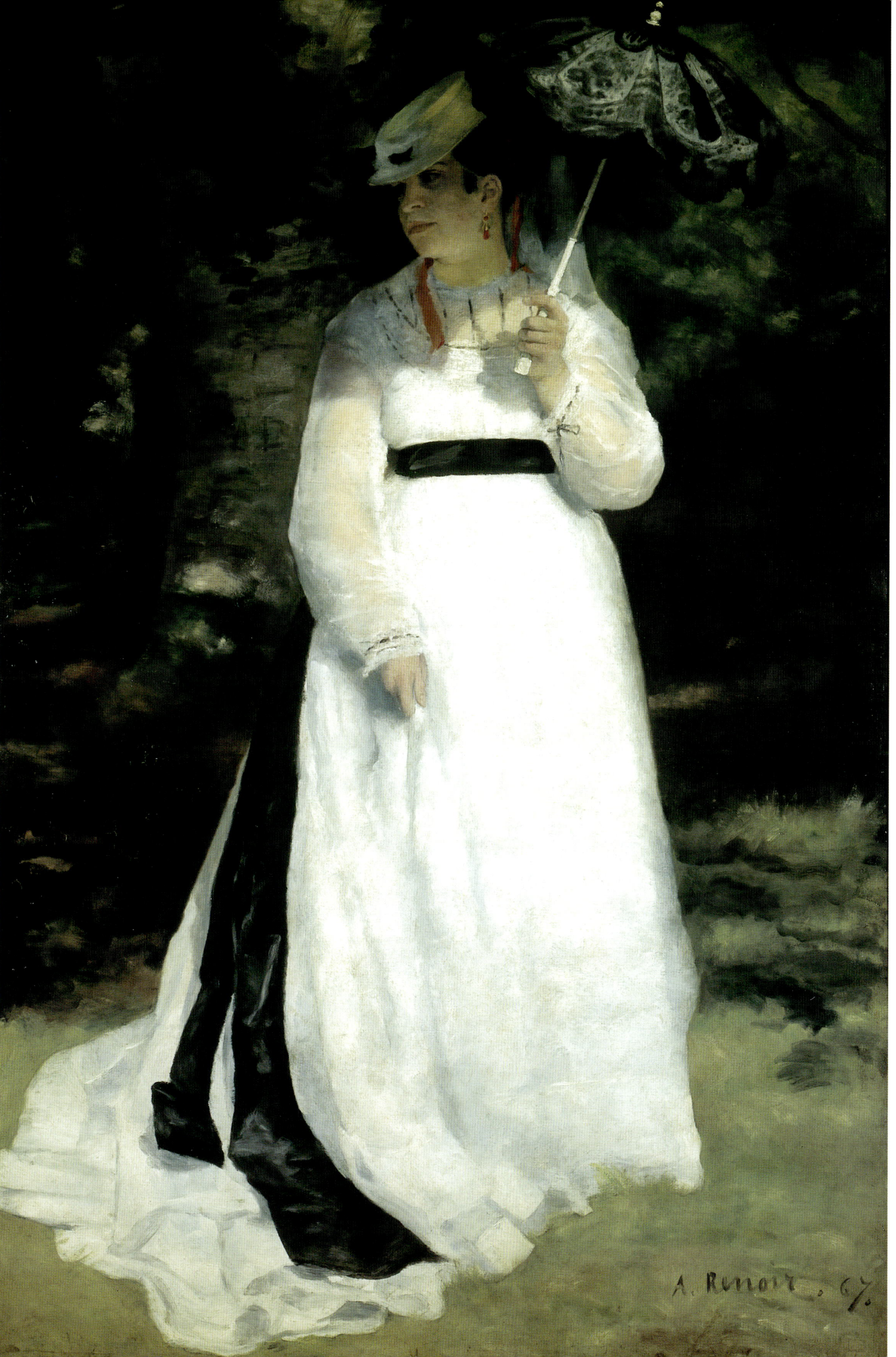

Pierre-Auguste Renoir, Lise with a Parasol *(1867). Renoir depicted his subject Lise Trehot in the natural setting of a public park. She appears to be on a summer stroll, enjoying the shade of the leafy trees and her parasol. Art critic Émile Zola saw the work at the official Salon and praised its modernity because Renoir blended elements of fashion and pleasure in the distinctive style of the times.*

Museum Folkwang, Essen, Germany. Oil on canvas ($72\frac{1}{2} \times 45\frac{1}{4}$ inches).

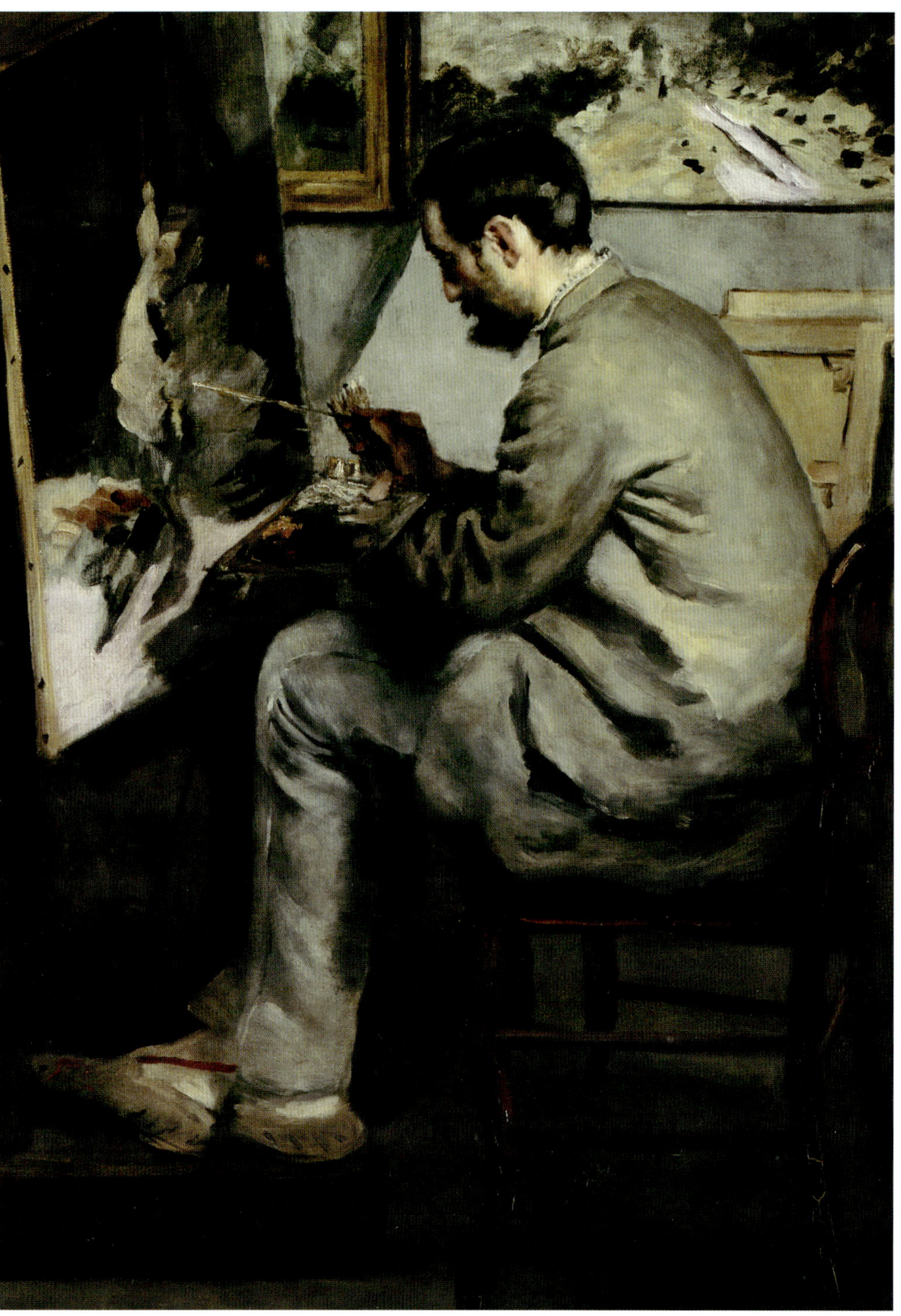

PIERRE-AUGUSTE RENOIR, Portrait of Frédéric Bazille Painting *The Heron with Wings Unfurled (1867). In 1862 Bazille enrolled in the studio run by Charles Gleyre. Along with his studio mates Claude Monet and Alfred Sisley, Renoir embraced the newest directions in contemporary art: the realism of Edouard Manet and Gustave Courbet and the naturalism of plein air painting advocated by the Barbizon School. Over the years the aspiring painters shared several studios, bouncing ideas off one another and giving each other encouragement. In the background of this portrait of fellow painter Frédéric Bazille, Renoir has replicated a snow scene by Monet.*

MUSÉE D'ORSAY, PARIS. OIL ON CANVAS (41 3/8×29 INCHES).

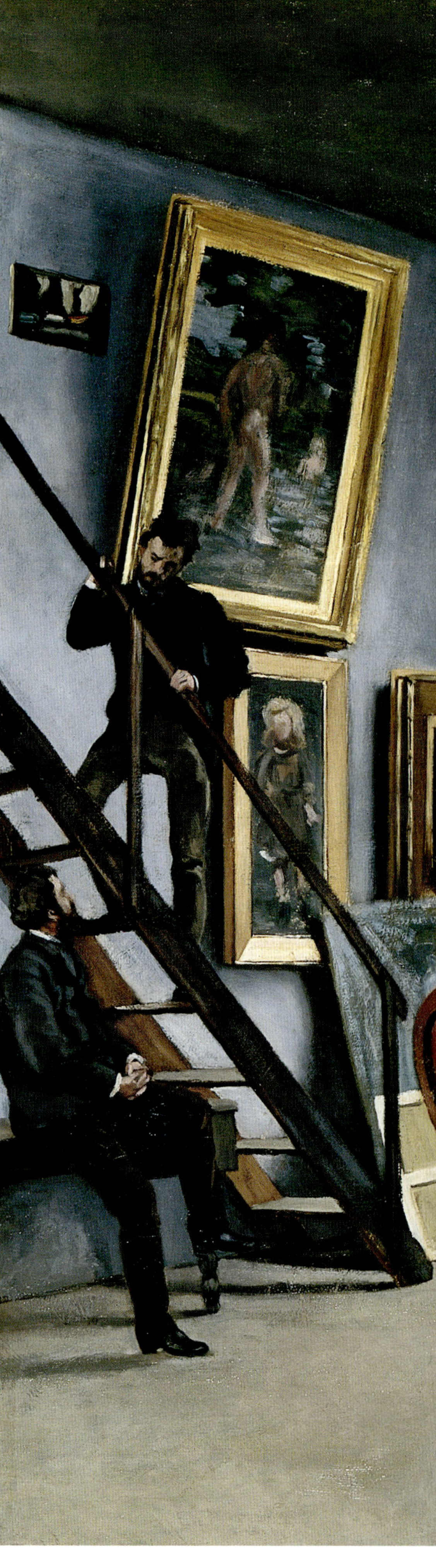

FRÉDÉRIC BAZILLE, The Studio on the rue de la Condamine *(1870). More than a group portrait or a record of the studio interior, this painting brings together an alliance of friends who were advocates of modern art. Bazille can be recognized by his unusual height, and he presents himself discussing the painting on the easel with Manet. Monet stands behind them. A still life Monet has painted is hung to the left of the piano. Critic Émile Zola stands on the stairs, while Renoir sits on a table below him.*

MUSÉE D'ORSAY, PARIS. OIL ON CANVAS (38 5/8×50 5/8 INCHES).

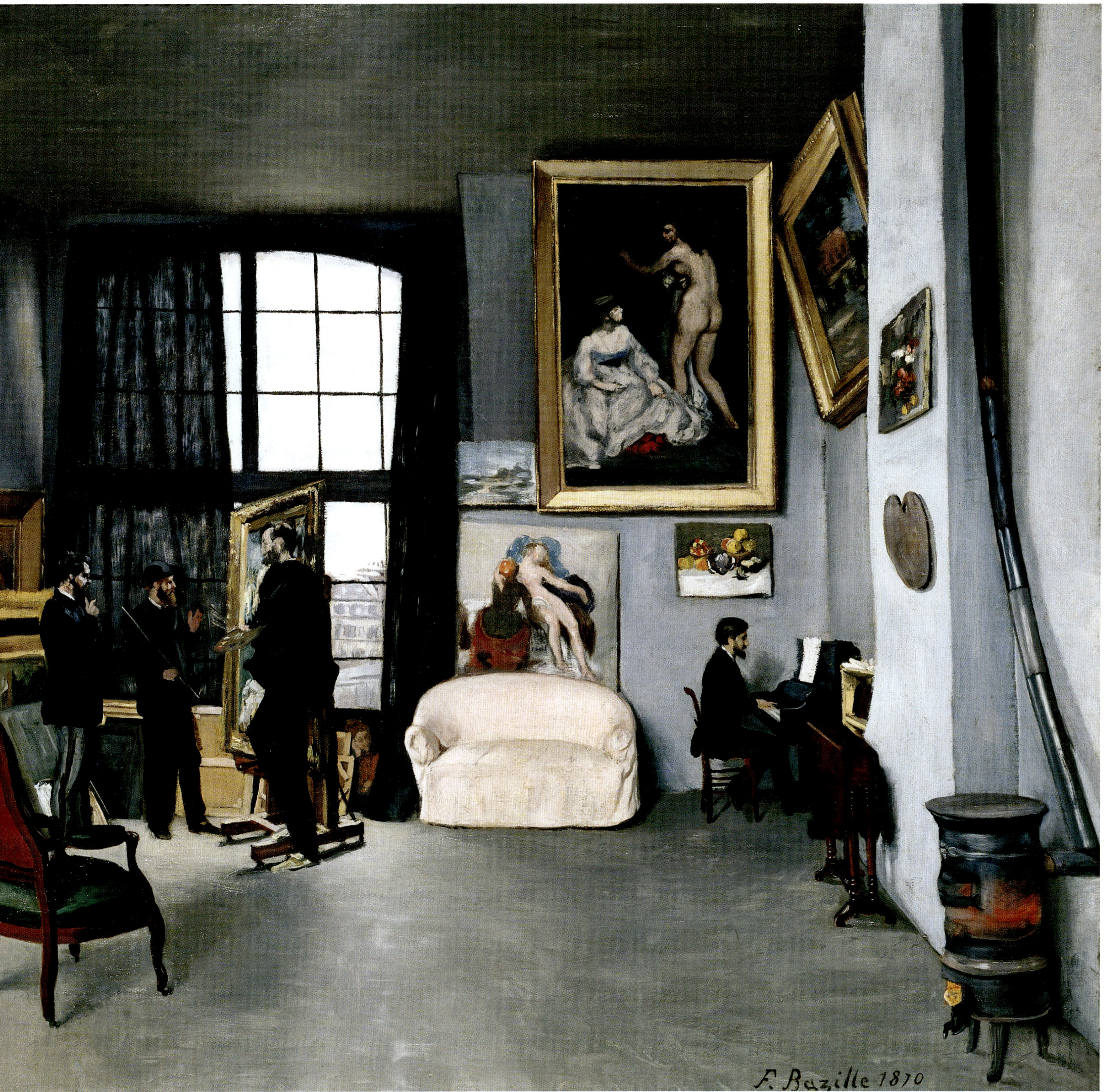
F. Bazille 1870

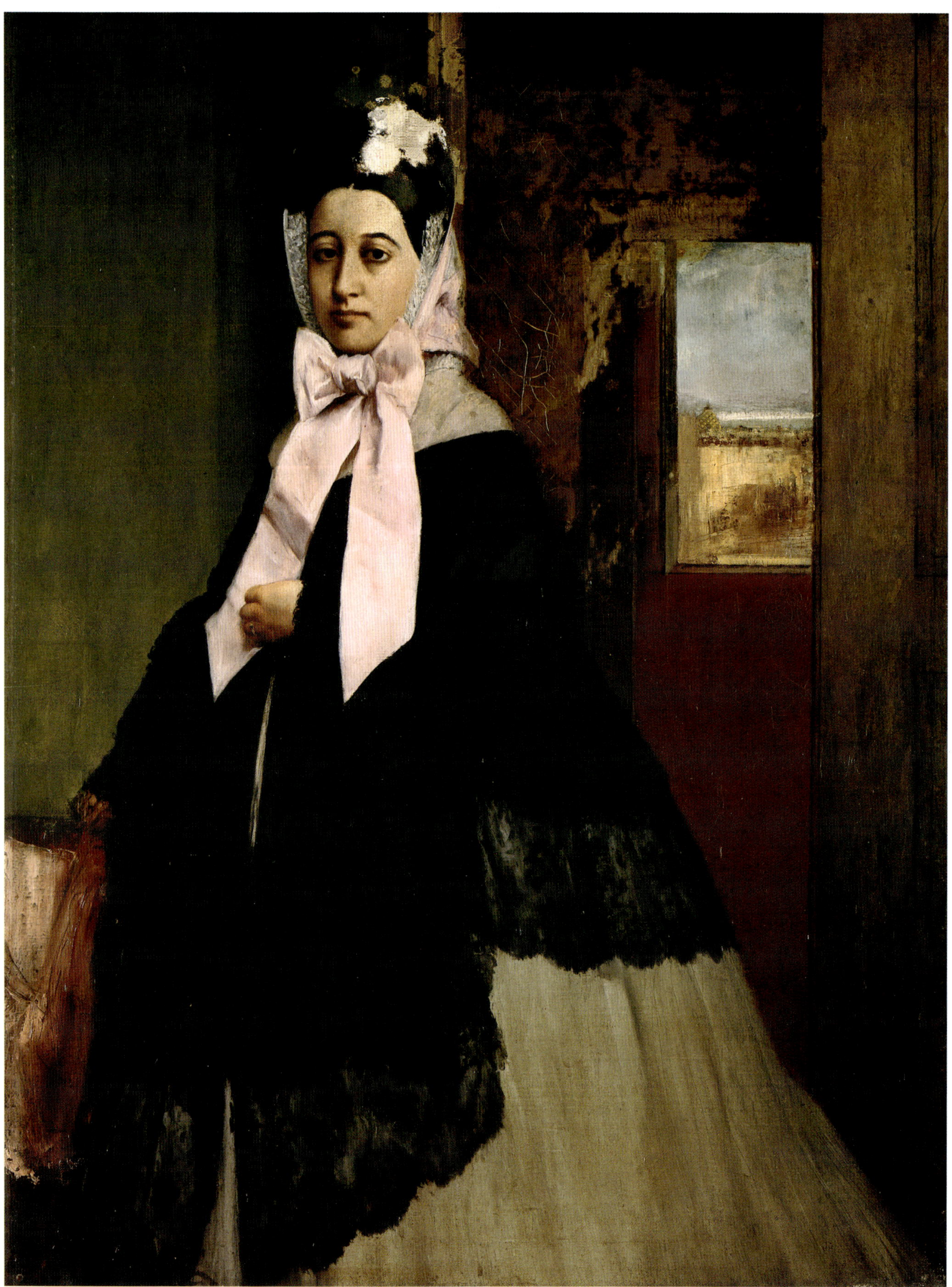

Hilaire-Germain-Edgar Degas, Portrait of Thérèse Degas *(1863). As a pupil of Louis Lemothe, Degas developed an admiration for presenting images precisely as they were. The depth of Degas's own skill can be seen in his early portraiture, in which he renders accurate likenesses of his family members. Here he presents his sister Thérèse. Her shawl suggests that she is prepared for a stroll outdoors; in fact, this is an engagement portrait, and her costume may hint to her impending departure from the family home.*

Musée d'Orsay, Paris.
Oil on canvas ($35 \times 26\frac{3}{8}$ inches).

Hilaire-Germain-Edgar Degas, Horses Before the Stands *(1866–68). Degas began to paint scenes at the racecourse around 1861. The challenging subject appealed to the analytical painter. Every aspect of horse racing was modern: a fashionable crowd, a leisure time activity, and the elements of motion and speed. In his daring approach to composition, inspired in part by Japanese prints and the new medium of photography, Degas boldly cut figures off at the border of his frame, giving the sense of spontaneous action.*

Musée d'Orsay, Paris.
Essence on paper mounted on canvas ($18\frac{1}{8} \times 24$ inches).

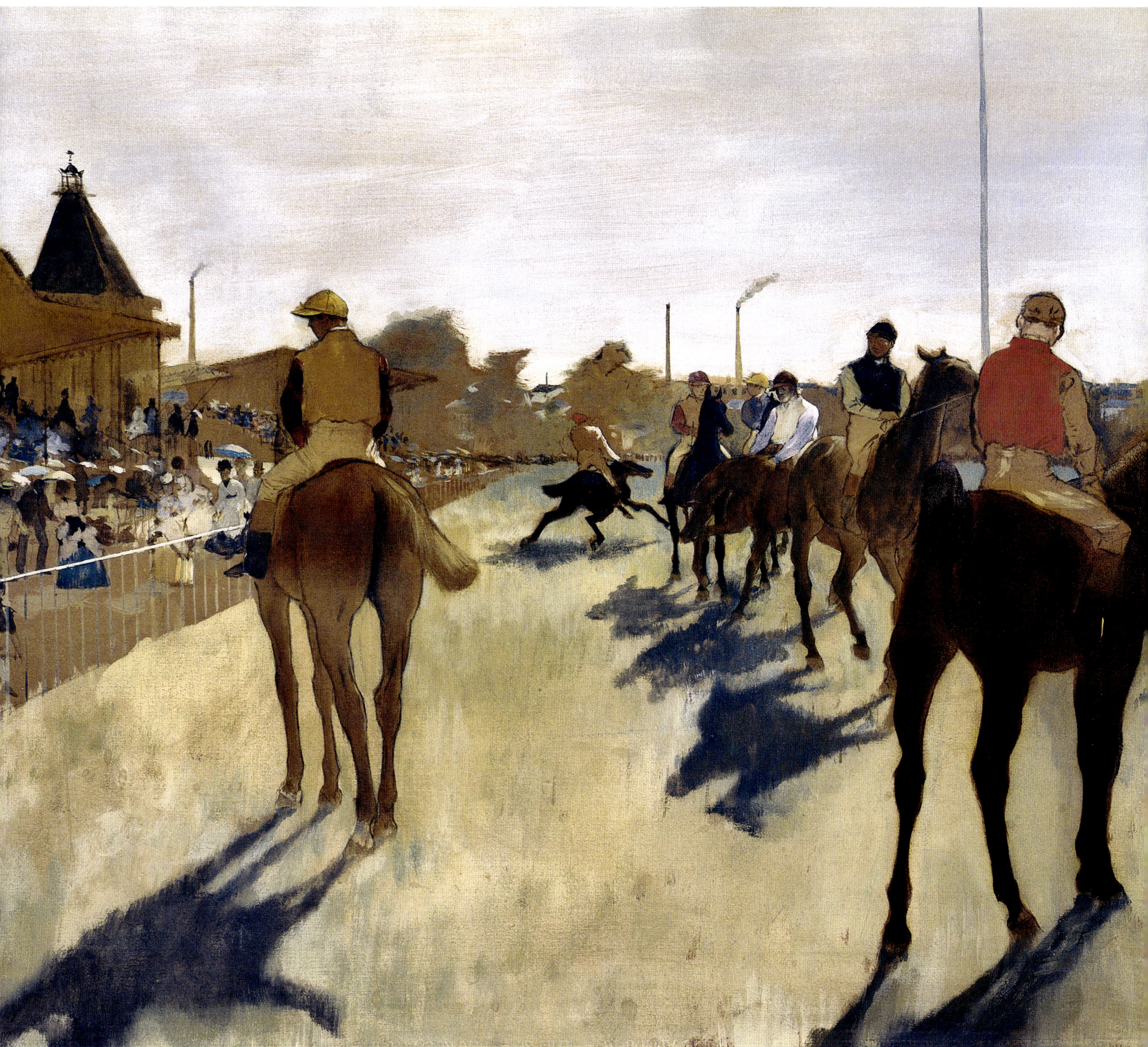

A Bold Experiment: The First Exhibition

If we must characterize them with one explanatory word, we would have to coin a new term: impressionists. *They are impressionists in that they render not the landscape but the sensation evoked by the landscape. The very word has entered their language: not* landscape *but* impression, *in the title given in the catalog for M. Monet's* Sunrise. *From this point of view, they have left reality behind for a realm of pure idealism.*

JULES CASTAGNARY, "THE EXHIBITION ON THE BOULEVARD DES CAPUCINES," *LE SIÈCLE,* APRIL 29, 1874

WHEN THE EXHIBITION of the Société Anonyme opened to the public on April 15, 1874, Claude Monet elicited the ire as well as the interest of the critics with his painting *Impression Sunrise* (1872). Late in life, recalling the sensation caused by the work, Monet explained its evocative title. "A landscape," he declared, "is only an impression," the instantaneous response of an artist to what he observes. He had been asked to affix a title to the work that portrayed a view across the harbor of Le Havre at dawn, with the boats moored at the docks enveloped in a silvery mist and a fiery sun casting orange reflections on the choppy, leaden water. Acknowledging that his subject was ephemeral—with the morning light on the water—rather than specific—with the harbor at Le Havre—Monet simply stated, "Put down *Impression.*" The conservative critics regarded the title as a provocation, challenging the conventional standards of art. *Impression Sunrise*—with its blunt brush strokes, pure unmixed pigments, and suggestive rather than descriptive approach to form—seemed unfinished, and a "sketch" was not deemed appropriate to exhibit for public view. Despite this, receptive critics recognized that Monet and his fellow artists could not be judged by the old standards. In a review for *Le Siècle,* Jules Castagnary pro-

CLAUDE MONET, Boulevard des Capucines *(1873–74). Monet portrayed lively energy in his bird's-eye view of the Boulevard des Capucines. Positioning his easel on a top floor of an apartment building, Monet studied the rhythmic patterns of pedestrian traffic and set his observations in the midst of surrounding buildings and trees under a volatile sky. The critic Jules Castagnary claimed he was unsure as to how to look at the painting because he found the point of view unsettling. However, Castagnary did praise Monet's skill at painting.*

THE NELSON-ATKINS MUSEUM OF ART, KANSAS CITY, MISSOURI. OIL ON CANVAS (31⅝×23¾ INCHES).

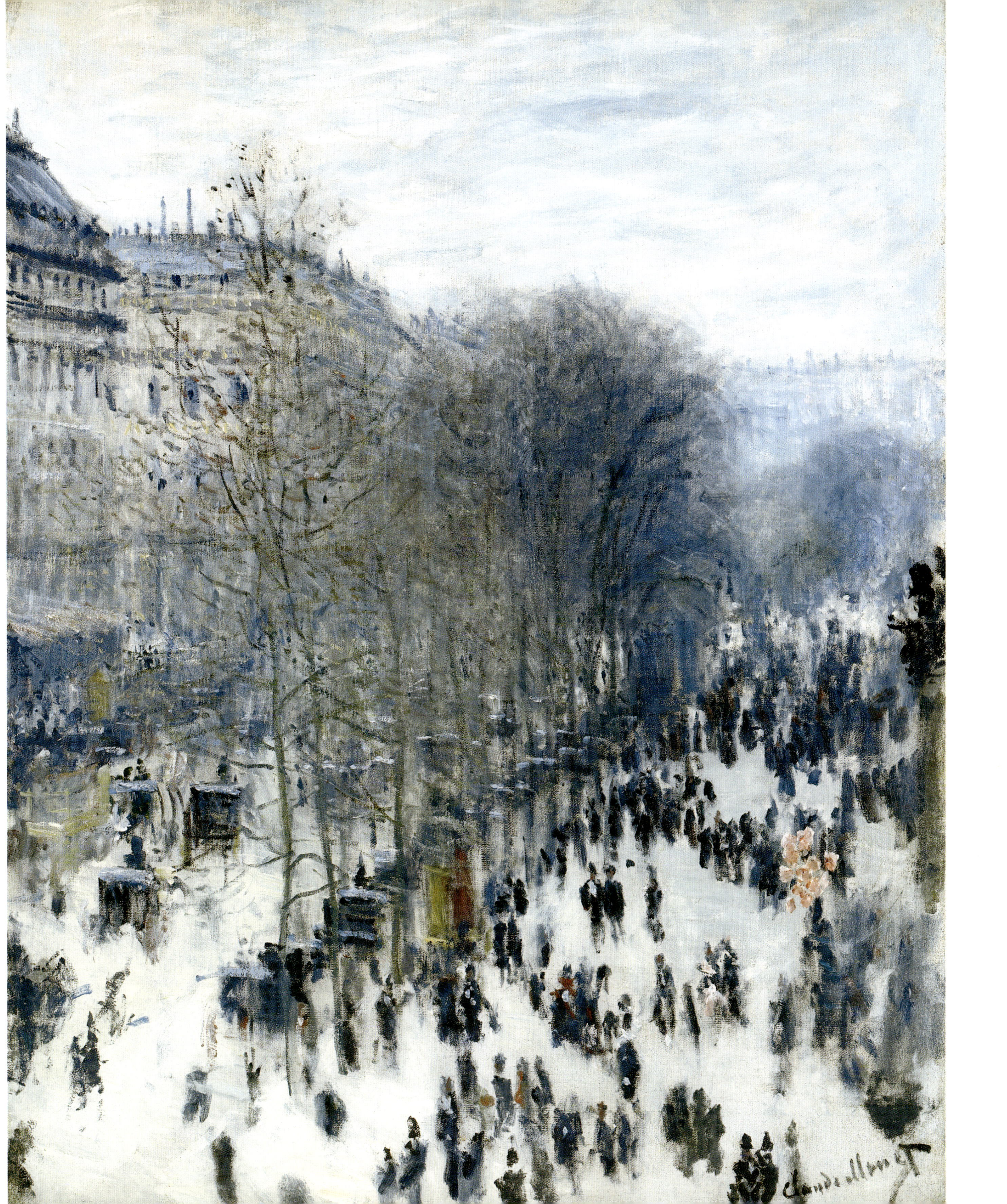

claimed that if a new term needed to be coined for these artists he would chose "impressionists," explaining that "they render not the landscape but the sensation evoked by the landscape."

The diverse nature of the works in the exhibition of the Société Anonyme proved difficult to characterize. Contrary to the implication of Castagnary's sensitive assessment, landscape was not the only type of painting represented. For instance, in addition to his seascapes and plein air views, Monet also offered the urban panorama *Boulevard des Capucines* (1873–74), a view overlooking one of the busiest avenues in Paris. Similarly, Camille Pissarro set his works both in the city and in the country, while Paul Cézanne presented a figure composition as well as plein air landscapes. Pierre-Auguste Renoir's *La Loge* (1874) portrayed a glamorous couple in a box at the opera, as much a part of the spectacle as the production on the stage. Hilaire-Germain-Edgar Degas also explored the world of modern entertainment, painting at the racecourse, the theater, and even in the dance studio. In contrast Berthe Morisot offered a glimpse of tranquil domestic life, posing her mother and sister in their homes. The 165 works in the exhibition were likewise diverse in media: oils, pastels, watercolors, and prints. Of the 30 artists in the exhibition, some were regular exhibitors at the official Salon. While most of the participants advocated modern-life subjects, and many emphasized visual sensation over accurate depiction in their approach, one common conviction united the artists of the Société Anonyme: the belief that contemporary art deserved an independent venue, free from the restrictions of tradition and convention.

The original name selected by the core group—Société Anonyme des artistes, peintres, sculpteurs, graveurs, etc. (literally, group of anonymous artists, painters, sculptors, printmakers, etc.)—indicated the members' commitment to inclusion as well as independence. The organization of the exhibition reflected the same goals. The society registered for a limited business charter on December 27, 1873. The charter defined the exhibition as a collective endeavor. For a reasonable fee, members could purchase a share of the operation, entitling them to submit two works to the exhibition. Unlike the official Salon, the works would be selected by the artists themselves rather than an appointed jury. Artists could set their own prices for purchase but were required to pay 10 percent of their profits into the corporation. All members were guaranteed equal rights and were expected to help promote and organize the exhibition. Although the charter strictly stated that membership entitled an artist to just two submissions, most of the participants were more generously represented; for example, Monet and Morisot each had nine works in the exhibi-

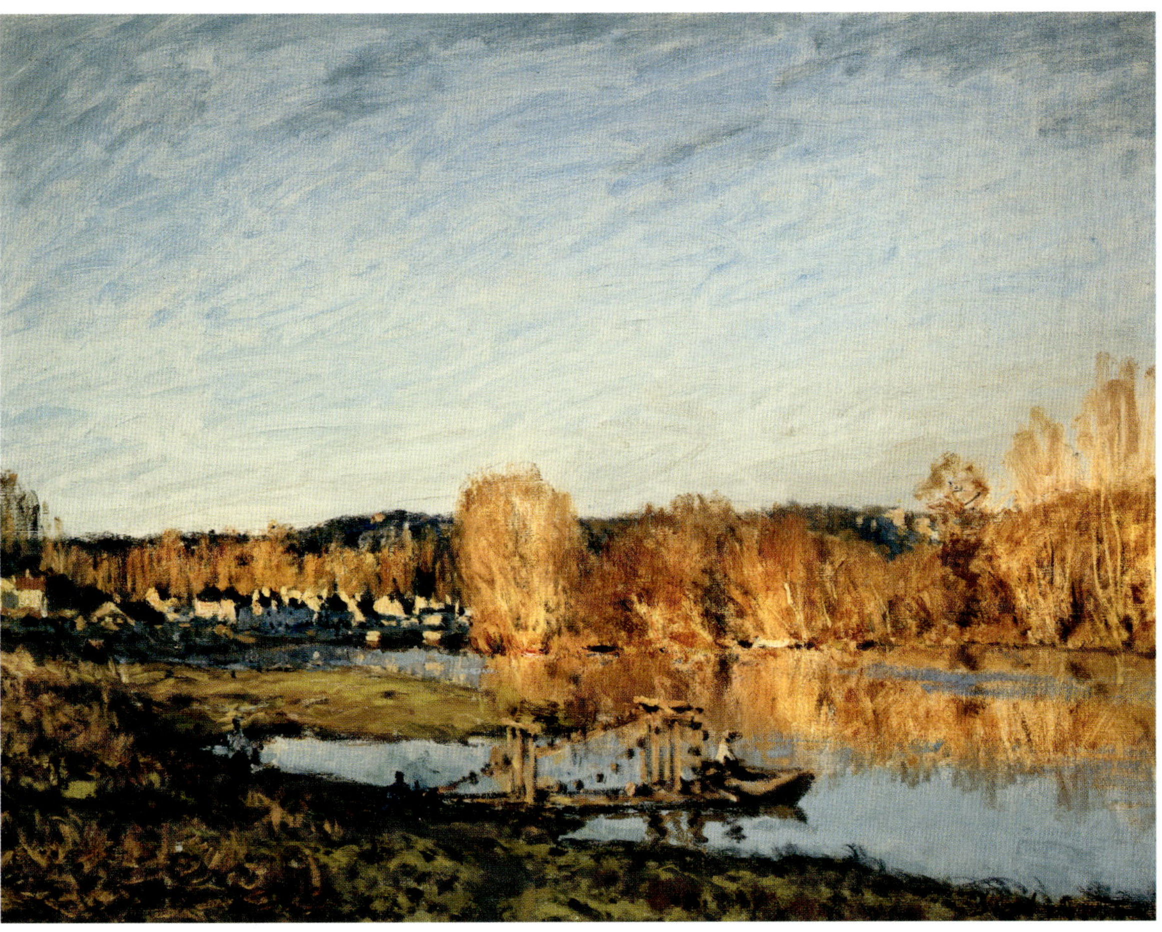

Alfred Sisley, Autumn: Banks of the Seine near Bougival *(1873). Sisley was a dedicated plein air painter. In this landscape he uses color to convey autumn. The band of trees along the shoreline are ablaze with russet-red leaves. The reflection of this color on the water is only slightly muted, contrasting with the pale blue water that repeats the color of the sky. Jean Prouvaire, a critic who admitted to only modest admiration of Sisley's work, found this landscape superior to other landscapes in the exhibition.*

Montreal Museum of Fine Arts. Oil on canvas (18¼×24⁵⁄₁₆ inches).

tion, and Degas had ten. In addition to the original 16 signatories, other artists were invited and no limits were placed upon what they were allowed to show. (Edouard Manet was invited to participate, but he refused.) The most notable feature of the exhibition was the trust placed in the individual artist to choose the works and in the public to attend and assess the exhibition.

The exhibition was held in three rooms of a studio leased by the photographer Felix Tournachon, known as Nadar. The studio occupied the upper floor of a new apartment building on the fashionable Boulevard des Capucines; Monet had painted his urban vista looking out the window. The manner in which the exhibition was installed furthered the group's dual objectives of independence and equality. A hanging committee, headed by Renoir, took responsibility for placing the pictures on the wall, but the order of appearance was chosen by lot to avoid favoritism. All of an artist's works appeared together, hung in two rows on the walls with the larger works above and the smaller below. This was a stark contrast to the practice of the Salon, where works were hung edge to edge, from waist height on the wall up to the ceiling.

The exhibition debuted two weeks in advance of the official Salon—a deliberate strategy that drew critical attention—and it ran for a month. The doors were open every day from 10 A.M. to 6 P.M., but additional evening hours from 8 P.M. to 10 P.M. brought the exhibition a wider audience. A small entry fee was charged with an even smaller price for a catalogue that listed the participants and their submissions. When the exhibition closed on May 15, around 3,500 visitors had attended. Some of the works had startled the public, some had delighted them, and a number had been sold. But the most important aspect of this bold experiment was the creation of a public venue where artists could present their works directly to an audience for review and purchase without an intermediary.

A Bold Experiment

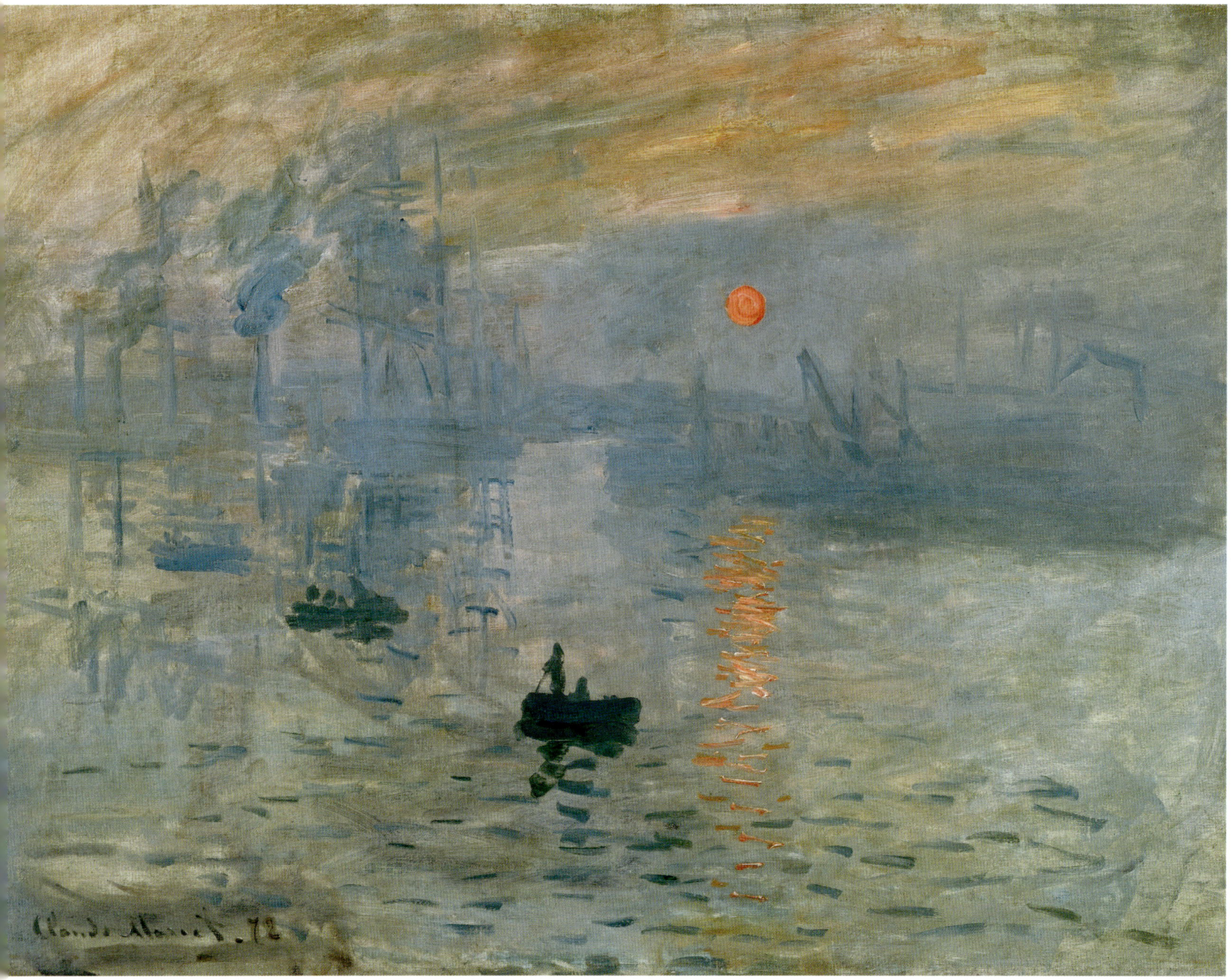

Claude Monet, Impression Sunrise *(1872). Monet regarded this painting as a collection of visual sensations: a burning-red sun, a misty atmosphere, and the black and violet silhouettes of boats bobbing on the water. Rather than identify the location of the scene, he chose to evoke a spectacular effect. The critics seized upon the title* Impression *to indicate that the works of Monet and his colleagues lacked the finish of accomplished Salon paintings.*

Musée Marmottan, Paris. Oil on canvas ($18\frac{7}{8} \times 24\frac{3}{4}$ inches).

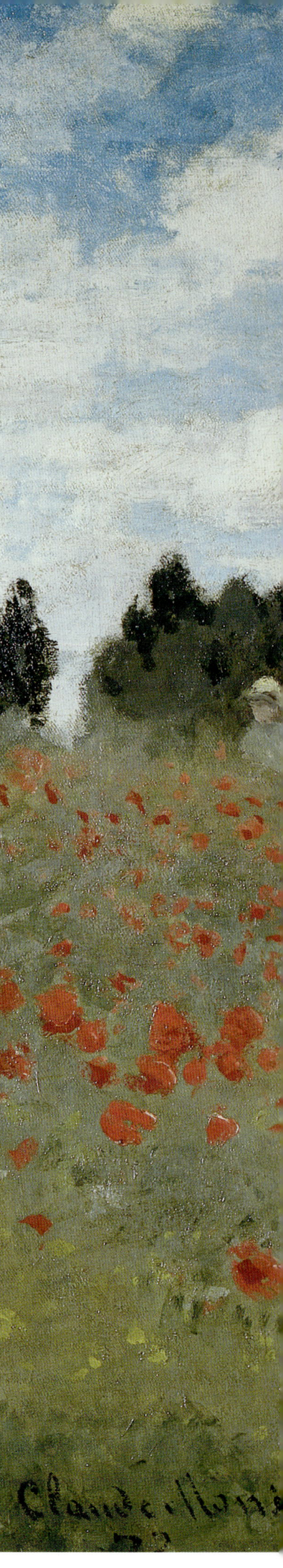

Claude Monet, The Poppy Field, near Argenteuil *(1873). Nine of Monet's works were at the exhibition of the Société Anonyme. In this one, his wife and son can be seen moving through a field of poppies. The grass and flowers sway gently in the wind, and the sky is studded with swiftly moving clouds. Monet's desire to capture the elusive effects of nature—light, motion, and temperature—transcended his interest in narrative subject, an idea that traditional critics found difficult to grasp.*

Musée d'Orsay, Paris. Oil on canvas ($19\frac{5}{8} \times 25\frac{5}{8}$ inches).

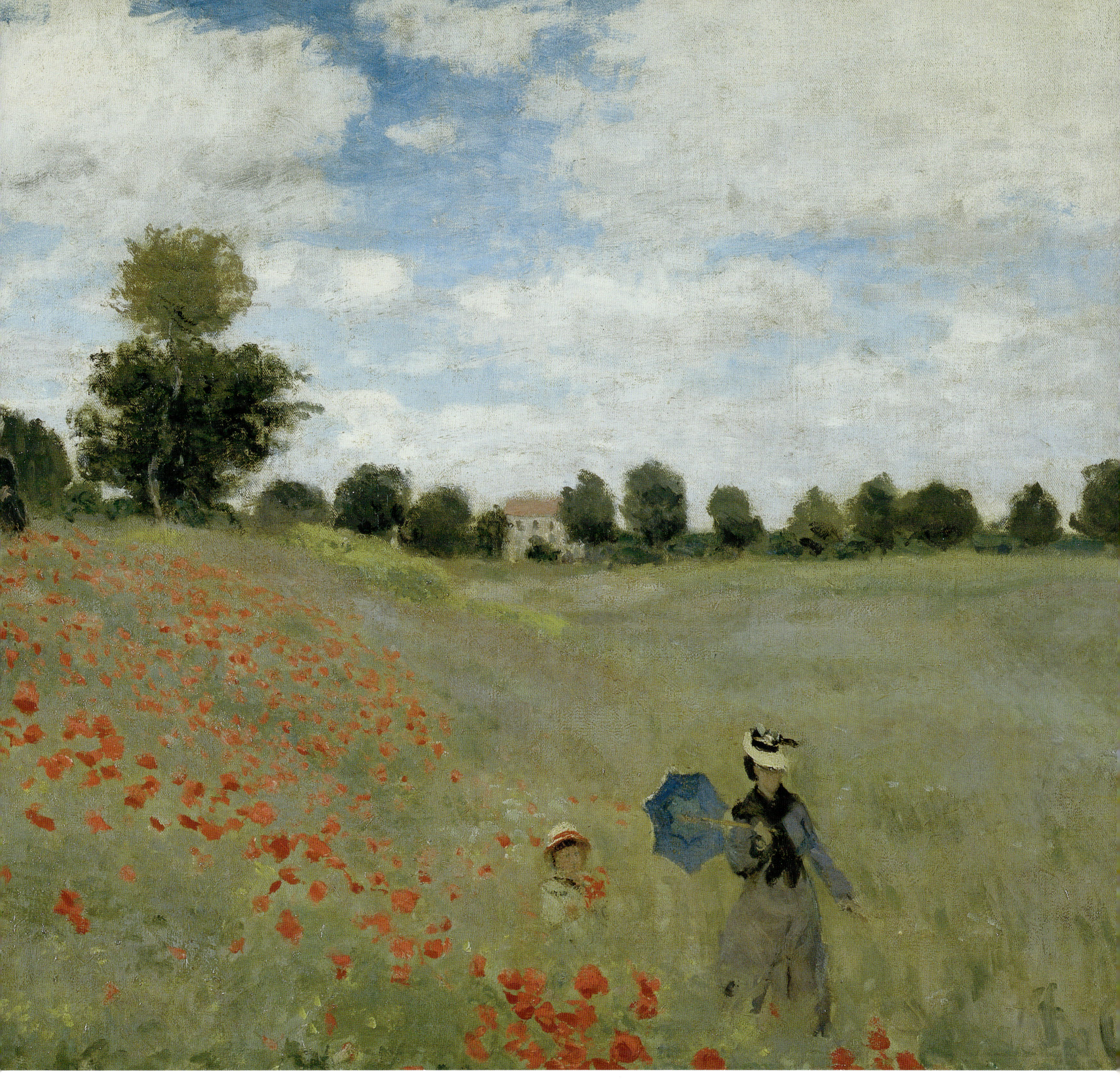

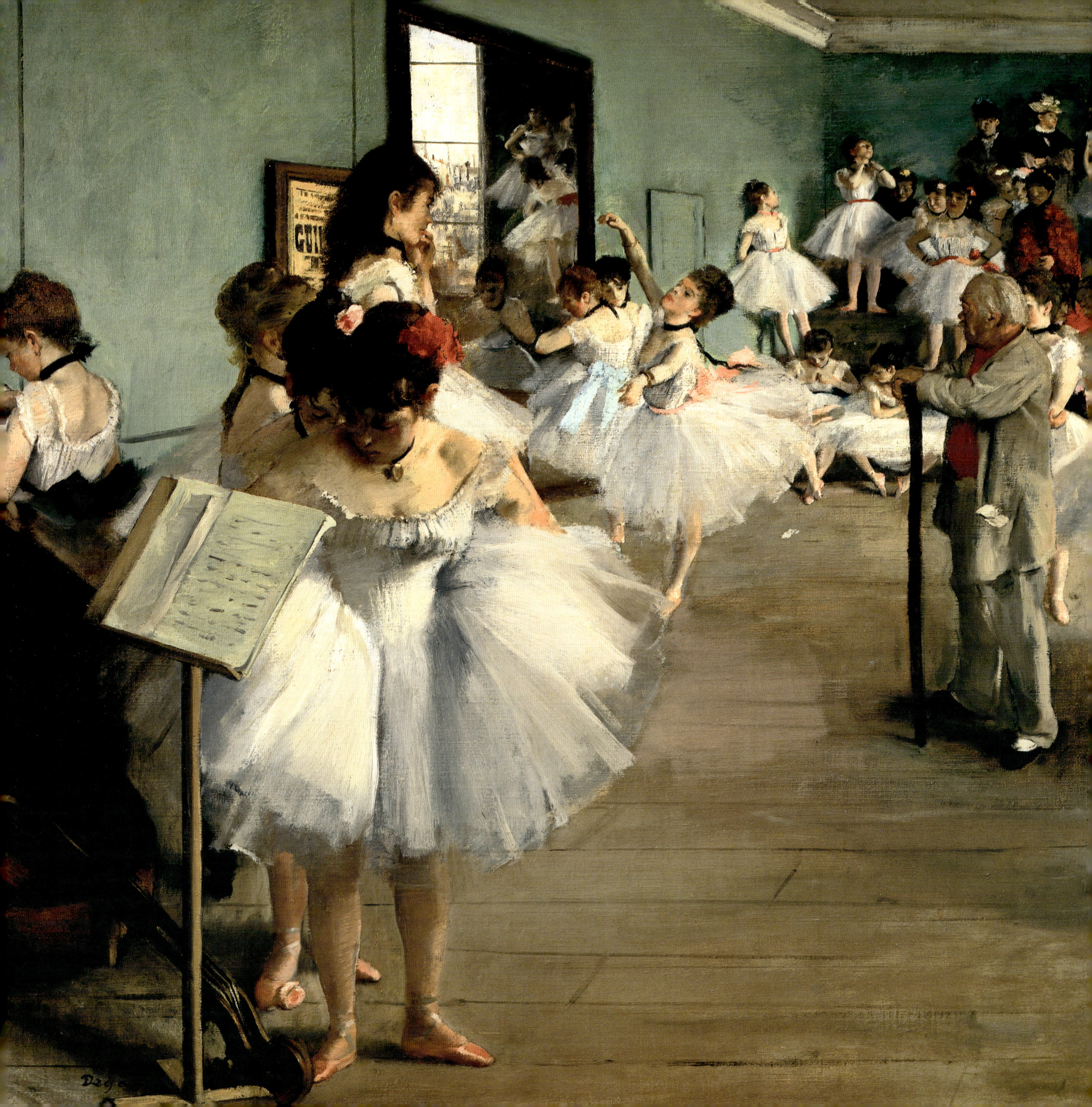

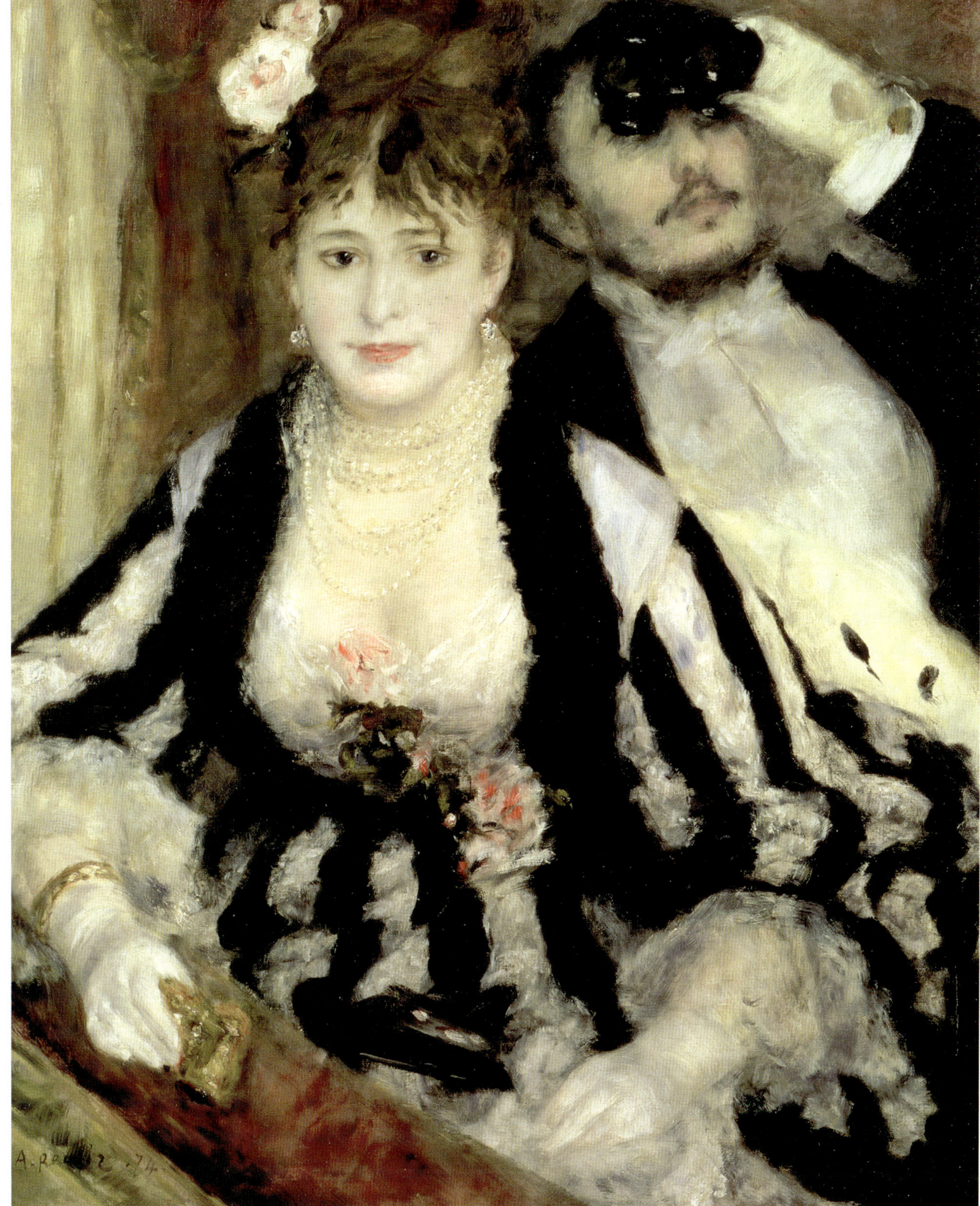

Hilaire-Germain-Edgar Degas (French, 1834–1917), The Dance Class *(c. 1874). Degas began to paint ballet dancers in 1872. He attended rehearsals, observed classes, and watched the dancers at the Paris Opera both from a seat in the audience and from the wings. His interest was the subtlety of movement rather than dance as an expressive art form. The turn of a foot or the bend of an elbow caught his eye as a swift and graceful motion, but he was equally intrigued by the awkward postures assumed by the dancers as they stretched or rested.*

The Metropolitan Museum of Art, New York. Oil on canvas ($32\frac{3}{4} \times 30\frac{1}{4}$ inches).

Pierre-Auguste Renoir, La Loge *(1874). Visits to the theater were part of sophisticated Parisian life. A loge, or theater box, was private, but it was also a showcase for the theater patron, who could be observed in fashionable and flattering evening dress. Renoir features a beautiful young woman in a dramatic dress looking directly at the viewer, while her companion points his opera glasses for a better look at another patron.*

Courtauld Institute Gallery, London. Oil on canvas ($31\frac{1}{2} \times 25$ inches).

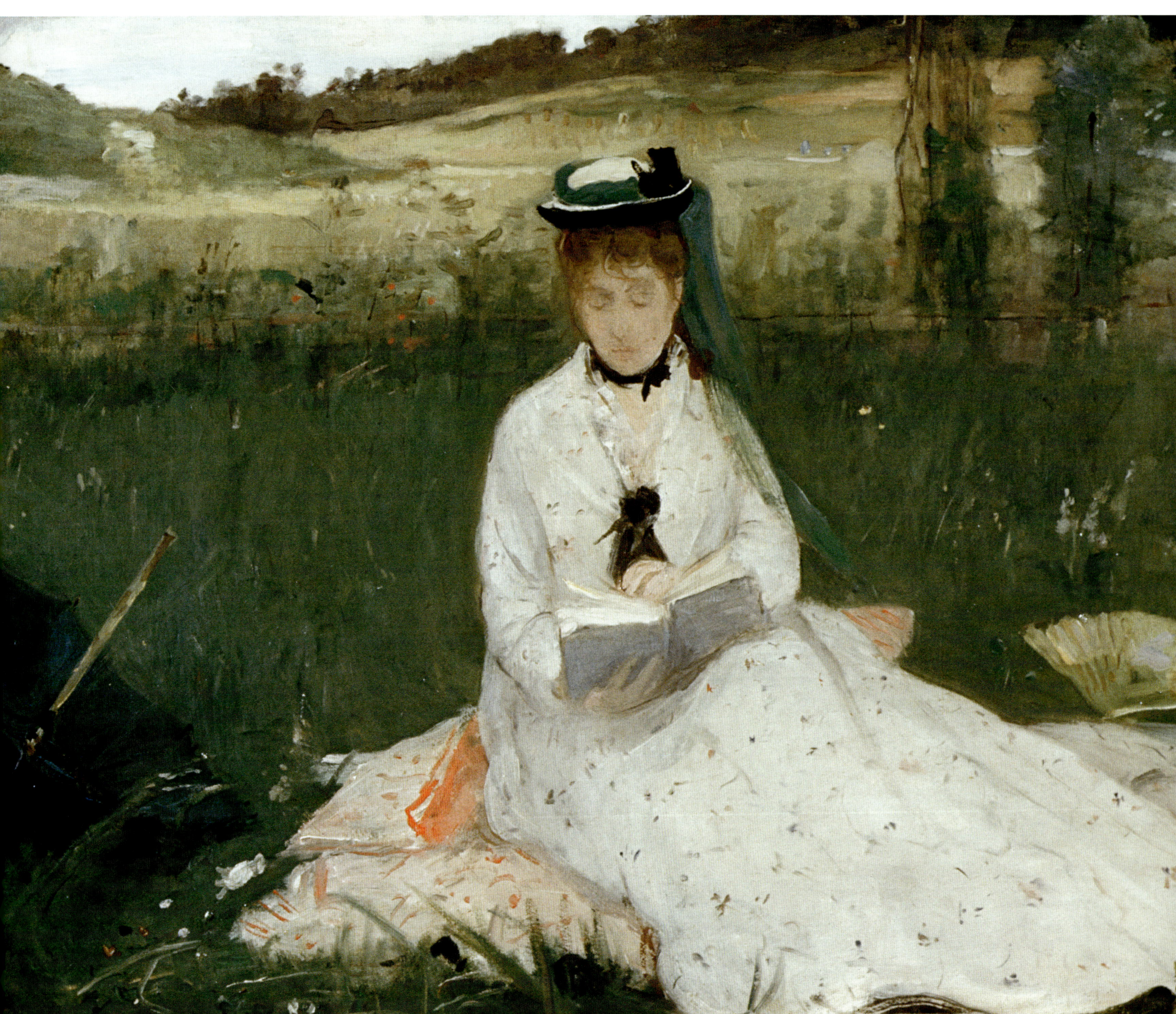

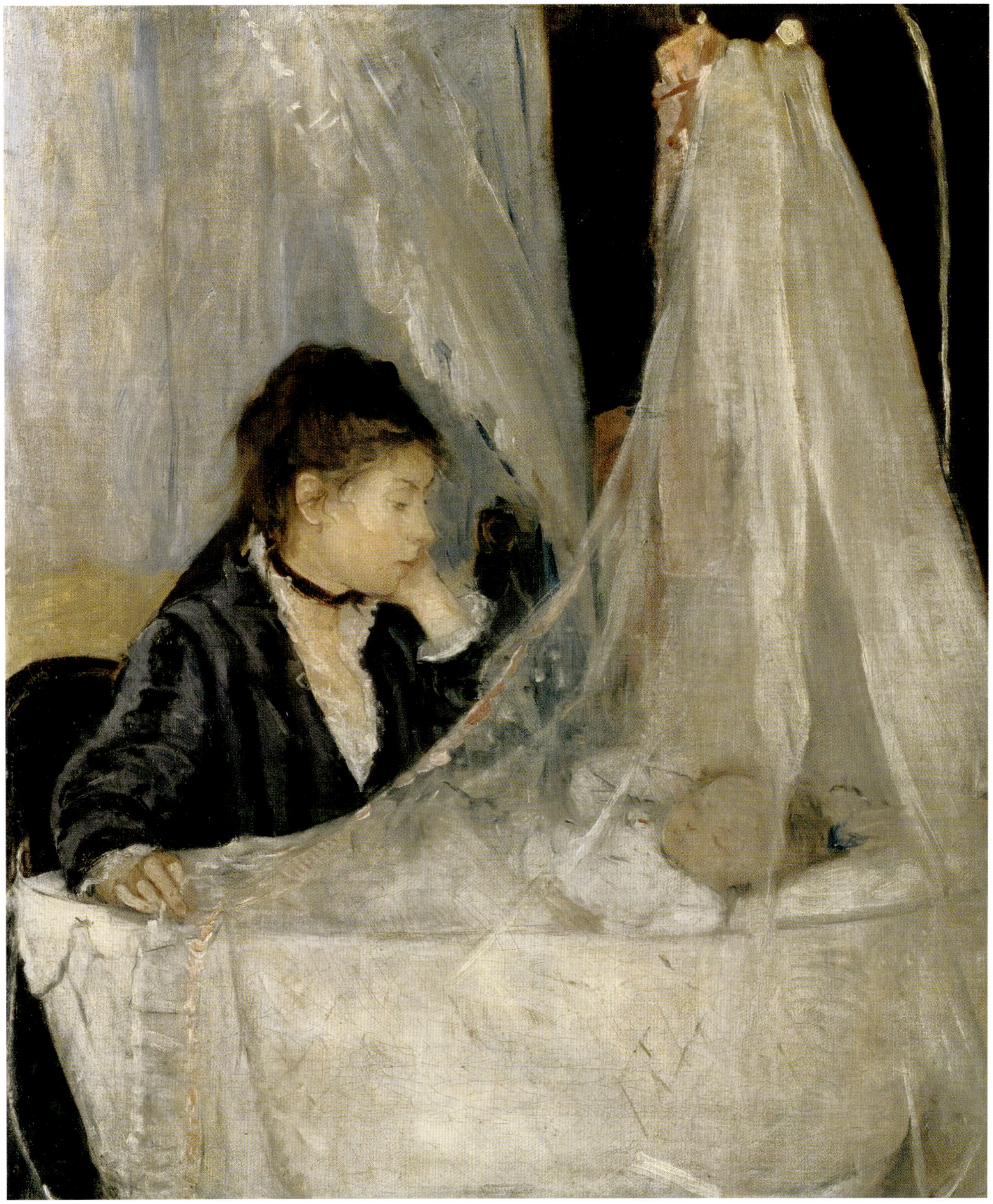

Berthe Morisot, Reading *(1873). In* Reading, *Morisot tackles a subject previously explored by Claude Monet and Pierre-Auguste Renoir: a contemporary woman in a park, enjoying a leisure activity. Featured here is Morisot's sister Edma. Edma wears a light, gauzy summer gown of the latest cut. A straw hat with a trailing scarf perched on the top of her head, an open fan, and a parasol complete her ensemble. Critics praised Morisot's work as graceful, confident, and even witty.*

The Cleveland Museum of Art. Oil on fabric ($18\frac{1}{8} \times 28\frac{1}{4}$ inches).

Berthe Morisot, The Cradle *(1872). Morisot's sister Edma modeled as the mother for* The Cradle. *The infant is Edma's own newborn Blanche. Morisot focused upon the day-to-day experiences of the lives of contemporary women. In presenting a mother watching her child sleep in a cradle, Morisot expresses the genuine absorption of a mother's attentions to her child's well-being without introducing an anecdote or an exaggerated sentimentality.*

Musée d'Orsay, Paris. Oil on canvas (22×18 inches).

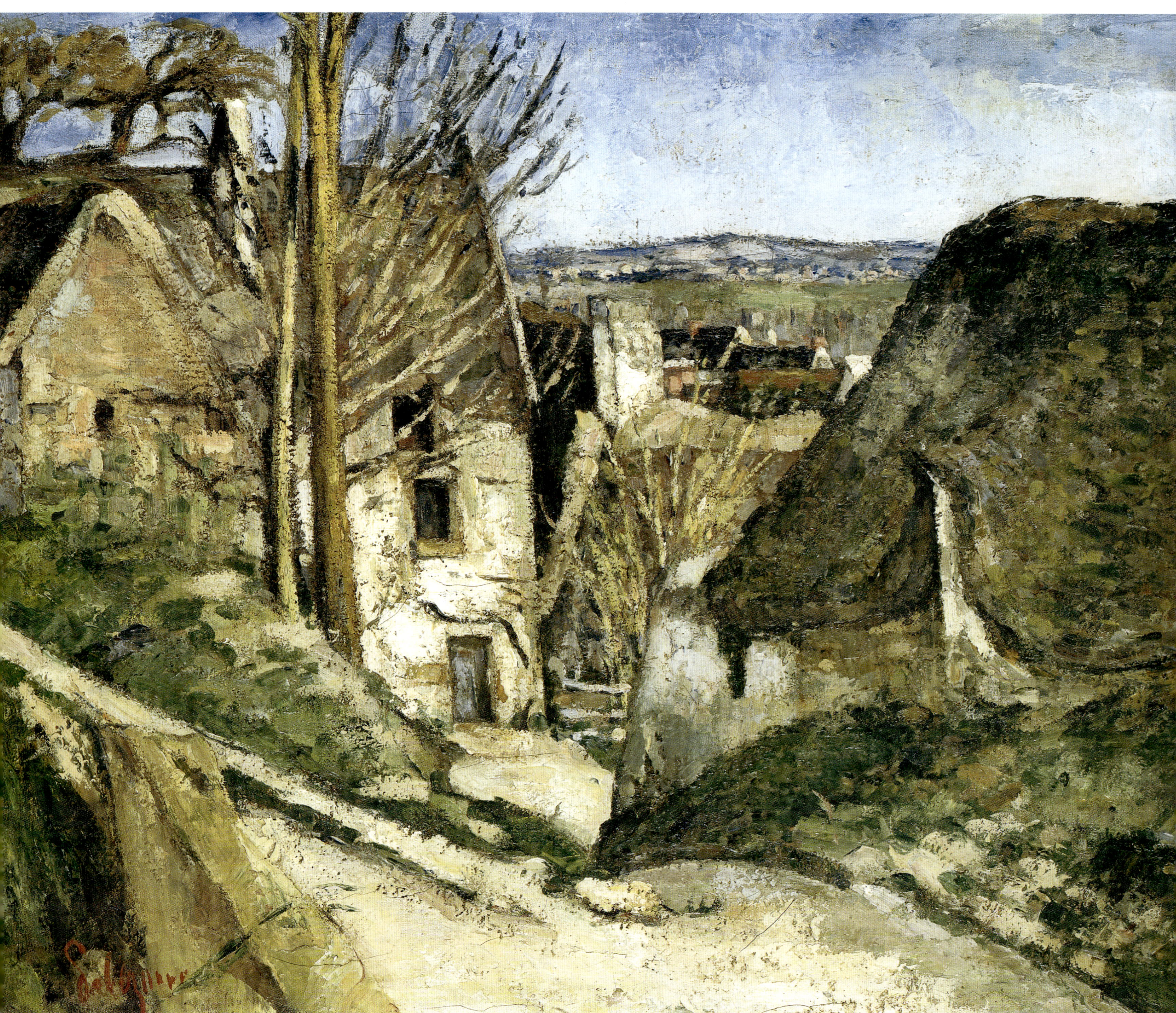

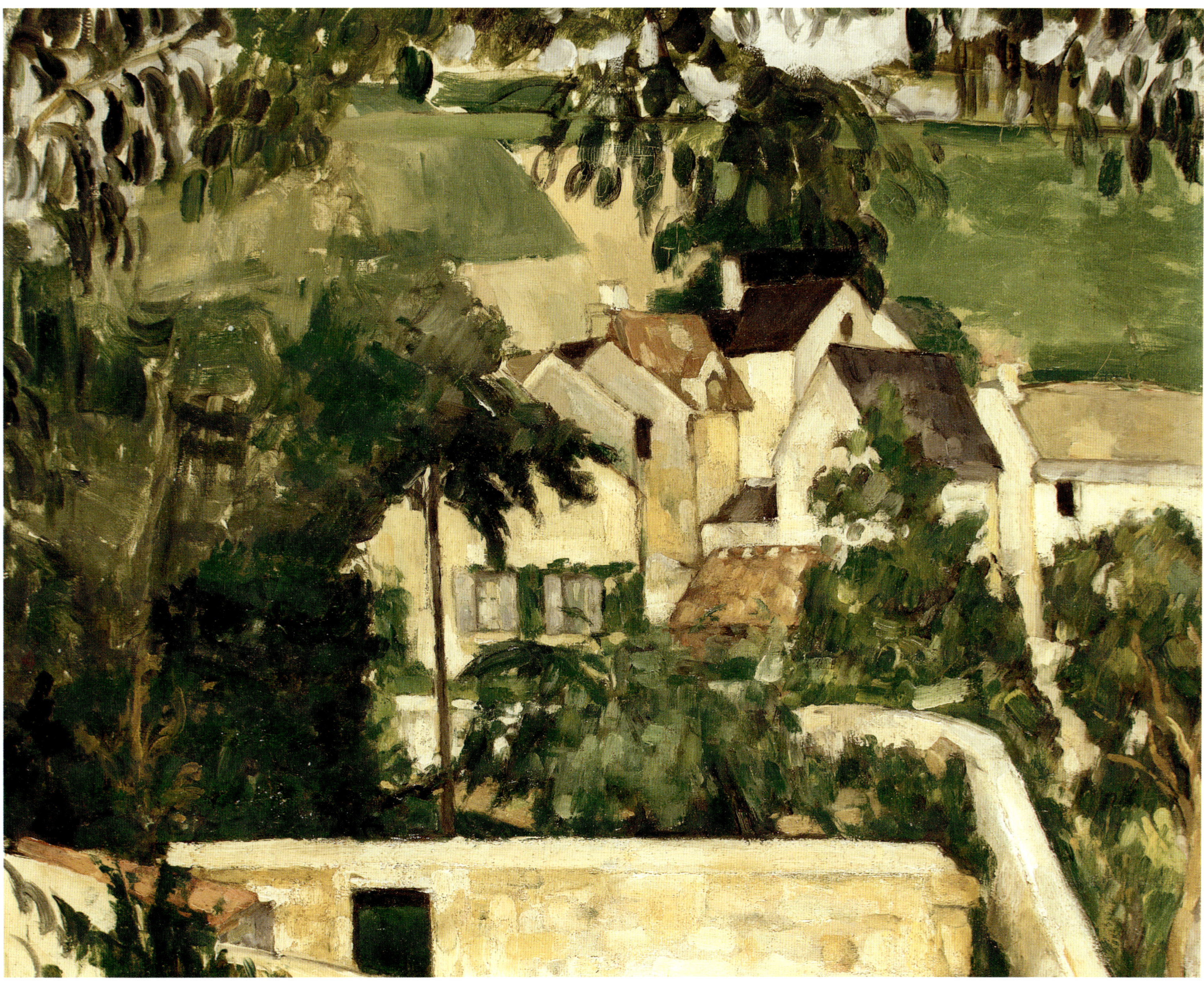

Paul Cézanne, The House of the Hanged Man *(1873). The title of this painting served only as a pretext for Cézanne's landscape. He applied his paint with a heavy hand and worked the surface with a palette knife. The resulting impasto (the thick paint application) and Cézanne's rigorously constructed composition marked a difference from the landscape approach of Claude Monet and Berthe Morisot that quickly characterized the Impressionist circle.*

Musée d'Orsay, Paris. Oil on canvas (21¾×26 inches).

Paul Cézanne, Study: Landscape at Auvers *(c. 1873). Of the three works that represented Cézanne at the first exhibition, this landscape earned the warmest reception. The critic Jean Prouvaire questioned the Salon jury's rejection of Cézanne, and critic Émile Zola exalted Cézanne. Shedding the dark palette of his earlier works, Cézanne was beginning to be attentive to the structure, rather than the appearance, of his subjects; he was starting to move away from the spontaneous imagery that critics linked with Impressionism.*

Philadelphia Museum of Art. Oil on canvas (18¼×21¾ inches).

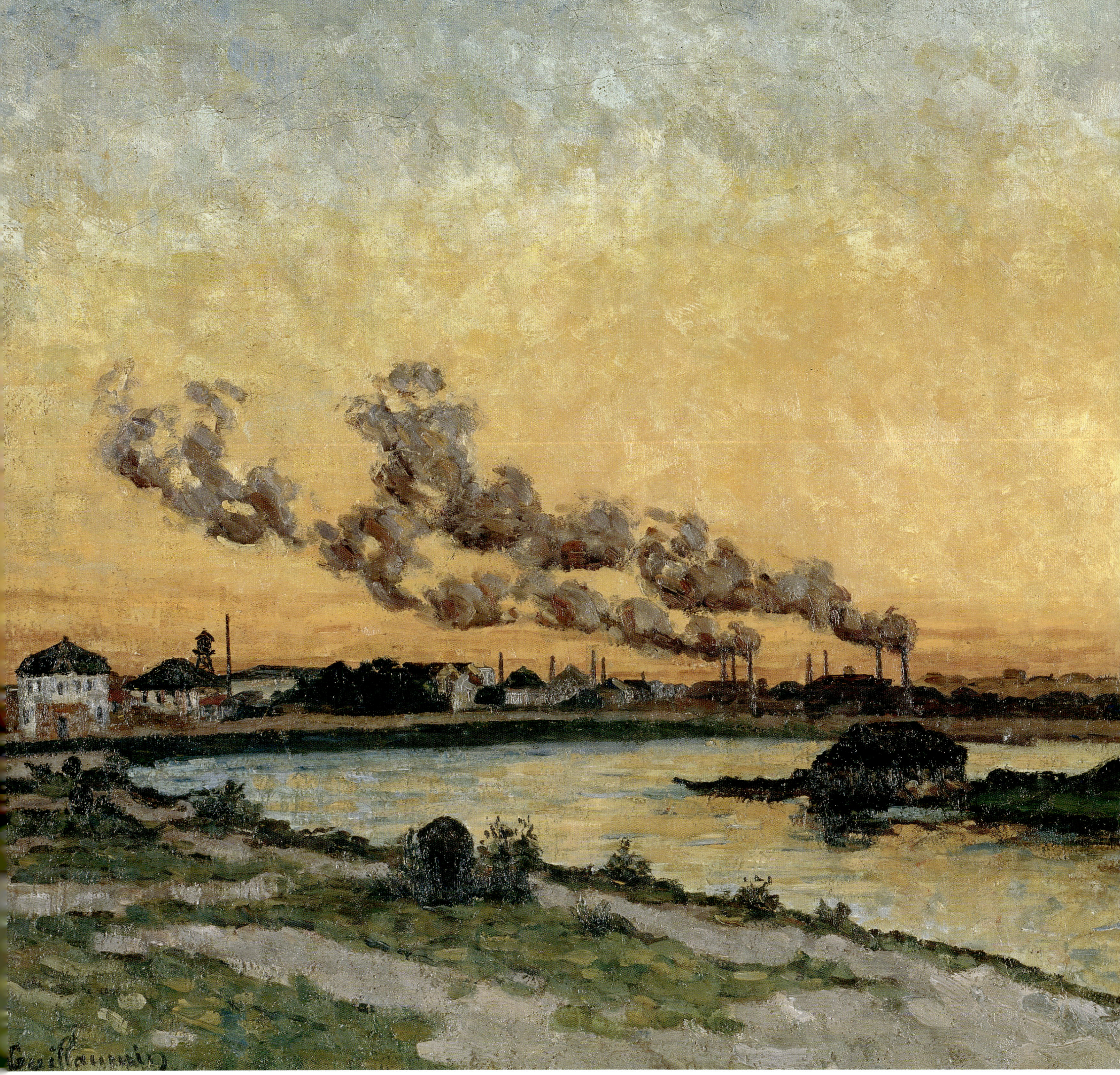
Guillaumin

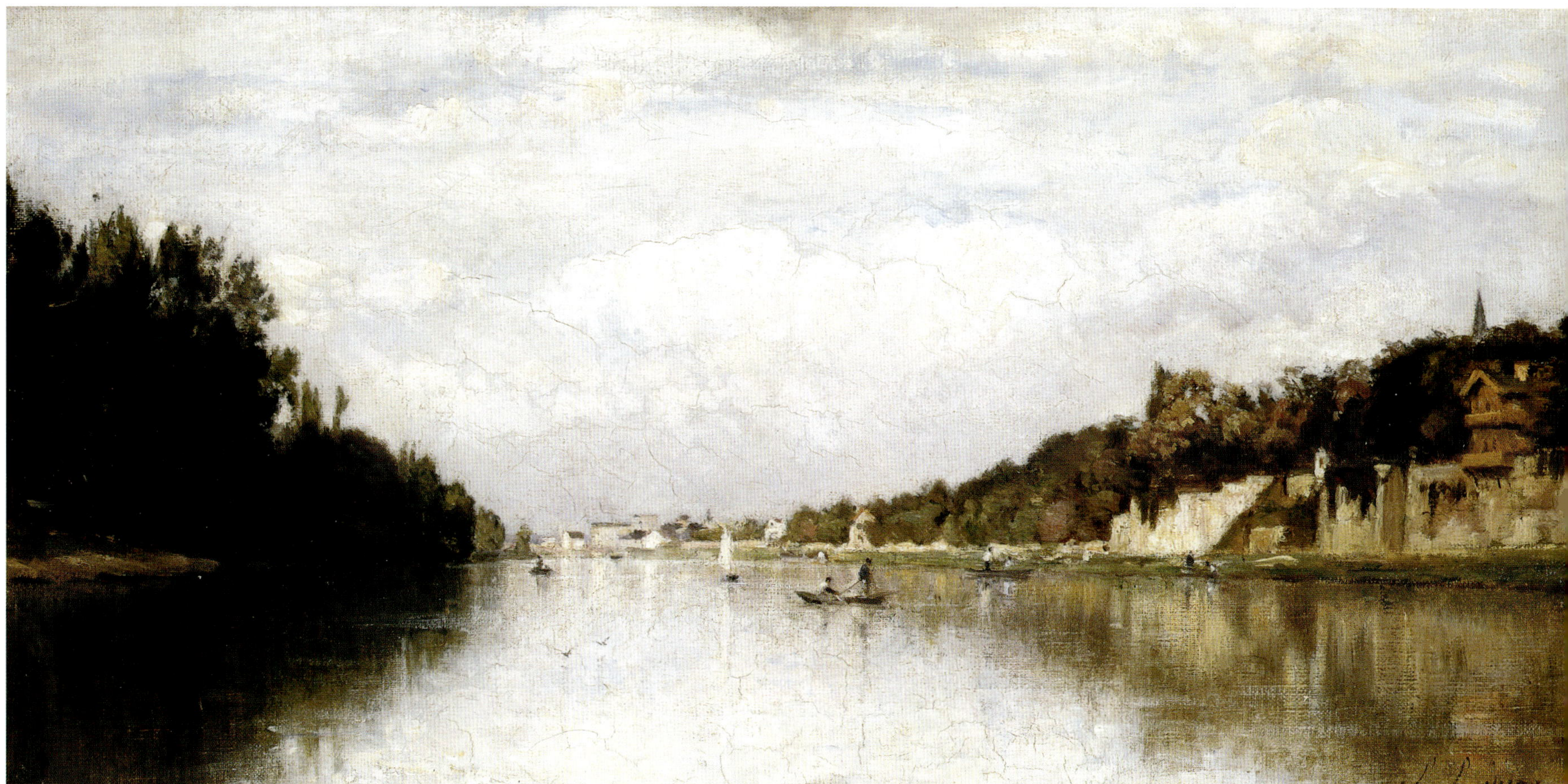

STANISLAS LEPINE, Banks of the Seine *(1869). Lepine only exhibited with the Impressionists in the first exhibition. Among his three works was* Banks of the Seine, *a serene view of the river from a point on the water that allowed Lepine to include both banks. His attentive rendering of reflections on the water—distinct at the highly lit right shore and obscured on the left—is similar to Claude Monet's and Camille Pissarro's river views.*

MUSÉE D'ORSAY, PARIS. OIL ON CANVAS (11⅞×23 INCHES).

JEAN-BAPTISTE ARMAND GUILLAUMIN, Setting Sun at Ivry *(1873). Guillaumin's view of Ivry embraces both nature and industry. The setting sun colors the broad sky, giving full play to temporal light effects. But the factory smokestacks billow steamy plumes that dissolve into the atmosphere, adding to the visual sensation. It was characteristic of members of the Impressionist circle to accept the modern landscape as they found it without idealization or judgment. Technology—in the form of factories and smokestacks—was simply another fact of contemporary life.*

MUSÉE D'ORSAY, PARIS. OIL ON CANVAS (25½×31⅞ INCHES).

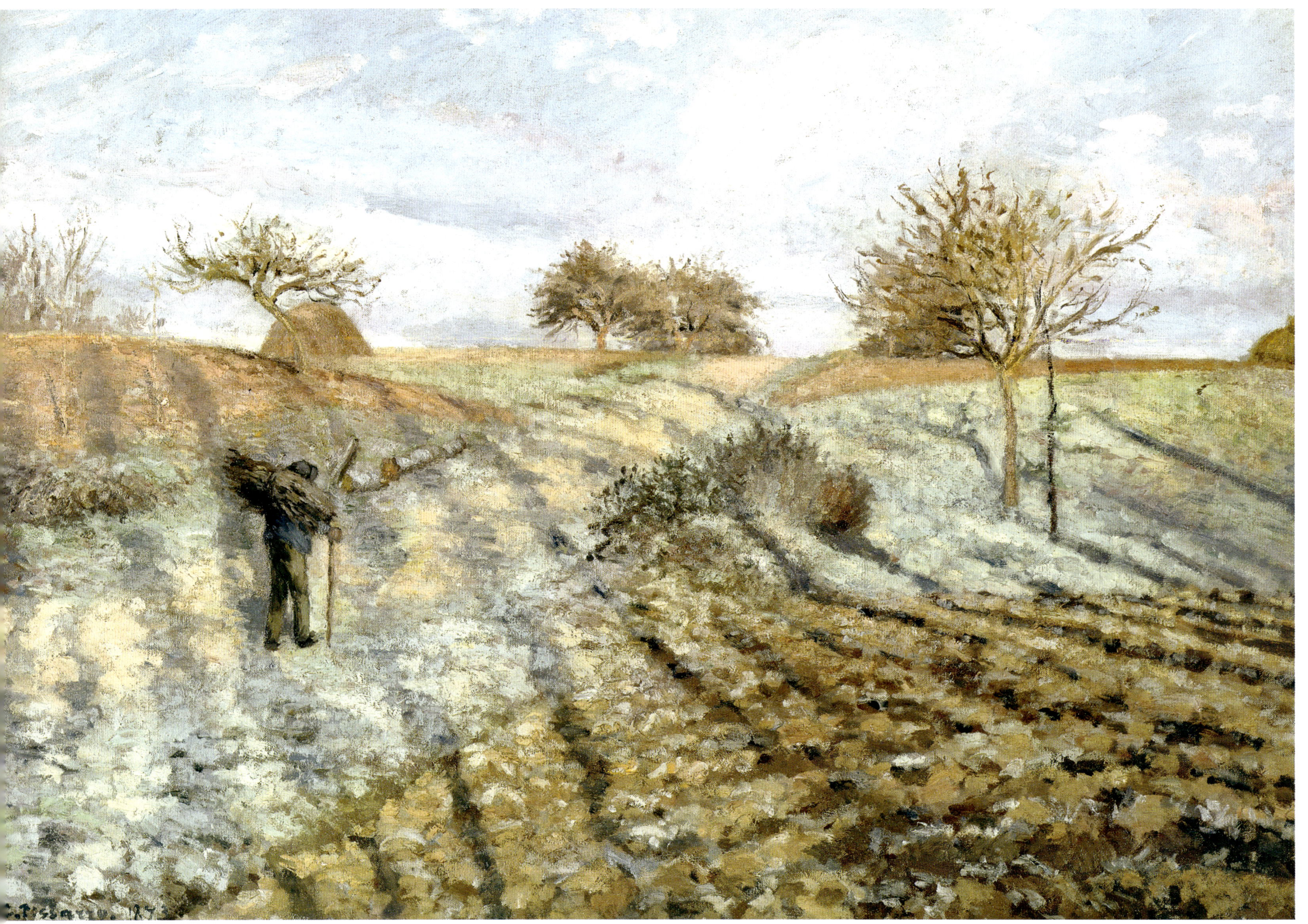

Camille Pissarro, Hoarfrost *(1873). With cool colors and a whitish glaze, Pissarro portrays the effects of frost upon a plowed field. The aqua sky appears deceptively warm and bright, but the bent figure, carrying his load of branches, is heavily garbed against the chilly air. This work received mixed critical responses, especially from critic Jules Castagnary, who praised some aspects of the painting but disliked others.*

Musée d'Orsay, Paris. Oil on canvas (25⅝×36⅝ inches).

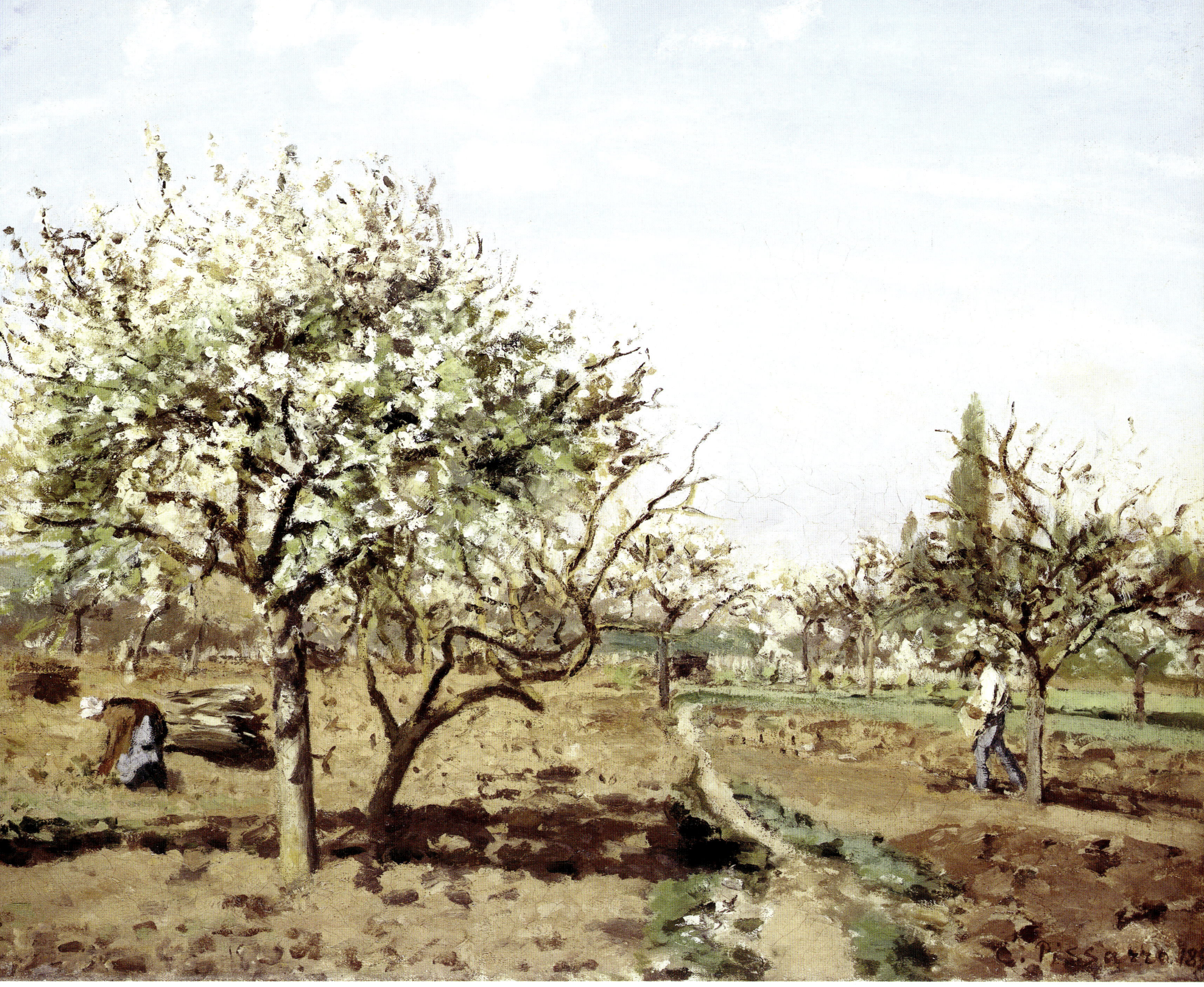

Camille Pissarro, Orchard in Bloom, Louveciennes *(1872). Pissarro resided in Louveciennes, a village roughly 15 miles west of Paris, in 1869. He sought refuge in London during the outbreak of the Franco-Prussian War but returned after the Armistice in 1871. In his view of an orchard in bloom, the delicate handling of the pale sky streaked with thin clouds strikes the atmospheric effect of cool spring air. The muted shadows on the ground and the bright flower petals on the trees shimmering in the sun heighten the sensation.*

National Gallery of Art, Washington, D.C. Oil on canvas (17¾×21⅝ inches).

Widening Influence: Second, Third, and Fourth Exhibitions

I do not want to predict what the future holds for the artists of the rue le Peletier; will they pass for masters one day? They might; then Degas will take the place that Ingres holds now, while that of Delacroix is saved for Claude Monet, the dazzling colorist of the group.

Arthur Baignères, *L'Echo Universel,* April 13, 1876

The first exhibition of the Société Anonyme succeeded in bringing a circle of independent and progressive artists to public and critical attention, but it was a commercial failure. The sales of works had been modest, and as a result, the percentage paid back to the chartered corporation did not provide enough to cover the cost of each member's initial share. In December 1874, the Société Anonyme declared bankruptcy and dissolved its charter. Claude Monet, Berthe Morisot, Pierre-Auguste Renoir, and Alfred Sisley held a joint auction of their previously exhibited works. The gallery owner Paul Durand-Ruel organized the sale, but the profits fell far short of the artists' expectations. Despite these difficulties, the core group decided to hold another exhibition. Durand-Ruel agreed to host it in his gallery on the rue le Peletier. As before, they invited others to participate. When the list of submissions was complete, there were 19 artists included, 11 fewer than in the first exhibition. But, with 250 works on display, each individual artist was well represented, and with the original circle dominating the selection—Degas with 24 works, Monet with 18, Morisot with 17—they established an even stronger public identity. Once again, Manet was invited but declined, deciding instead to mount a solo exhibition of his work in his own studio.

There was a striking range of diversity in subject and style, most notably among the core members. Along with his plein air landscapes, Monet pre-

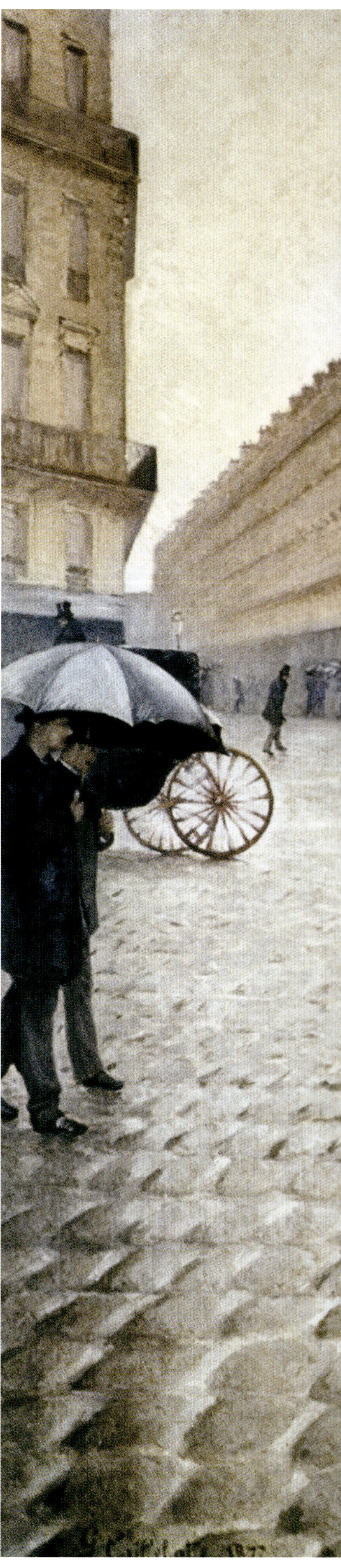

Gustave Caillebotte, Paris Street; Rainy Day *(1877). In* Paris Street; Rainy Day, *Caillebotte caught the temperament of modern-day Paris. The broad span of the boulevards, the impressive forms of the apartment blocks, and the elegant composure of the figures appear as urban icons. The effect of the misting rain on a gray day has the credible force of first-hand observation. Critic Émile Zola admired the epic scale of this painting and predicted that Caillebotte would prove to be the boldest innovator in the group.*

The Art Institute of Chicago. Oil on canvas (83½×108¾ inches).

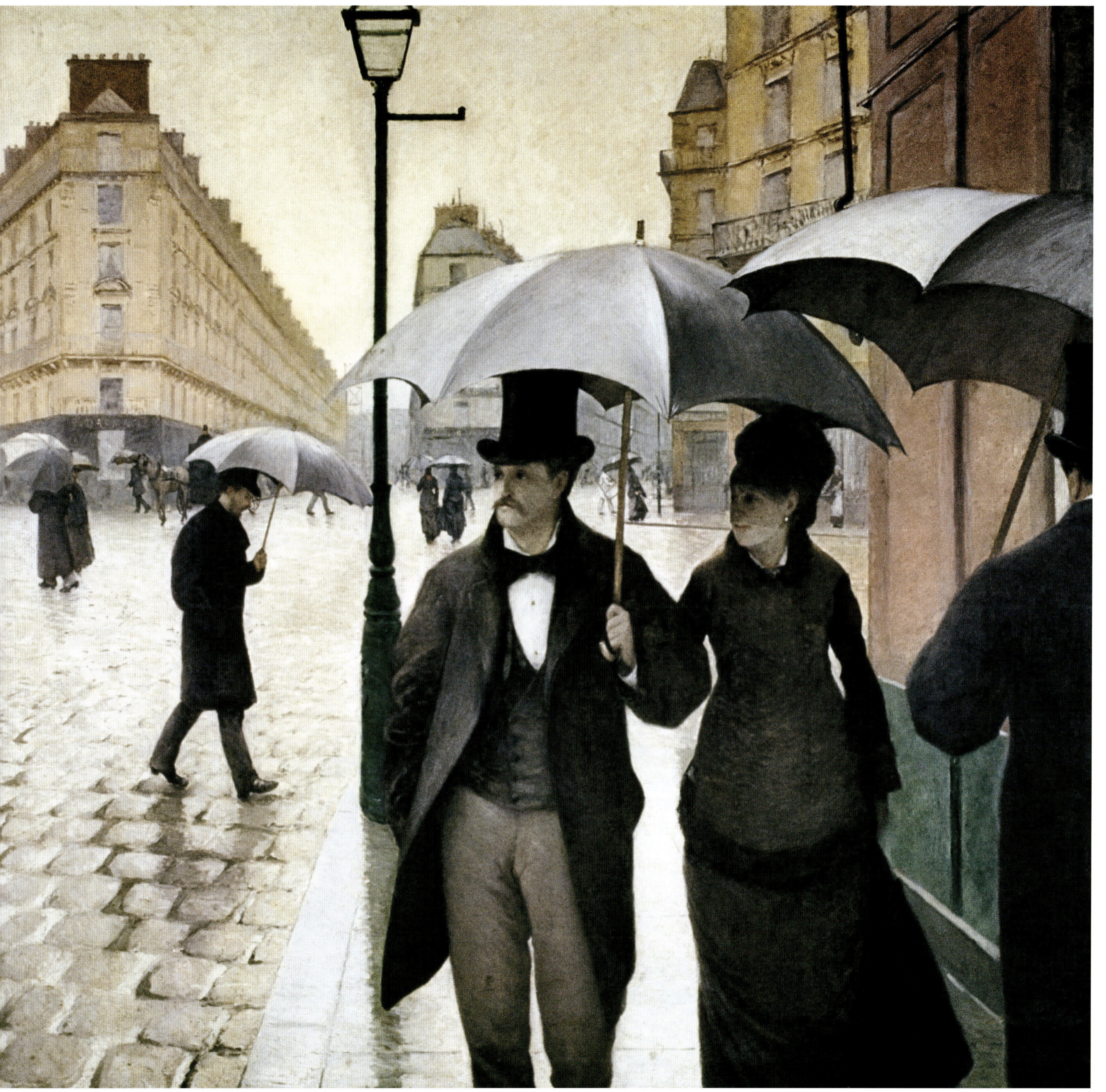

sented *Japonnerie (La Japonaise)* (1876), a fanciful portrait of his wife Camille in a bright red kimono. Degas demonstrated a keen eye for realist observation in *The Cotton Exchange at New Orleans* (1873), which he painted while visiting his American relatives. The fresh atmosphere and deft brushwork seen in Morisot's *Hanging the Laundry out to Dry* (1875) prompted conservative critic Albert Wolff to single her out as an interesting participant in a group he otherwise dismissed as "Five or six lunatics, including one woman." The second exhibition also marked the Impressionist debut of Gustave Caillebotte. Born into a wealthy family and trained as a naval architect, Caillebotte was fascinated with the changing image of the modern city. His subjects provided a true record of urban life: workmen sanding hardwood floors; a man at a balcony railing looking out on a broad avenue of pristine new apartment buildings.

The exhibition attracted the expected skepticism from the conservative sectors, which was balanced by strong endorsement from writers Edmond Duranty, Stéphane Mallarmé, and Émile Zola. Mallarmé linked the Impressionists with Manet's own struggle for a modernist art, while Duranty's pamphlet "The New Painting: Concerning the Group of Artists Exhibiting at the Durand-Ruel Galleries" established their achievement as an exciting and timely development in the course of the arts. Writing for the international journal *Le Message de l'Europe,* Zola declared, "One cannot doubt that we are witnessing the birth of a new school," which he predicted would eventually triumph over academic tradition.

Early in 1877, Caillebotte hosted a dinner party for Manet, Monet, Pissarro, Degas, Renoir, and Sisley. A third exhibition was discussed, and with Caillebotte's initiative—as well as his generous financial support—the group mounted an extensive publicity campaign. They found five spacious rooms in a new apartment building on rue le Peletier, just off the fashionable Boulevard Haussmann and across the street from Durand-

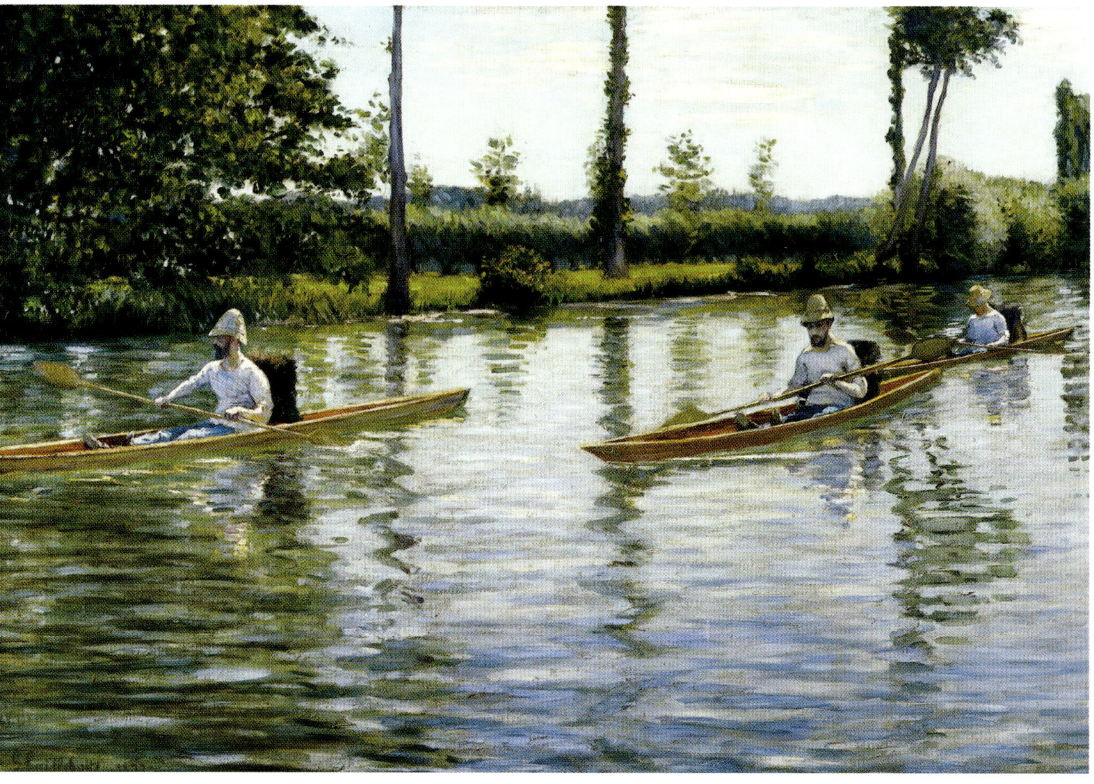

GUSTAVE CAILLEBOTTE, Boating on the Yerres (Perissoires sur l'Yerres) *(1877). From his boyhood, when he and his brothers rowed on the Yerres River near their family's country home, Caillebotte loved water sports. After focusing on the street scene for several years, Caillebotte approached boating scenes for his compositions. He created a sophisticated and subtle tension by painting multiple axes; in this case, the horizon and reflections are countered by the diagonal paths of the boats.*

MILWAUKEE ART MUSEUM. OIL ON CANVAS (40¾×61⅜ INCHES).

Ruel's gallery, and Caillebotte paid the rent with the understanding that he would be reimbursed from the profits. Eighteen artists agreed to participate, and despite adamant persuasion, Manet again declined. More than 240 works were featured, with the core members having the fullest representation. Again, the third exhibition included a wide variety of subjects and media. Degas presented his monotypes highlighted with pastel, and Cézanne offered portraits, figure compositions, still lifes, and landscapes. But the urban spirit dominated. Renoir's *The Ball at the Moulin de la Galette* (1876) featured attractive people enjoying a popular beer garden on a sunny day. The brisk pace and polished elegance of Caillebotte's *Paris Street; Rainy Day* (1877) matched the views of the street seen from the windows of the gallery. Among the 30 works by Monet were 5 paintings of the Saint-Lazare train station. Early that year, Monet had set his easel in the terminal to capture the effects of smoke and steam produced by the locomotives. He defined the paintings as a series based on repeated observations rather than narrative or chronological sequence. Writing a strongly supportive review, the critic Georges Rivière asserted that color and "not the subject itself . . . distinguishes the Impressionist from other painters," but the third exhibition emphasized urban identity as much as visual sensation. Although critical reception was rising, sales from the third exhibition had been disappointing, and an auction of unsold works held a month later provided little revenue.

Nevertheless, in September 1877, the group began to plan a fourth exhibition for the following spring, but to avoid conflict with the International Exposition scheduled for May 1878, they postponed it until April 1879. The fourth exhibition, held in a suite of rooms in a building on the Avenue de la Opera, saw a further reduction in the number of participants—now 15—represented by at least 240 works. There were notable absences among the core members; Renoir, Morisot, and Cézanne did not participate. However, there were significant debuts. Paul Gauguin, a stock agent who had recently taken up painting, had submitted his works too late to be listed in the catalogue, but they were shown nonetheless. After admiring her work in the Salon, Degas convinced Mary Cassatt to join. Her intimate portrayal of women's lives added a dimension to the subject of female modern life pioneered by Morisot, and through the course of the exhibitions, Cassatt was the sole American participant. Again the works had a clearly modernist orientation, and Degas argued that the group should take the name D'Artistes indépendants, realistes, and impressionistes. But the circle resisted any confining identity, preferring to remain independents.

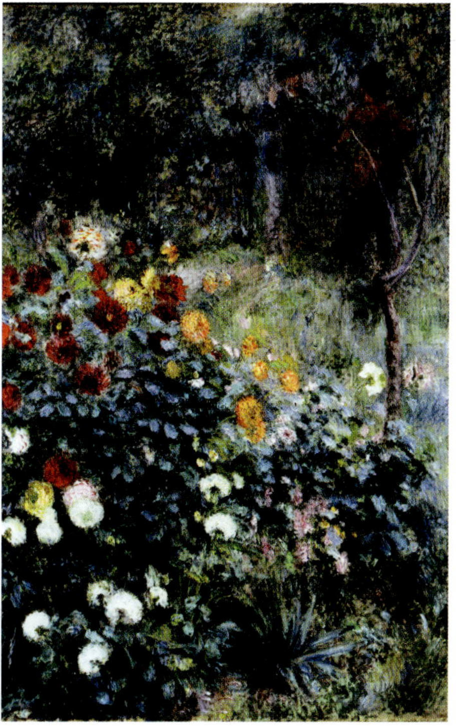

Pierre-Auguste Renoir (French, 1841–1919), The Garden in the rue Cortot, Montmartre *(1876). For a brief time, Renoir rented a studio in Montmartre. He chose it for its location near the Moulin de la Galette, where he was painting a scene of customers enjoying a warm afternoon in the beer garden. The studio also had a neglected garden, and Renoir painted its profusion of flowering dahlias with pure, bright dabs of pigment. Although the features of the men in the background are indistinct, they are believed to be Claude Monet and Alfred Sisley.*

Carnegie Museum of Art, Pittsburgh. Oil on canvas (59¾×38⅜ inches).

THE SECOND EXHIBITION 1876

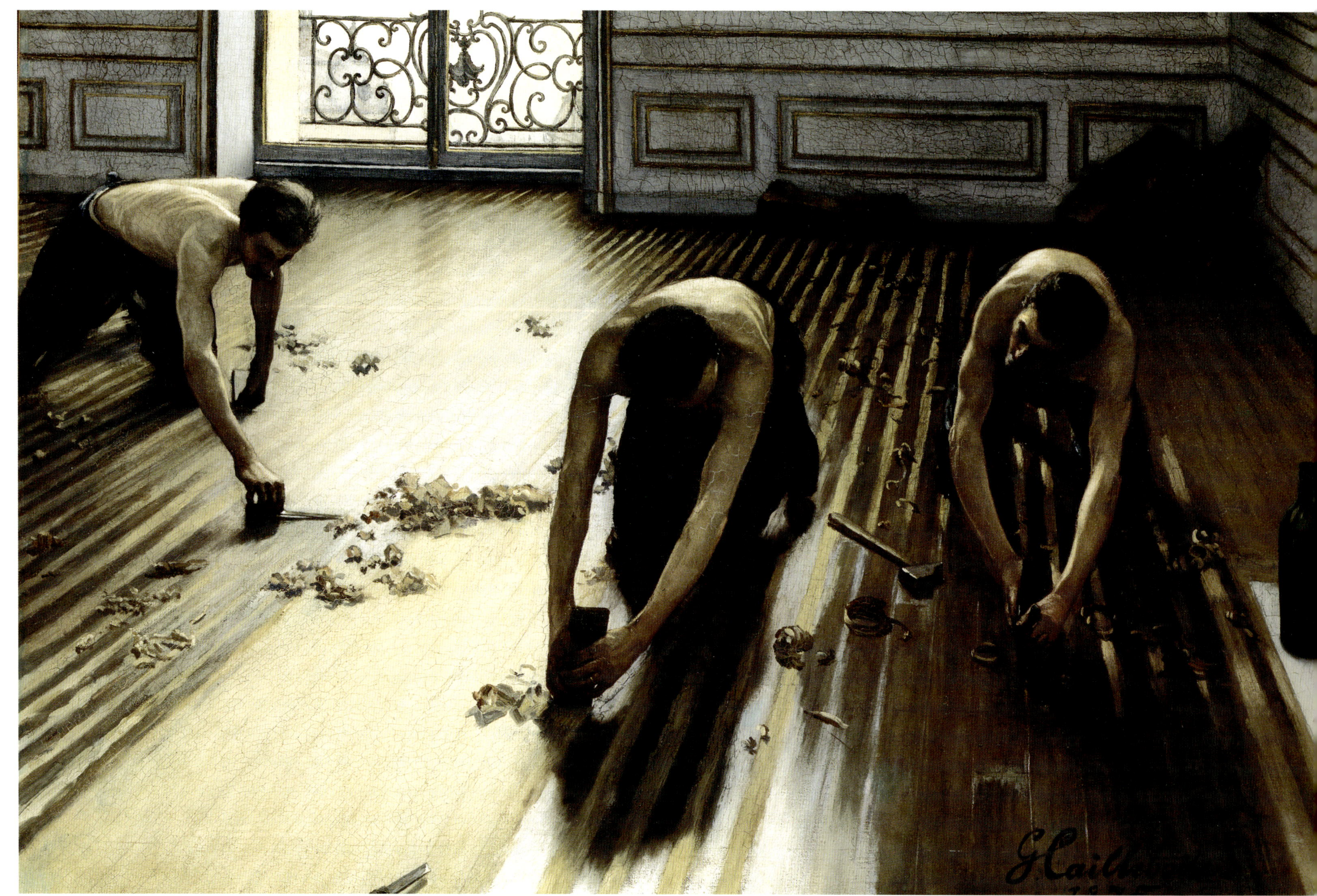

GUSTAVE CAILLEBOTTE, The Floor Scrapers *(1875). Caillebotte first associated himself with the Impressionists in the second exhibition. With* The Floor Scrapers' *daring perspective and uncompromising subject, it became the target of harsh criticism. But critic Philippe Burty observed that Caillebotte's representation of the workers was absolutely faithful, a true image of the reality of working life.*

MUSÉE D'ORSAY, PARIS. OIL ON CANVAS (39⅜×57¼ INCHES).

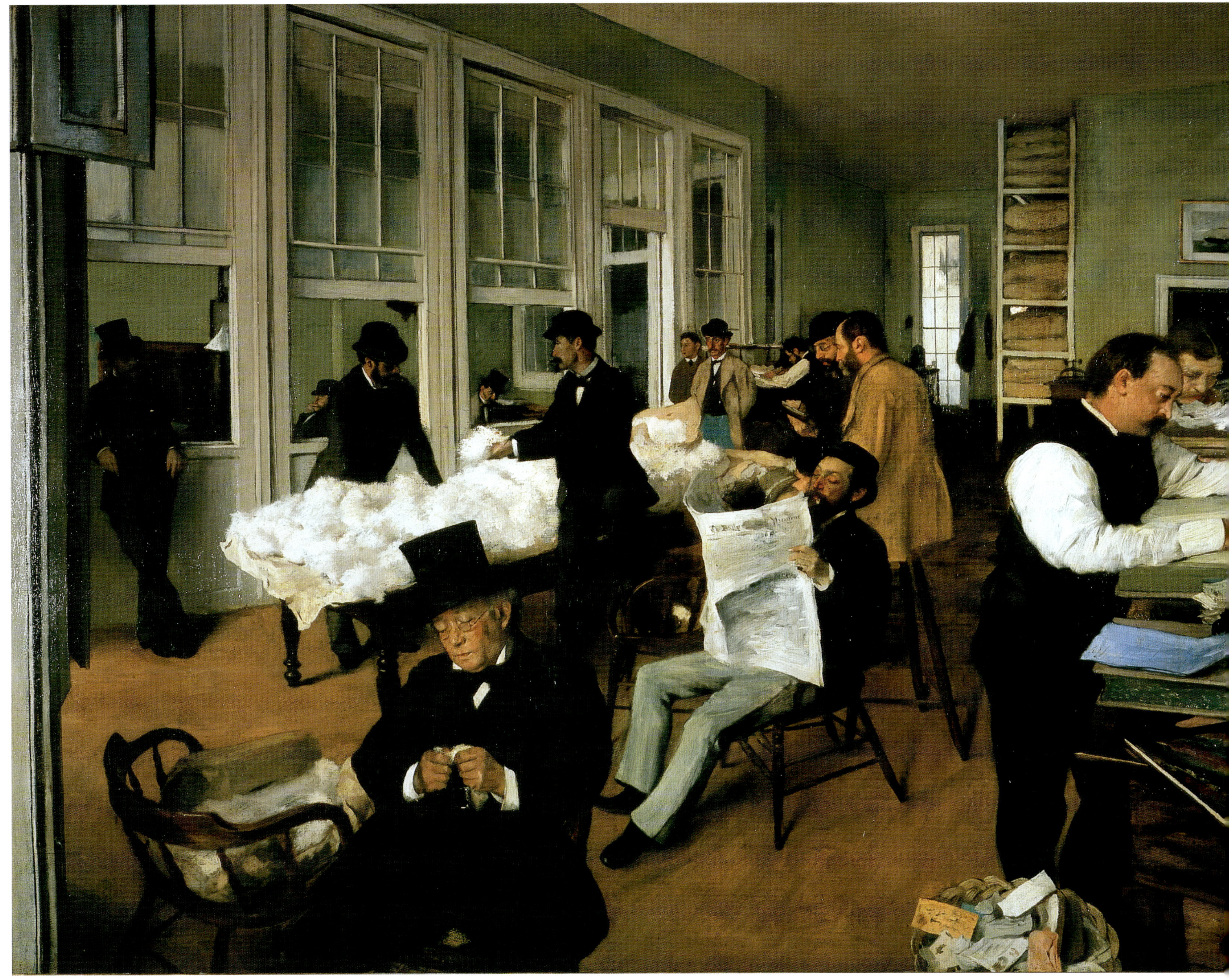

Hilaire-Germain-Edgar Degas, The Cotton Exchange at New Orleans *(1873). Degas visited his maternal family in New Orleans in 1872. His slice-of-life depiction of the Cotton Exchange contains several family portraits, including his brother Achille resting against the open window at the left and their uncle Michael polishing his spectacles in the foreground. No detail escaped Degas's scrutiny, from the dealers inspecting the quality of the cotton to the clerks hovering over paperwork at their desks.*

Musée Municipal de Pau, France. Oil on canvas (28¾×36¼ inches).

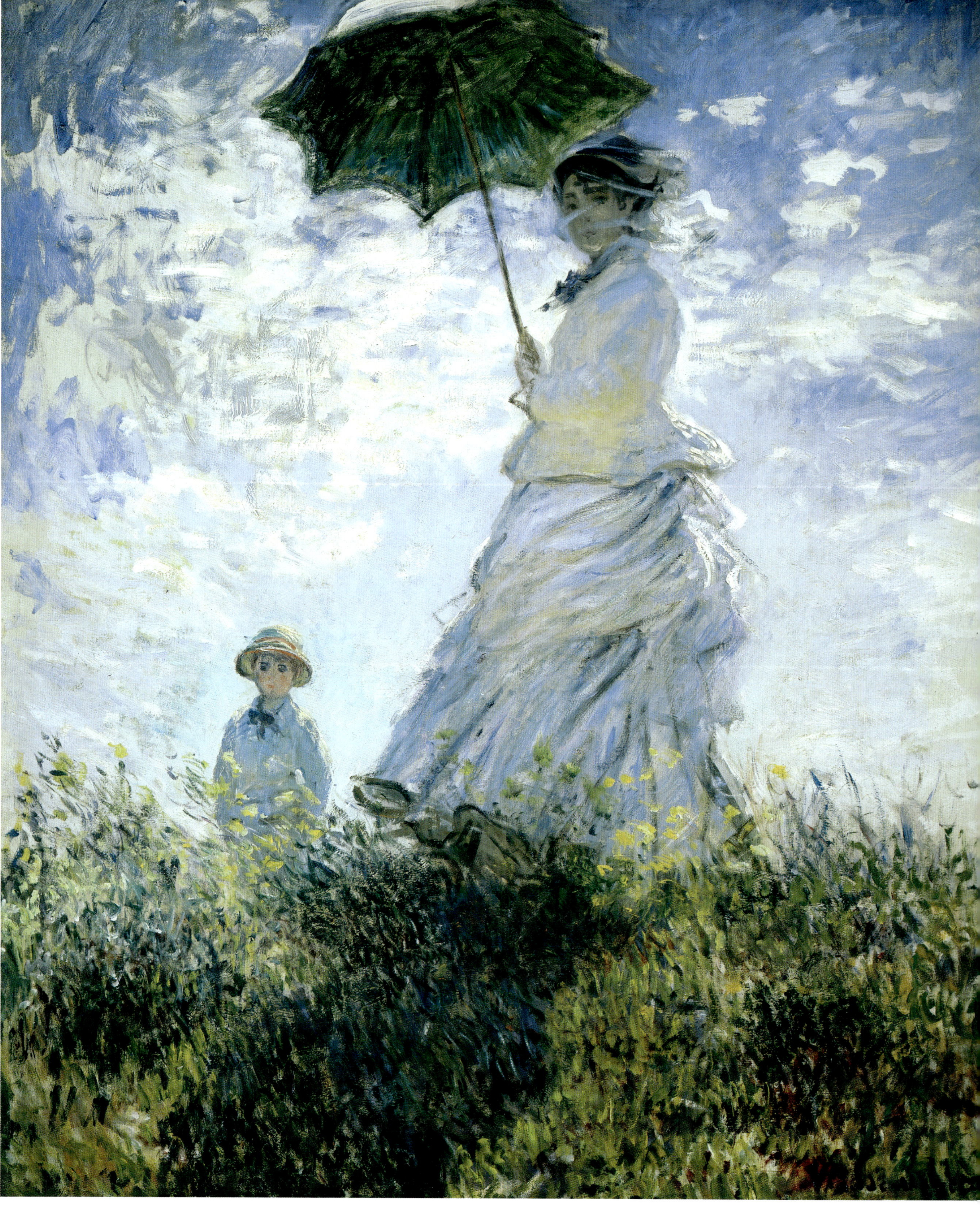

Claude Monet, Woman with a Parasol—Madame Monet and Her Son *(1875). Monet's fascination with painting figures in the setting of natural light continued after he moved with his family to a suburban home in Argenteuil. Here he presents Camille standing on a hilltop with their son Jean. The breeze whips her flowing skirts and wraps her veil around her face. The grasses and wild flowers sway at their feet, revealing that motion and the shimmering effects of light motivate Monet's artistic expression.*

National Gallery of Art, Washington, D.C. Oil on canvas (39⅜×31⅞ inches).

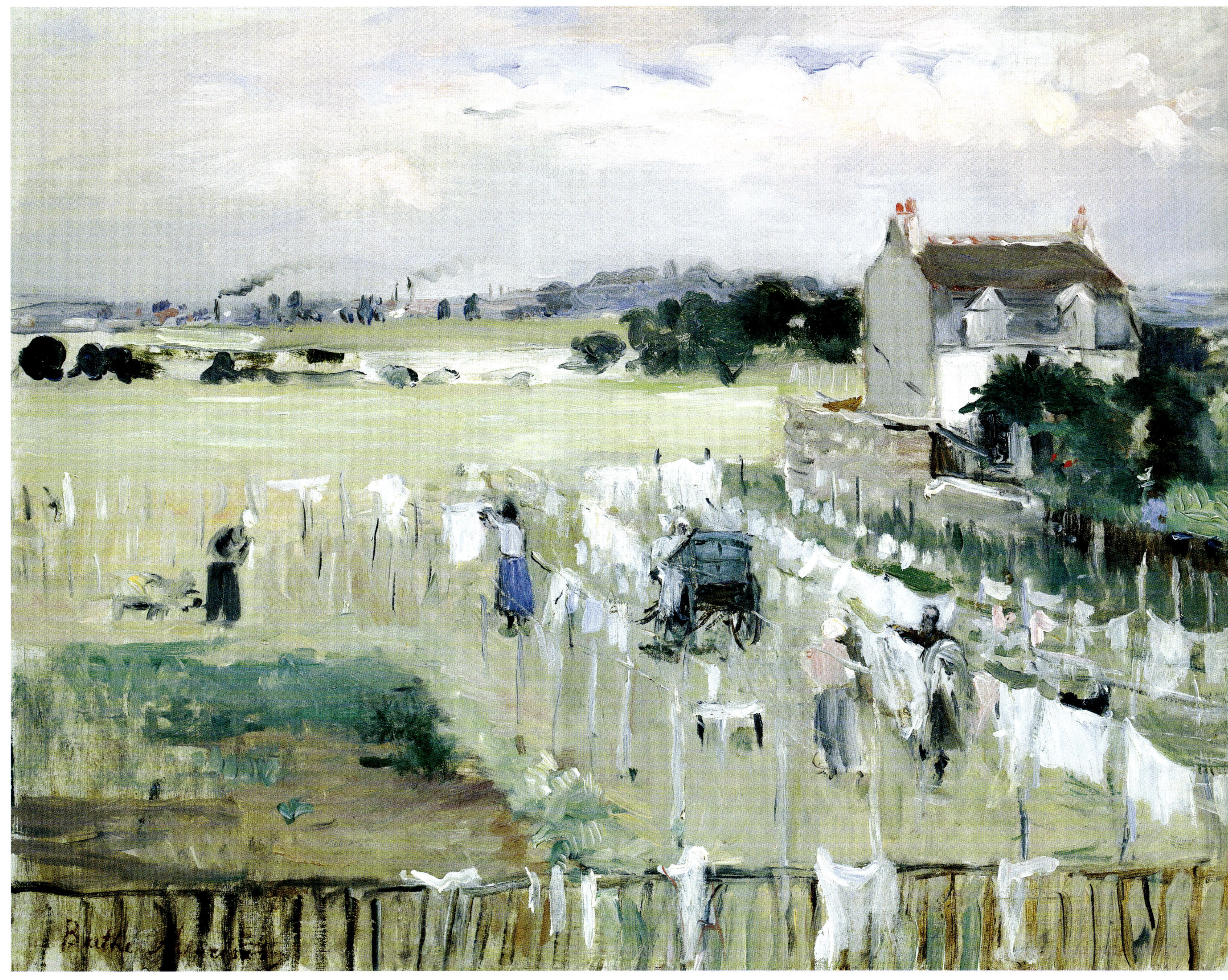

BERTHE MORISOT, Hanging the Laundry out to Dry *(1875). With a deft touch and a pale yet subtle palette, Morisot transformed a boring subject into a dazzling study of light and color. The critics singled out this work for special praise, most notably remarking upon Morisot's command of color. Her gender was also noticed by some critics.*

NATIONAL GALLERY OF ART, WASHINGTON, D.C. OIL ON CANVAS (13×16 INCHES).

THE THIRD EXHIBITION 1877

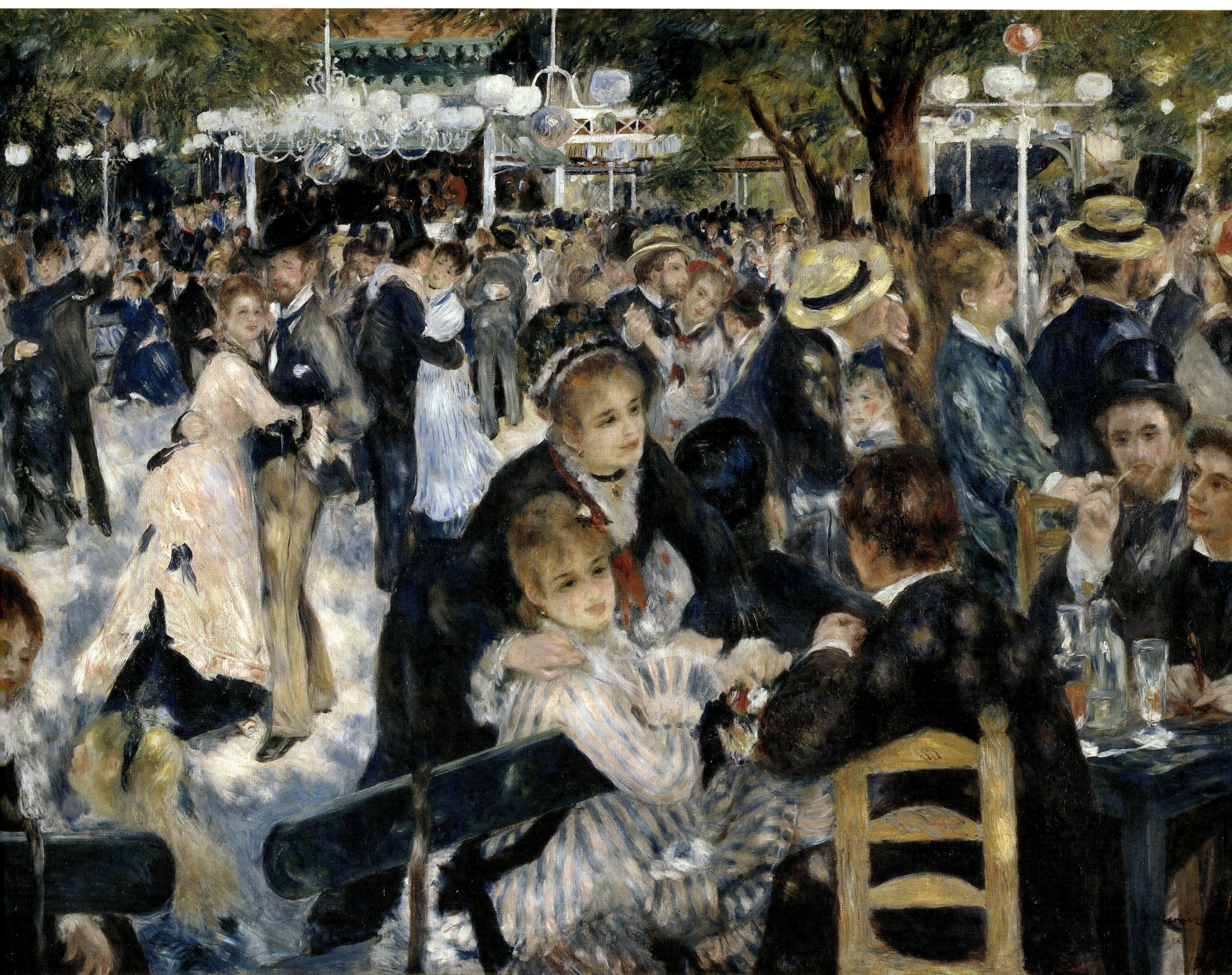

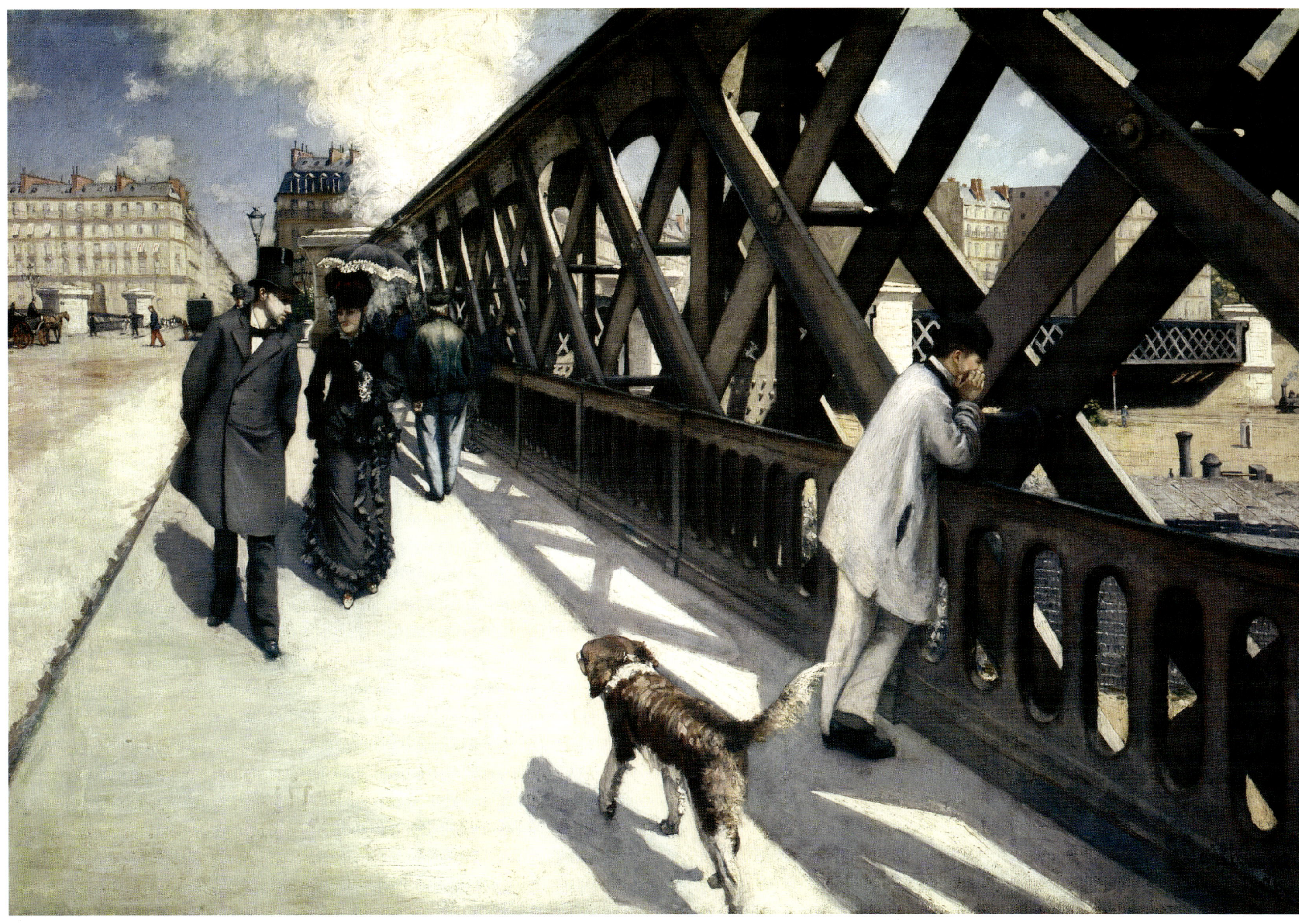

GUSTAVE CAILLEBOTTE, Le Pont de l'Europe *(1876). The strong diagonal of the massive iron trusses pulls the viewer's gaze along the pedestrian path, as if joining in the random actions of Parisians out for a stroll. The cool tones of Caillebotte's palette enforce the sense of the city's fabric—built of stone, iron, and concrete—even in the light of a mild, sunny day.*

MUSÉE DU PETIT PALAIS, GENEVA. OIL ON CANVAS (49⅛×71⅛ INCHES).

PIERRE-AUGUST RENOIR, The Ball at the Moulin de la Galette *(1876). On the northern outskirts of Paris, the hilly district of Montmartre remained partly rural through the later decades of the 19th century. Old windmills dotted the landscape, and the Moulin de la Galette, a lively beer garden, attracted young clientele. In his view of the café, Renoir expresses the sensuous pleasure of drinking, dancing, and flirtation in the open air, with sunlight filtering through the trees on a warm summer day.*

MUSÉE D'ORSAY, PARIS. OIL ON CANVAS (51½×69 INCHES).

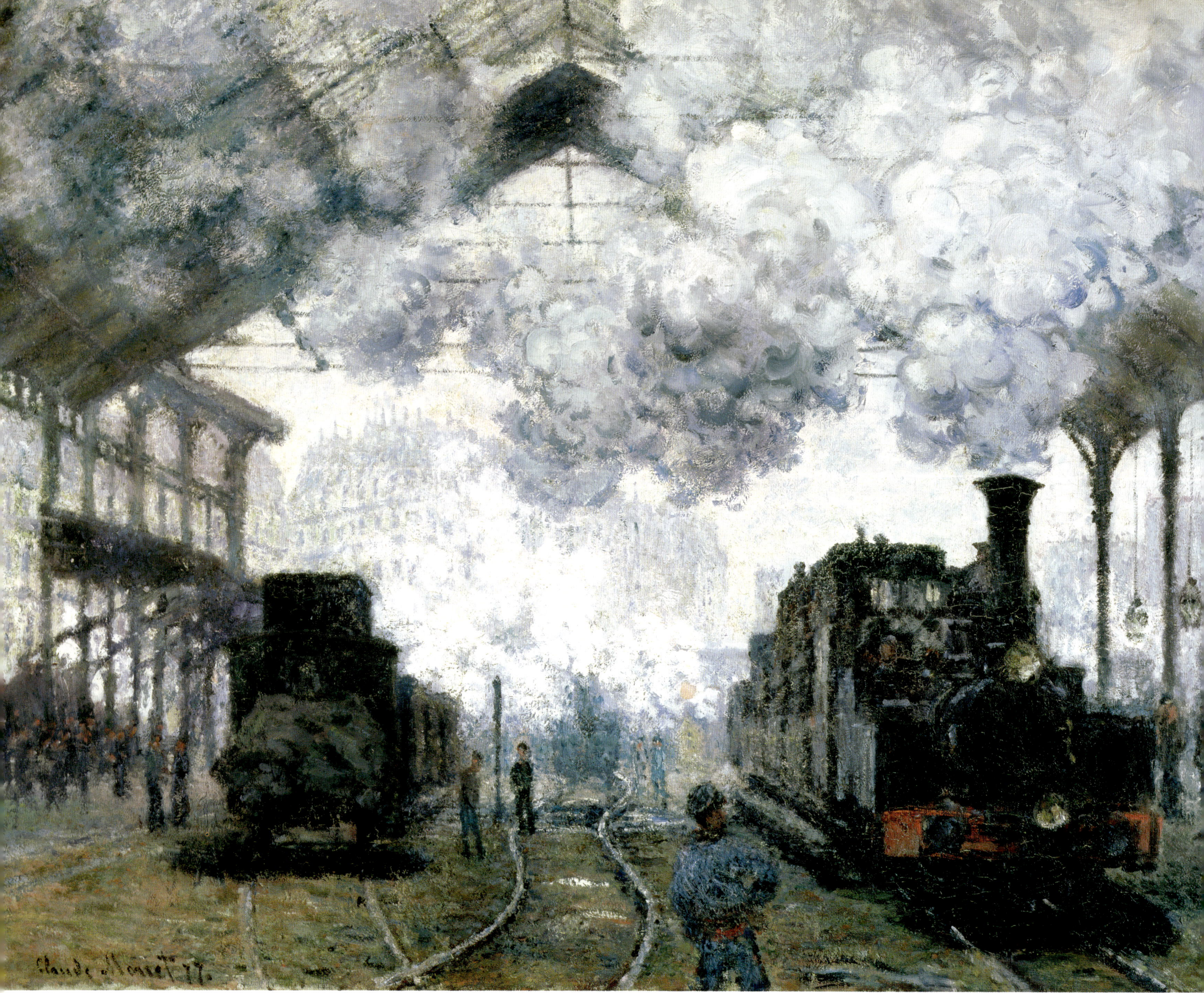

Claude Monet, Saint-Lazare Station, Paris *(1877). Early in 1877, Monet began to paint in and around the Saint-Lazare train station in Paris. The constant movement of the trains and the crowd, as well as the billows of smoke and clouds of steam that rose to the glass canopy above the tracks, provided an infinite variety of atmospheric effects to paint. Between January and April, Monet completed nearly a dozen canvases in the first of his painting series, and he presented three of them in the third exhibition.*

The Fogg Art Museum, Harvard University, Cambridge, Massachusetts. Oil on canvas ($32\frac{1}{4} \times 39\frac{3}{4}$ inches).

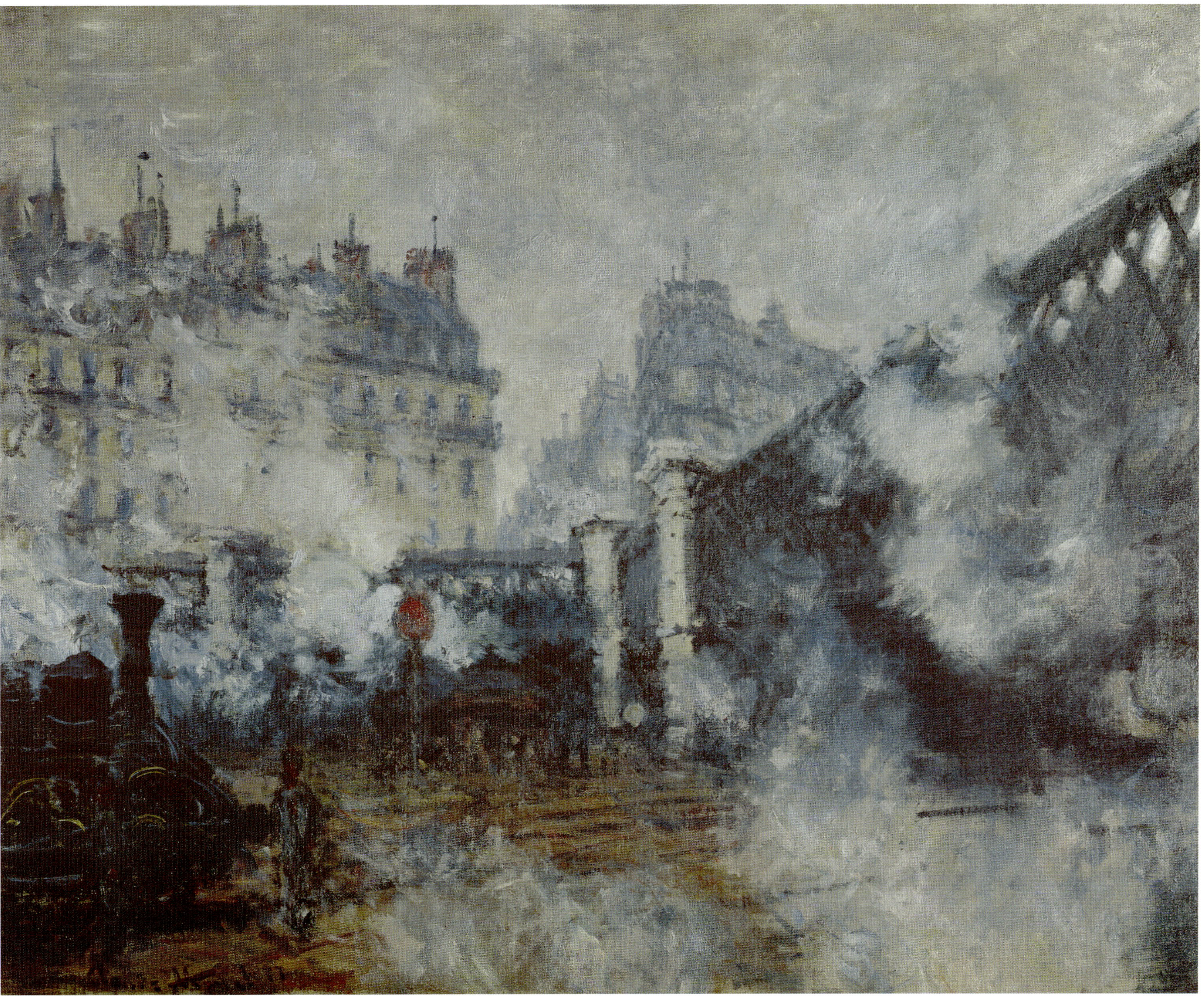

CLAUDE MONET, Pont de l'Europe (Gare Saint-Lazare) *(1877). Monet set his easel outside the station to catch the effect of the steam engines roaring down the tracks just below Pont de l'Europe. The rising smoke transforms the gritty urban scene, and Monet portrayed this in a shimmering palette of violet, pink, and silver. Monet strongly believed that the series of pieces that he created at the train station worked as an ensemble.*

MUSÉE MARMOTTAN, PARIS. OIL ON CANVAS (25¼×31⅞ INCHES).

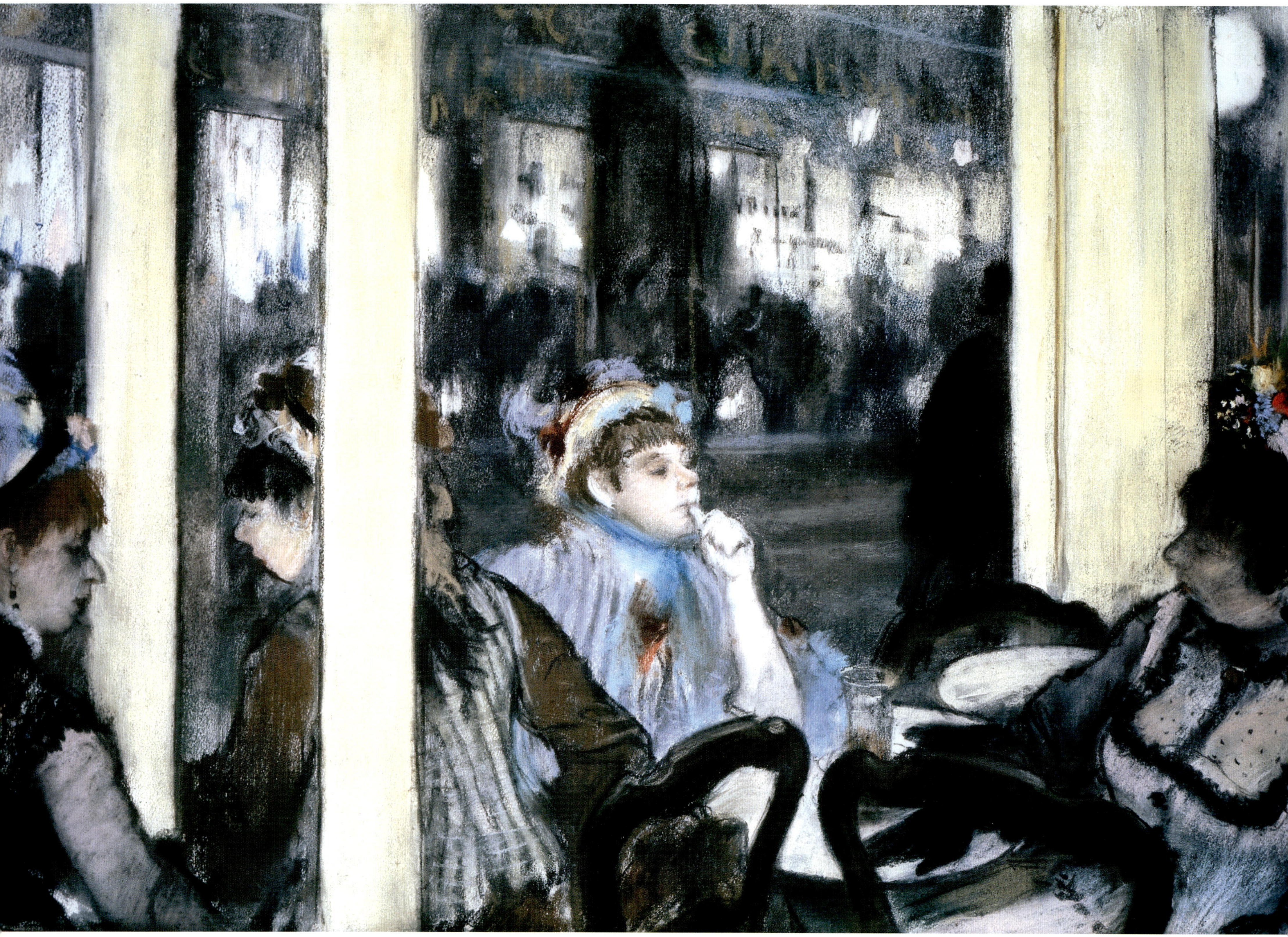

HILAIRE-GERMAIN-EDGAR DEGAS, Women in Front of a Café, Evening *(1877). Unlike the other members of the circle, Degas had little interest in seeking subjects outside the realm of urban Paris. In this, he embodied poet Charles-Pierre Baudelaire's idea of the* flaneur, *the man at home—and at leisure—in the city, who observed every aspect of modern life. Here he highlights a monotype—a single reproduced image—with bright strokes of pastel.*

MUSÉE D'ORSAY, PARIS. PASTEL OVER MONOTYPE ($16\frac{1}{8} \times 23\frac{5}{8}$ INCHES).

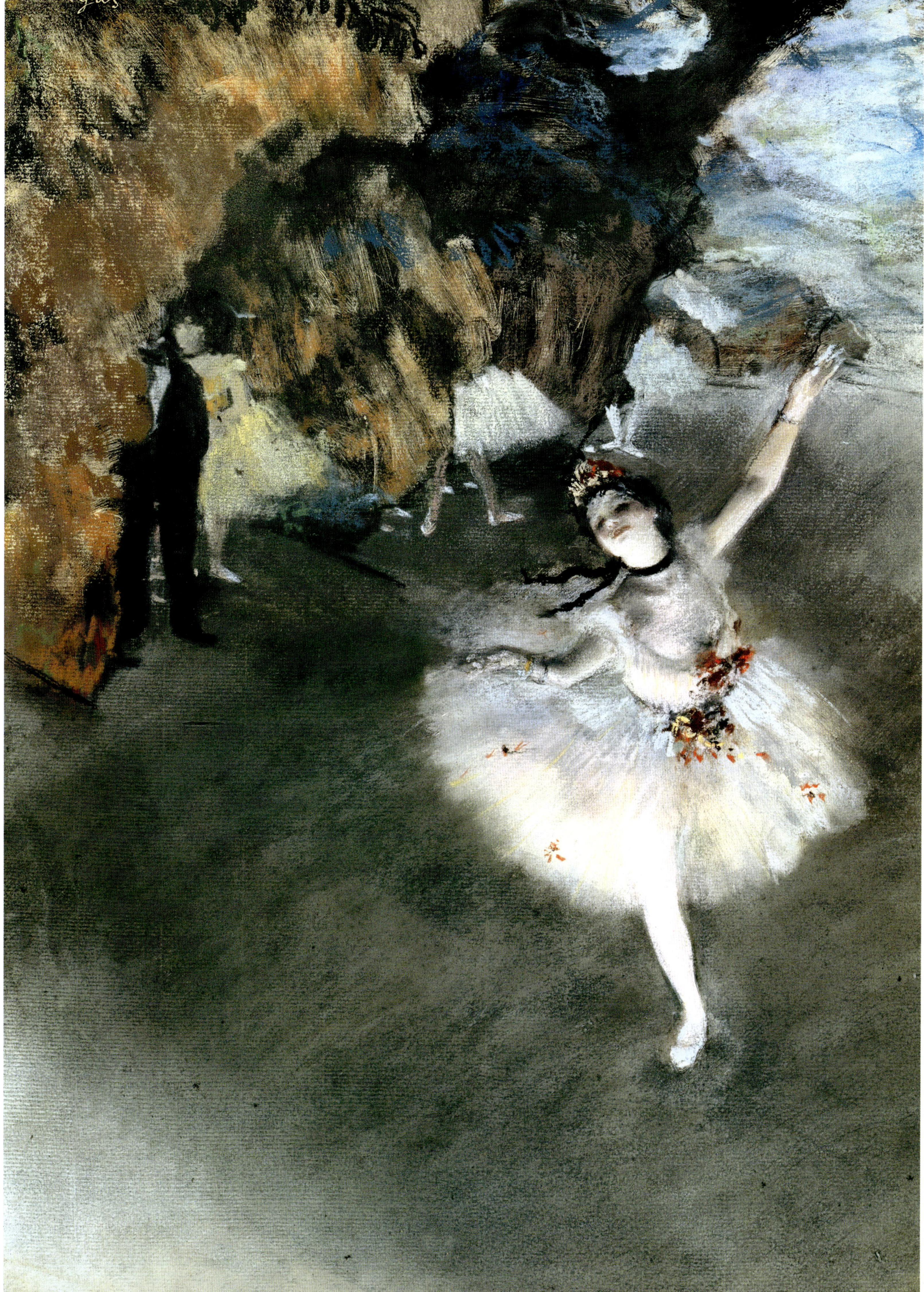

Hilaire-Germain-Edgar Degas, The Star (L'Étoile) *(1878). Degas selected an elevated point of view for this painting. The dancer's skirt seems to vanish under the stage lights, which cast pale violet shadows on the smooth, powdered skin of her bare arms and chest. Degas followed the rapid movement of the dancer across the stage with swift and sure calligraphic strokes.*

Musée d'Orsay, Paris. Pastel on paper (23⅝×17⅜ inches).

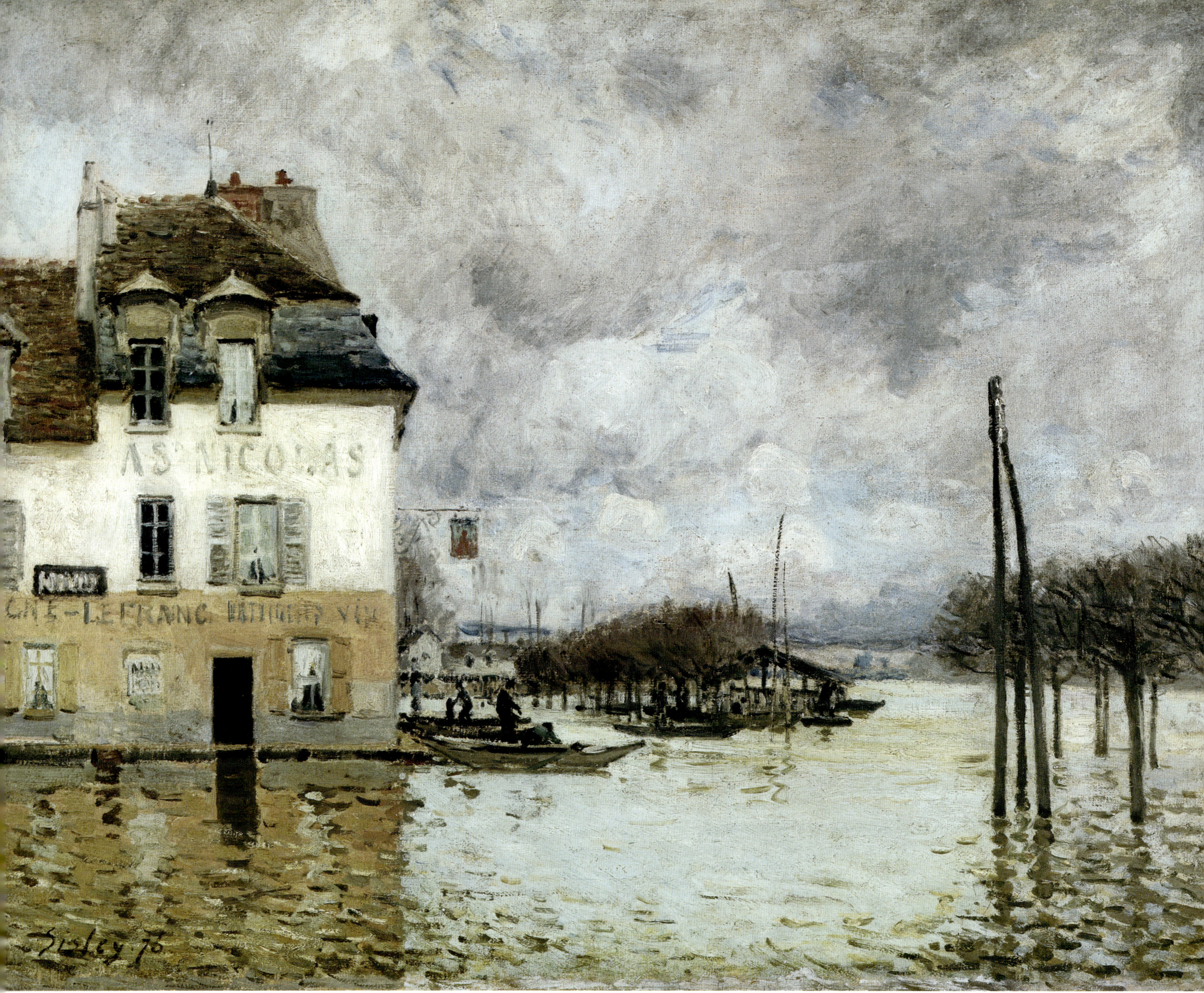

ALFRED SISLEY, Flood at Port-Marly *(1876). The catalogue of the third exhibition lists the entry* Inondations, *and the critic Charles Bigot mentions two works depicting floods by the artist, but neither have been identified. This painting—with its nuanced, blue-gray palette—may have been in the exhibition, and it serves to illustrate Sisley's command of the heavy, moisture-laden atmosphere and the clear reflections on the high, trembling waters.*

MUSÉE D'ORSAY, PARIS. OIL ON CANVAS (23⅝×31⅞ INCHES).

THE FOURTH EXHIBITION 1879

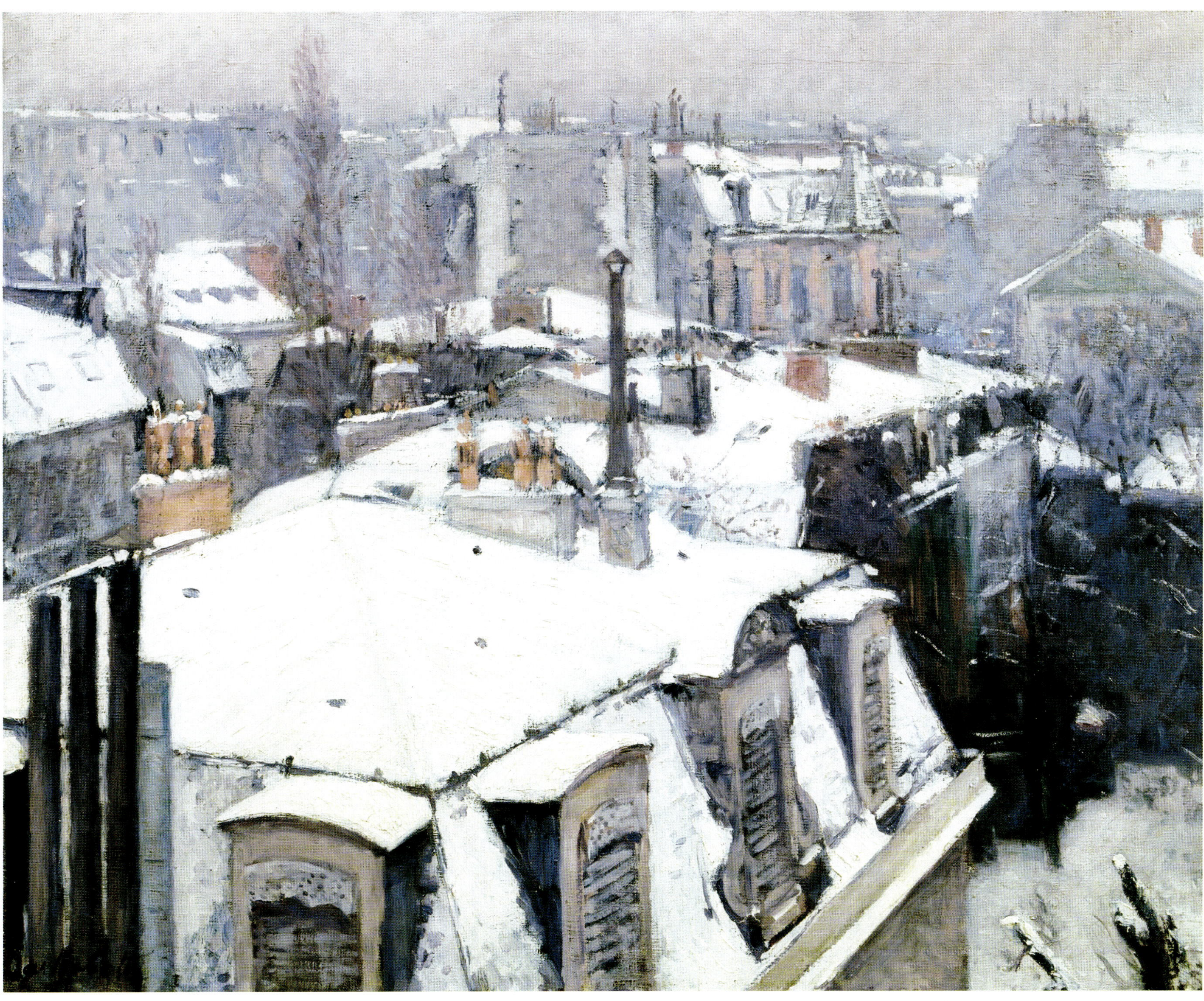

GUSTAVE CAILLEBOTTE, Rooftops in the Snow, Paris *(1878). With 23 works, Caillebotte was well-represented at the fourth exhibition. His most daring work provided a view—perhaps from a balcony or attic window—across Parisian rooftops covered with snow. For the most part, the rooftops are nondescript, punctuated only by chimney stacks and dormer windows, but the unfolding view, high across the city, has a distinctively urbane aesthetic.*

MUSÉE D'ORSAY, PARIS. OIL ON CANVAS (25⅝×31⅞ INCHES).

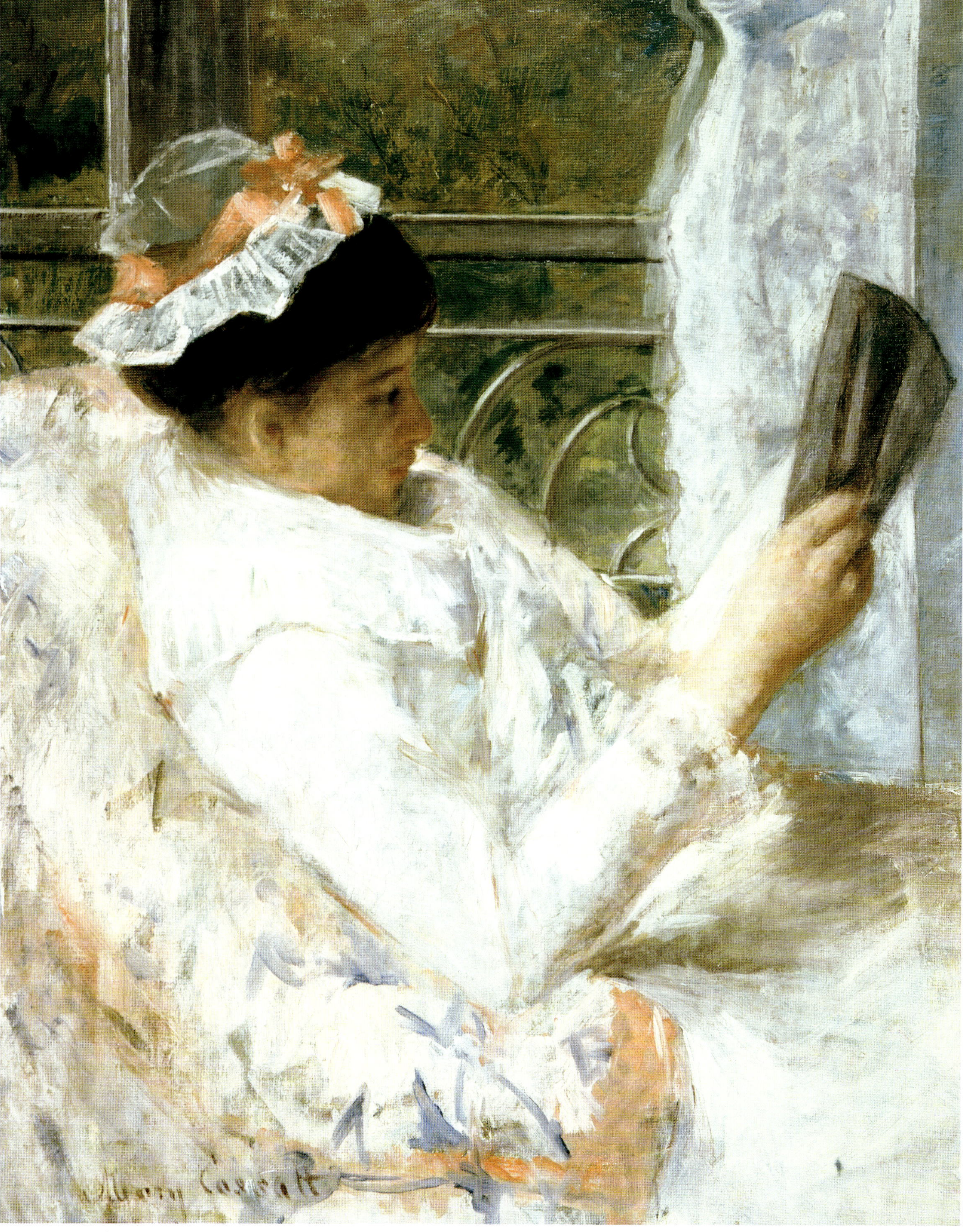

MARY CASSATT, Woman Reading *(1878). In 1874 Degas saw a work by Cassatt at the official Salon, and a few years later he urged her to exhibit with the Impressionists. She became the first and only American in the circle. Cassatt concentrated on the seemingly simple daily activities of a middle-class woman's life: welcoming friends for tea, answering letters, and reading. The critics found her work fresh and real, demonstrative of her mastery of color as well as the domestic subject.*

JOSLYN ART MUSEUM, OMAHA, NEBRASKA. OIL ON CANVAS (32¼×23½ INCHES).

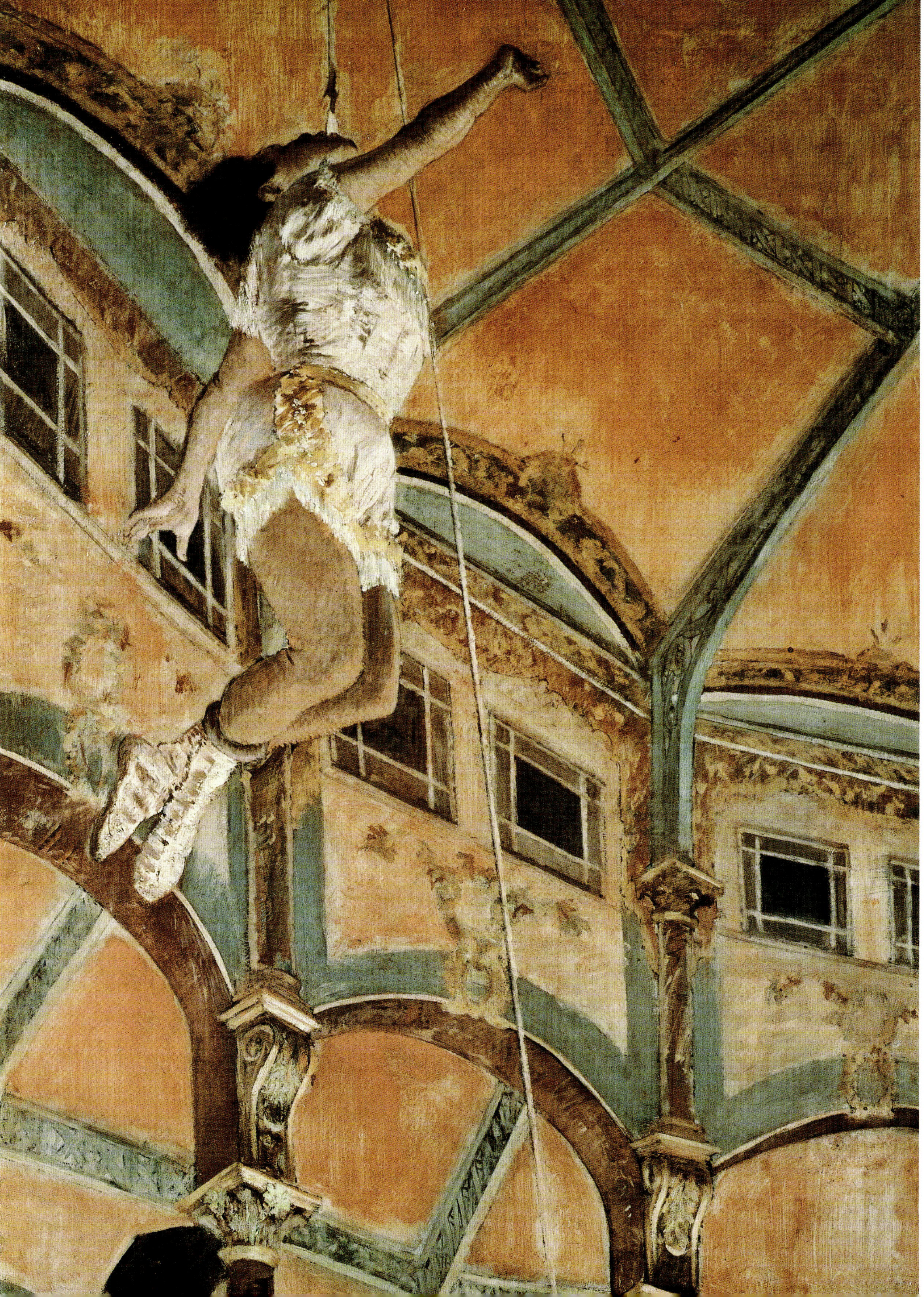

Hilaire-Germain-Edgar Degas, Miss La La at the Cirque Fernando *(1879). Degas prepared at least four studies of the famed aerialist La La performing her trademark stunt: hanging by her teeth at the end of a rope. His finished painting captures the breathless excitement of the moment, when the crowd looks up to see her dangling high above their heads. The critic Armand Silvestre commended Degas's firm and accurate drawing.*

The National Gallery, London. Oil on canvas (46×30½ inches).

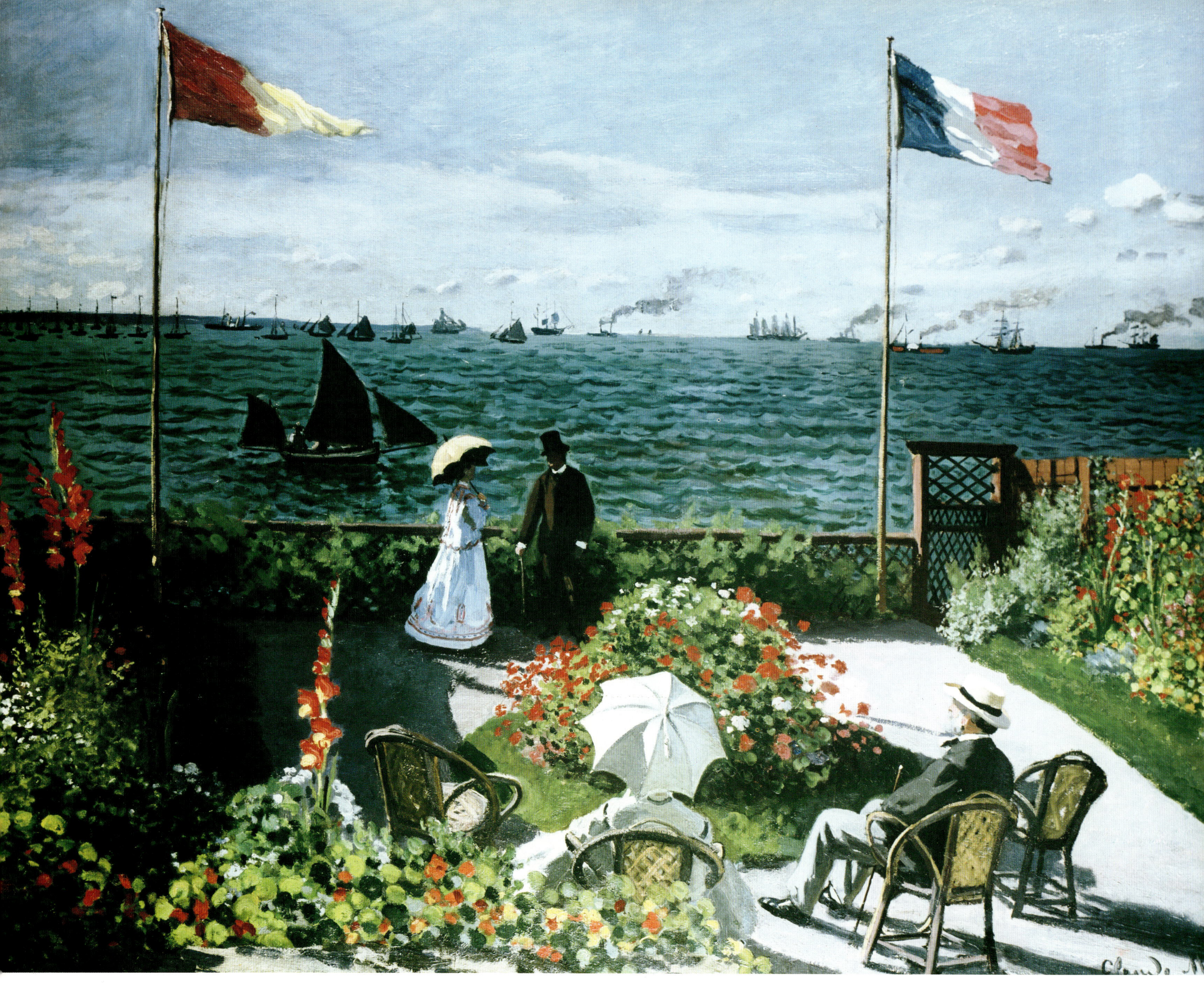

CLAUDE MONET, Garden at Sainte-Adresse *(1867). With motion and color, Monet expresses the experience of enjoying a view of the sea from a terrace in the coastal resort at Sainte-Adresse. The flags flutter in the wind, and thin clouds move swiftly across a bright sky. The sun strikes the terrace, illuminating the sheen of the women's parasols and the vivid flowers. Although the painting includes portraits of several of Monet's relatives, his attention was focused on visual sensations.*

THE METROPOLITAN MUSEUM OF ART, NEW YORK. OIL ON CANVAS (38⅝×51⅛ INCHES).

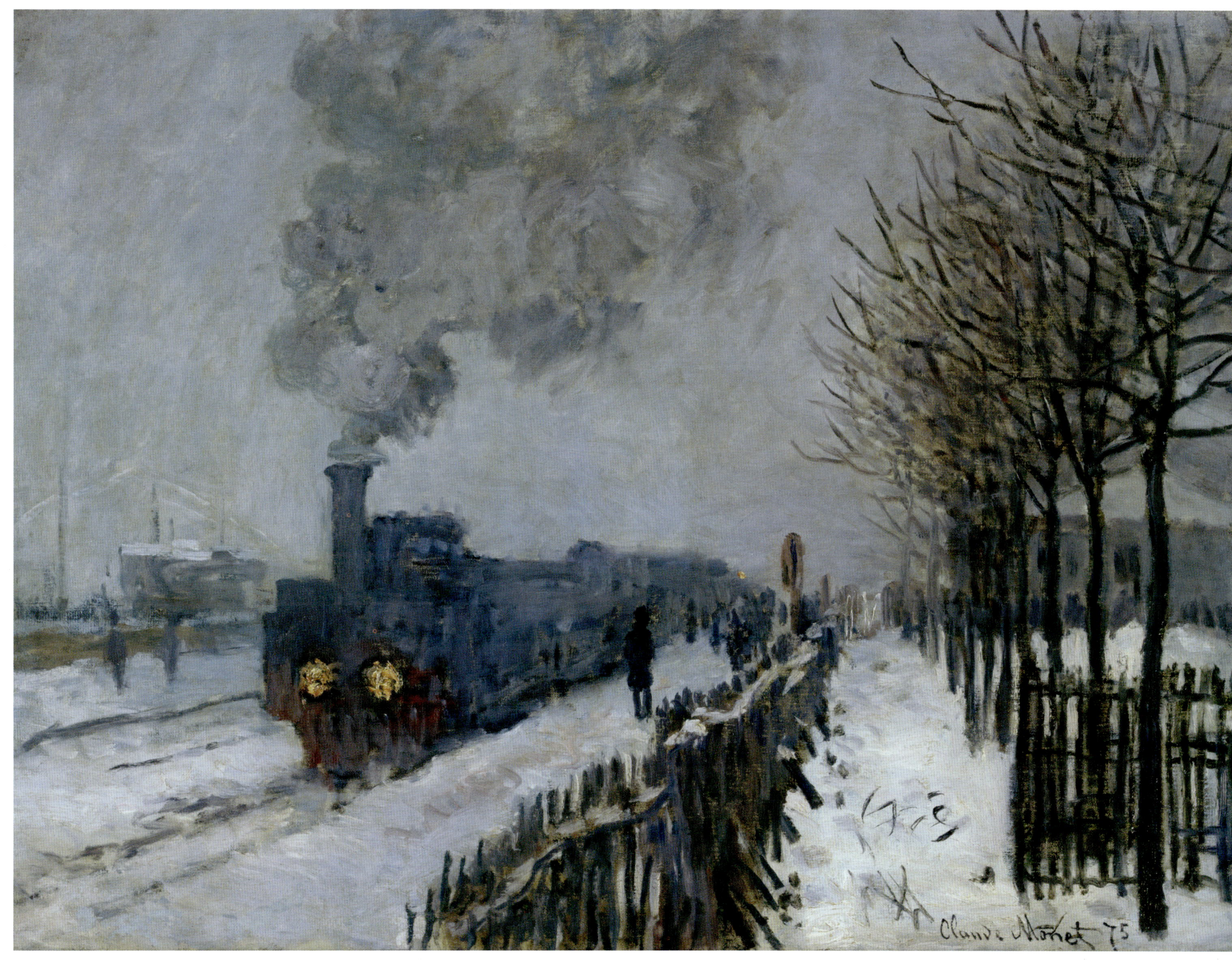

CLAUDE MONET, Train in the Snow *(1875). It is speculated that this was the painting presented in the fourth exhibition as* Paysage d'Hiver. *The subtle tonality reveals Monet's fascination with painting in the winter. The snow-covered ground, the steel gray sky, and the icy frost on the bare limbs of the trees convey the damp and frigid atmosphere. The billowing smoke from the locomotive challenges Monet to further modulate his tones and capture the effect of steam dissolving in the moisture-laden air.*

MUSÉE MARMOTTAN, PARIS. OIL ON CANVAS (23¼×30¾ INCHES).

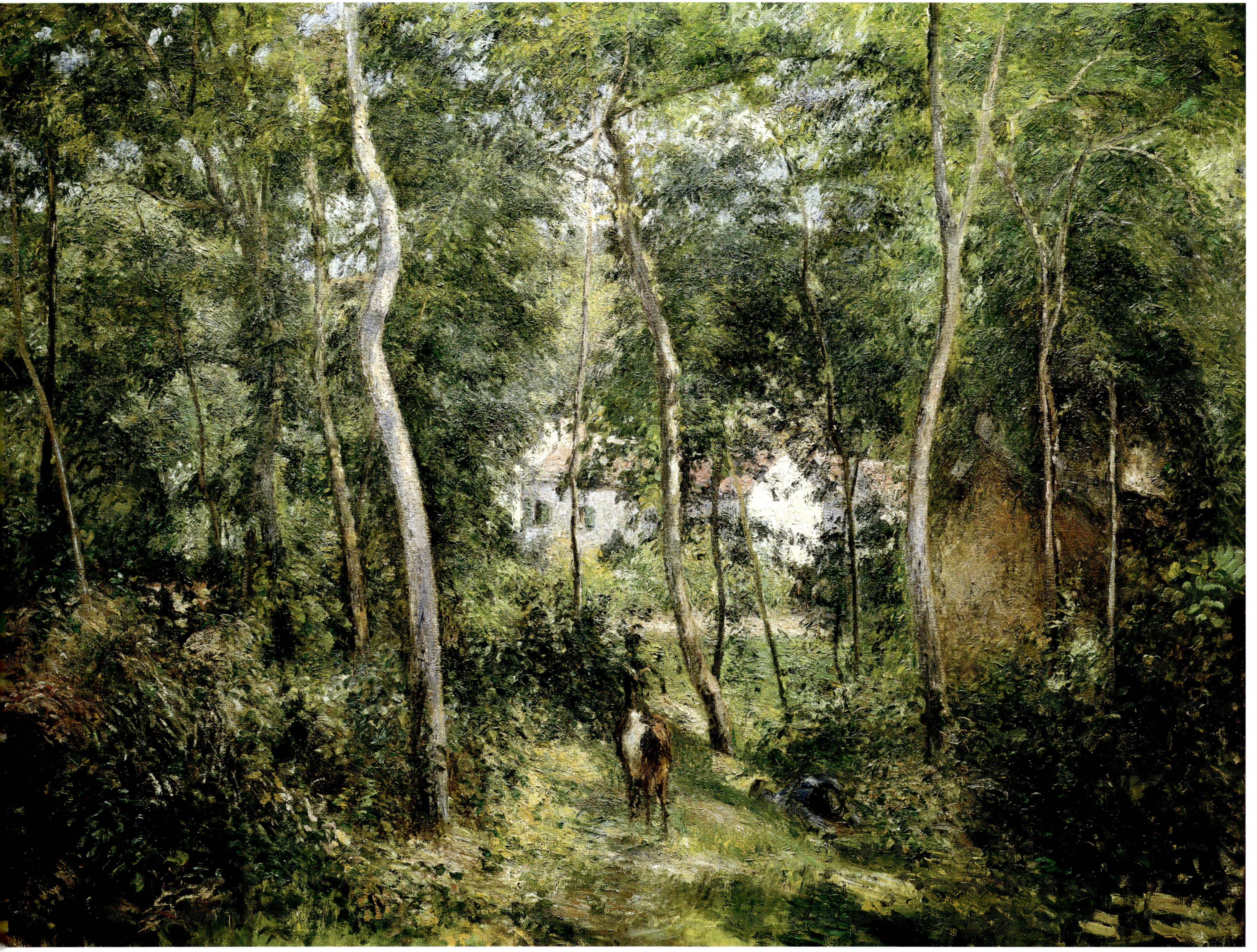

Camille Pissarro, Edge of the Woods *(1879). Pissarro submitted two versions of this work, which is also known as* Undergrowth in Summer, *to the fourth Impressionist exhibition. The paint is lightly dabbed on the surface to render the dense growth of foliage. The whitewashed walls and red-tile roof of a cottage can be seen in the distance through the tree trunks, just as patches of blue sky can be glimpsed through the branches, simulating the visual experience of a walk in the woods.*

The Cleveland Museum of Art. Oil on canvas (49⅝×63¾ inches).

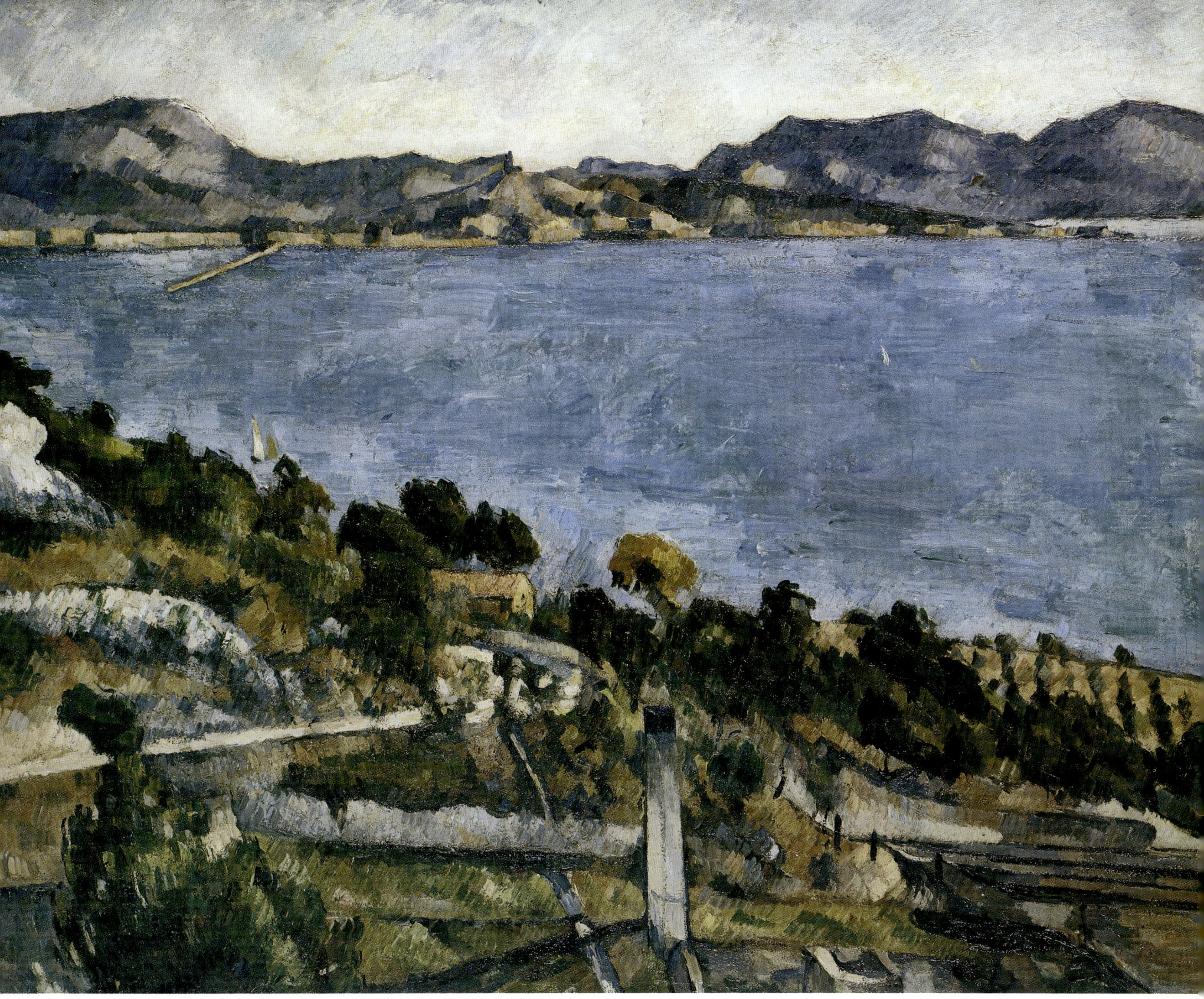

Paul Cézanne, L'Estaque: View of the Bay of Marseilles *(c. 1878–79).*
L'Estaque is a small coastal village on the Mediterranean to the west of Marseilles. Cézanne's mother owned a house there, and the painter visited several times to paint views of the bay. He deliberately flattened the planes of the panoramic landscape. Noting that the blinding illumination of the sun reduced all forms to silhouettes, Cézanne presented the features of the view as simple forms.

Musée d'Orsay, Paris. Oil on canvas (21⅞×28¾ inches).

SHIFTING ALLIANCES: FIFTH, SIXTH, AND SEVENTH EXHIBITIONS

The exhibitors are naturally divided into two groups: those who actually merit the name Independents because they bring a new note, an original accent, to their art, and those who only timidly separate themselves from established traditions.

CHARLES EPHRUSSI, *LA CHRONIQUE DES ARTS ET DE LA CURIOSITÉ,* APRIL 16, 1881

FROM THE OUTSET, the core circle of Impressionists had an unspoken agreement that if an individual artist chose to show their work at the official Salon, they would decline participation in the independent exhibition for that year. In 1880 Pierre-Auguste Renoir had two works accepted by the Salon jury and, as he had in the previous year, chose the official venue over the Impressionist exhibition. To raise his professional profile—and to boost his income—Claude Monet also submitted two works for the jury's scrutiny. One was rejected, but *Lavacourt* (1880), a more conventional plein air view over the Seine, was accepted. However, both Renoir and Monet were disappointed with the way their paintings were hung at the Salon and wrote a letter of complaint to the Minister of Fine Arts.

Hilaire-Germain-Edgar Degas and Gustave Caillebotte shared responsibility for organizing the fifth Impressionist exhibition but argued over every detail. They clashed over the group's name: Degas insisted on Groupe des artistes independents, which appeared on the promotional posters, but the catalogue simply announced Catalogue de la 5me Exposition de Peinture. Caillebotte demanded that the names of participating artists be advertised, Degas fought him on that point, and Berthe Morisot and Mary Cassatt requested that their names not be listed. They also argued about the alternative exhibitions sponsored by *La Vie Moderne*, a journal founded by Georges Charpentier, a publisher who had become Renoir's most important patron.

After much discord, the fifth exhibition opened on April 1, 1880, in an unfinished building on the corner of rue de Pyramids and rue Saint

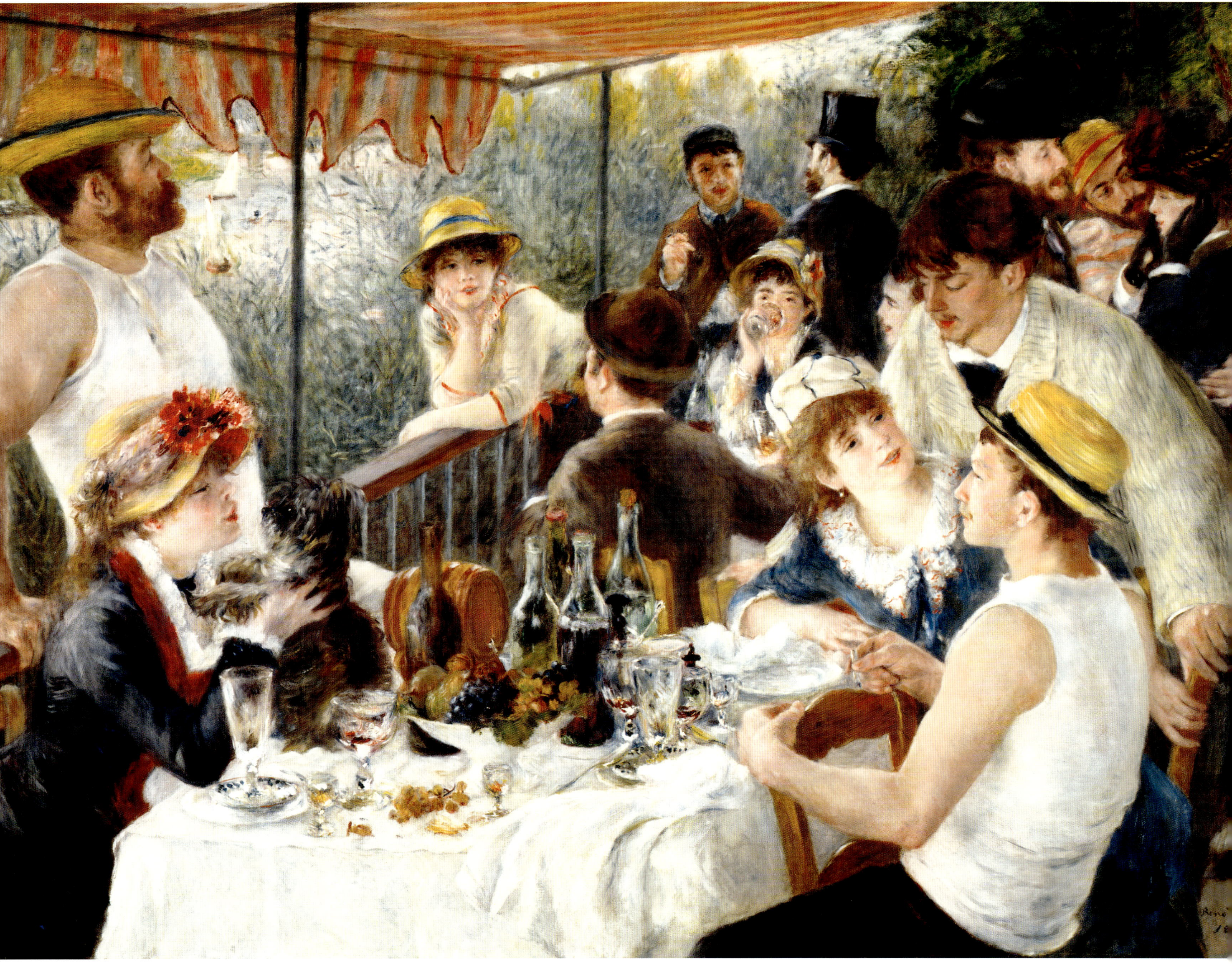

Pierre-Auguste Renoir, The Luncheon of the Boating Party *(1880–81). Renoir used costume, color, and setting to convey the pleasures of a sunny afternoon among friends. His palette has a golden glow; for instance, the women's fair skin flushes in the warmth of the sun. The straw hats and bare arms of some members of the party signal the rising heat. Renoir set his painting at an establishment he knew well—the upper terrace of the Restaurant Fournaise—and he portrayed his friends and his future wife (in the lefthand corner) among the company.*

The Phillipps Collections, Washington, D.C. Oil on canvas (51×68 inches).

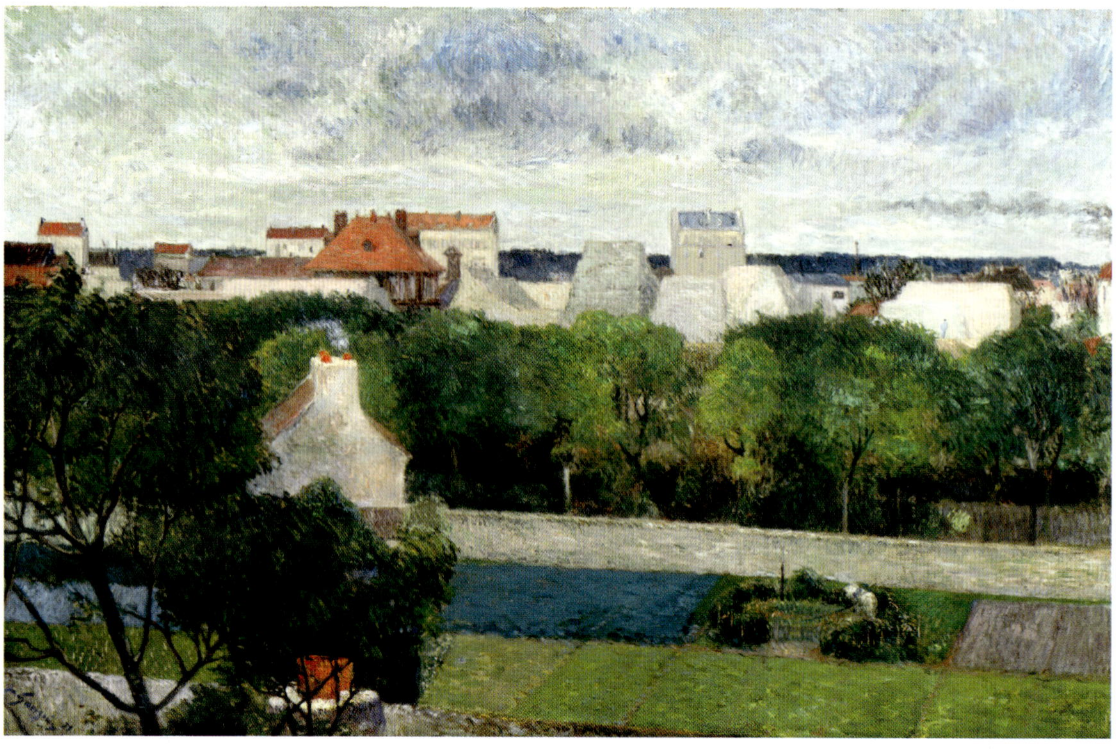

Honoré. Critics questioned the wisdom of choosing the location, noting that during the day the sounds of construction were intrusive. Writing in the conservative journal *Le Voltaire,* Gustave Goetschy wrote, "The sounds of hammer blows come simultaneously from every floor, causing the awful portraits by Caillebotte to constantly shake." Other critics complained as well, citing the poor lighting and bad installation. The novelist Joris-Karl Huysmans, an early champion of the group, observed that the realist approach of the major participants—specifically Degas, Cassatt, Pissarro, and Caillebotte—made the exhibition rather conventional. He reflected that "Caillebotte has rejected the system of Impressionist strokes . . . ; he has limited himself to following the orthodox techniques of the masters." For the public the colorful, spontaneous approaches of Monet and Renoir had defined a "classic" idea of Impressionism that was not in evidence at the fifth exhibition. Henry Havard, a critic for the journal *Le Siècle,* wrote, "let us acknowledge that Impressionism is dying."

Undeterred by internal conflict and flagging support, the artists involved with the fifth exhibition scheduled the sixth one to run through the month of April (1881). The space secured for the installation brought the artists back to the site of their first exhibition in the building on the rue des Capucines. However, Nadar's spacious and lofty studio was no longer available, and the works were hung in five small rooms on a mezzanine deep in the back of the building. Connected by narrow corridors, the rooms were cramped; they had low ceilings and were cluttered with furniture. Most critics decried the dim lighting and crowded installation. Again Renoir exhibited his work at the Salon; Monet refrained from having his work considered for either exhibition. Confrontations with Degas prompted Caillebotte to complain to Pissarro, writing "What is to become of our exhibitions?" Caillebotte believed that in the absence of Renoir and Monet, Degas was intent on overshadowing the remaining core members by including only his protégés. Ulti-

PAUL GAUGUIN, The Market Gardens of Vaugirard *(1879). Gauguin submitted eight works to the fifth Impressionist exhibition, including this landscape. With his broad areas of color and patchy application of paint, Gauguin has followed the example of Paul Cézanne and Camille Pissarro, emphasizing structure over atmospheric effect.*

SMITH COLLEGE MUSEUM OF ART, NORTHAMPTON, MASSACHUSETTS. OIL ON CANVAS (25⅝×39⅜ INCHES).

mately Caillebotte decided not to participate, and Pissarro, the only core member who would exhibit in all eight exhibitions, helped Degas with the plans.

In their reviews of the sixth Impressionist exhibition, critics took issue with the extreme realism of Degas's sculpture *Little Dancer of Fourteen Years* (1880; cast 1920). The original was made of wax (the statue is now known through versions in bronze), and Degas's use of gauze and satin to dress the figure crossed the line between reality and artistic illusion. The only work to earn consistent praise was Pissarro's *Pathway at Chou in March* (1878), an atmospheric landscape that revealed the painter's mastery of the now classic hallmarks of Impressionism: a deft touch and a fresh palette. The sixth exhibition brought a rare critical consensus: Progressive and conservative reviewers agreed that it was inferior to all the previous Impressionist exhibitions.

Continuing conflicts marred the planning stages for the seventh exhibition. Again Degas took the lead. He persuaded his friend Henri Rouart, a successful engineer and an amateur painter who had exhibited in all six prior exhibitions, to finance the project. Both Monet and Renoir were hesitant to return to the group, but Durand-Ruel, who now represented them, insisted that the exhibition needed their presence to restore its reputation. He offered to submit works he had in his stock. Both Gauguin and Caillebotte voiced strong objections to Degas's practice of filling the roster with his friends. Insulted, Degas refused to exhibit, and out of respect for Degas, Cassatt declined as well. In the end, only nine artists agreed to exhibit, but they were represented by more than 200 works. Installed in the large, well-lit upper gallery of the Salon du Panorama de Reichshoffer—the first floor of this popular entertainment spot on rue Saint Honoré housed a permanent display of the bloodiest battle of the Franco-Prussian War—the works filled the allotted space to capacity.

The catalogue was hastily prepared and handwritten, but the exhibition suggested a strong return to the initial Impressionist color and spontaneity. Renoir's *A Luncheon at Bougival* (1880–81), a delightful scene of a congenial boating party, elicited enthusiastic reviews, and Monet's *Ice Floes* (1880)—rejected by the Salon in 1880—was praised for its originality. Monet also exhibited his evocative *Setting Sun over the Seine at Lavacourt, Winter Effect* (1880), a suggestive river view reminiscent of the spectacle of reflected light seen in *Impression Sunrise* (1872). The earlier work, once so shocking, had come to define the essence of Impressionist style. Ernest Chesneau voiced this opinion, writing of the painter's ability to render the fleeting effects of nature: "That is what the painters aptly named 'Impressionists' aspire to and succeed in rendering for us; it is the memory that they wish to and know how to fix."

THE FIFTH EXHIBITION 1880

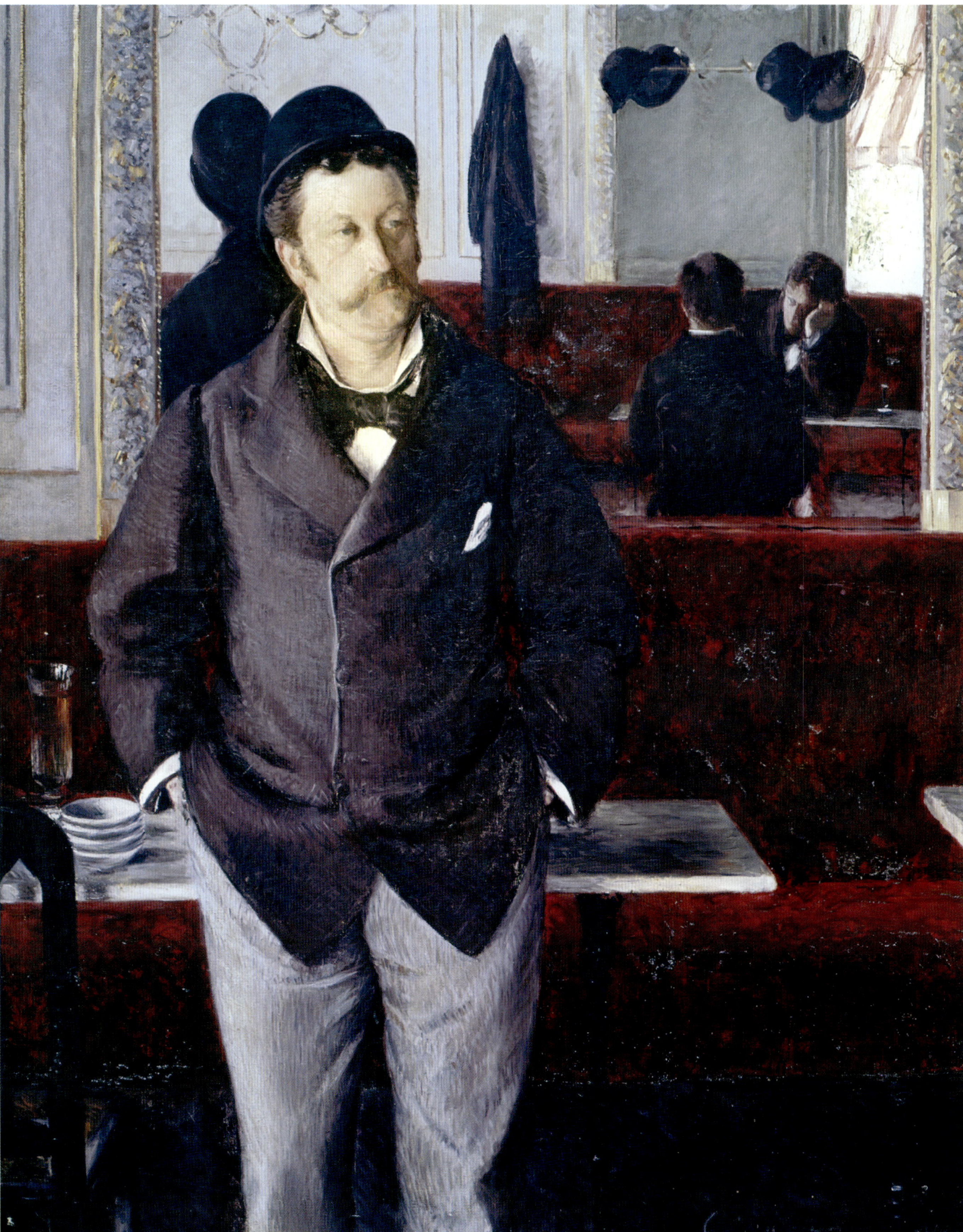

GUSTAVE CAILLEBOTTE, In a Café *(1880). Without Caillebotte's financial support, the Impressionist exhibitions might not have happened. In his art, he continued to explore the modern-life subject, often enhancing the sense of immediacy in his compositions by using reflections in mirrors to extend the illusion of space beyond the painting's frame.*

MUSÉE DES BEAUX-ARTS, ROUEN, FRANCE. OIL ON CANVAS (61×45¼ INCHES).

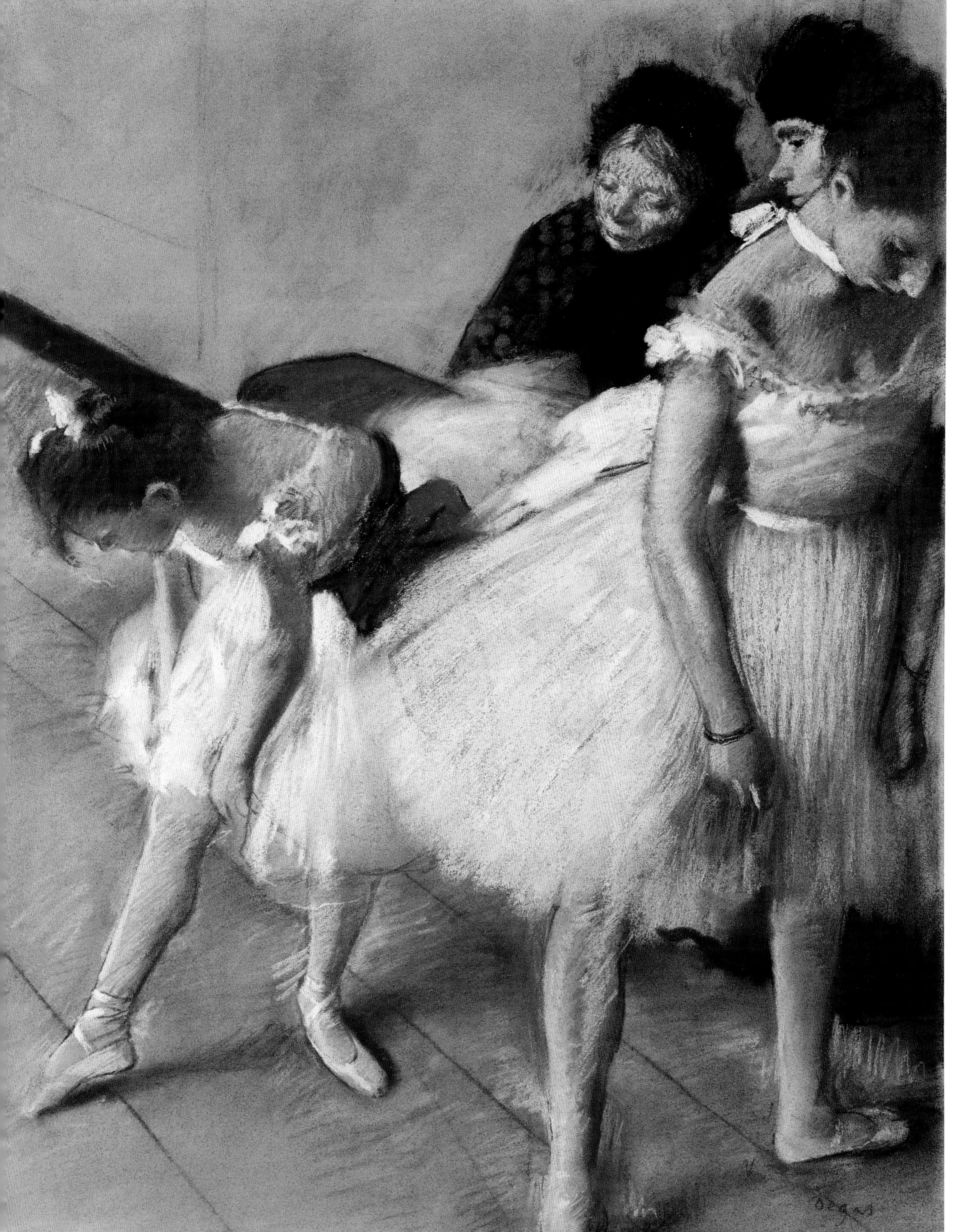

Hilaire-Germain-Edgar Degas, Examen de Danse (Dance Examination) *(1880). Pastel was a good medium for Degas's portrayal of dancers because, with each sure stroke, he described a gesture—the point of a foot, the arch of a neck—as swiftly as it was made in life. To suggest the weight or insubstantiality of form—from the dancers' sturdy limbs to their flowing skirts—he varied the pressure of his touch.*

Denver Art Museum. Pastel on paper (24½×18 inches).

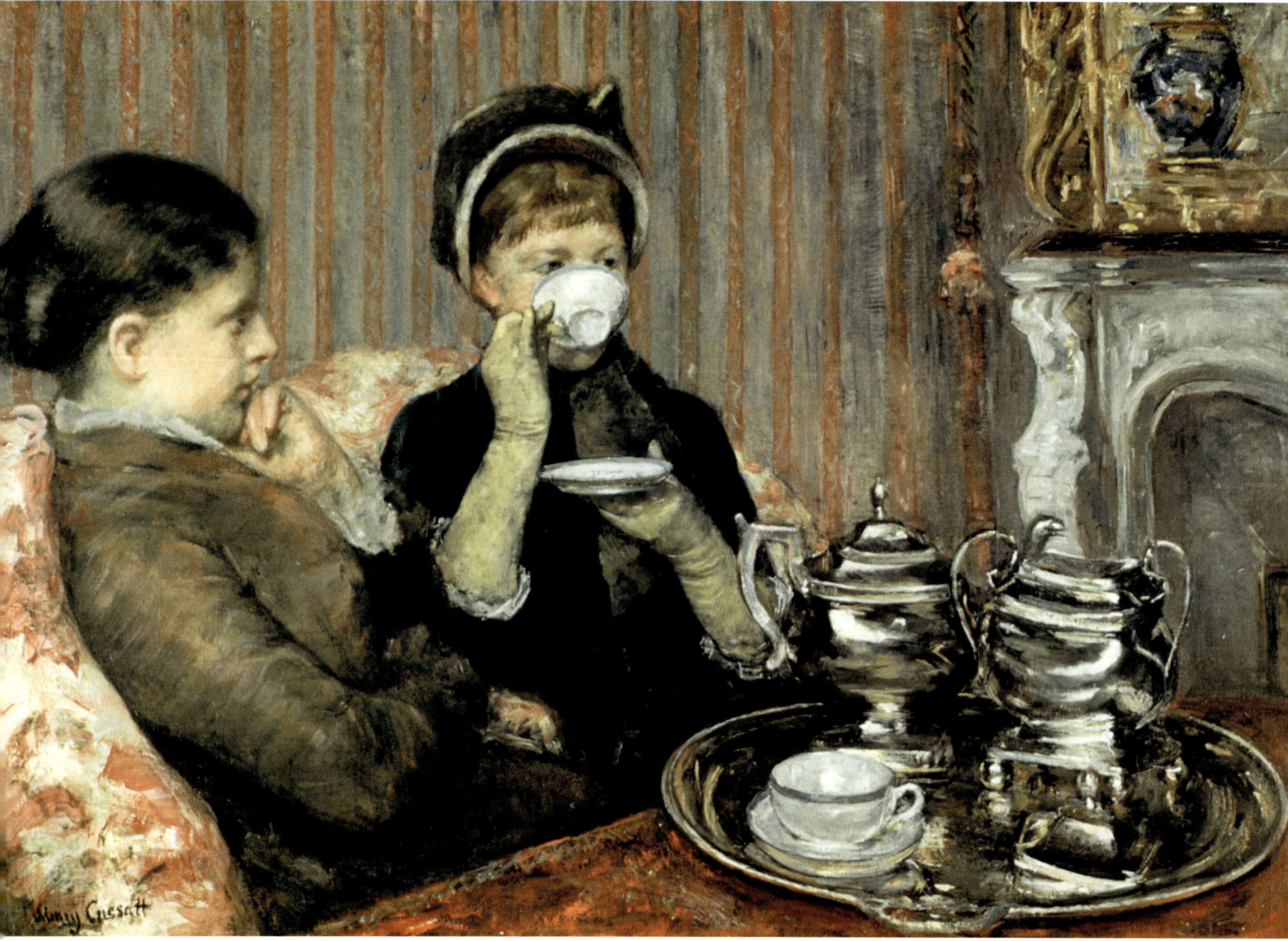

MARY CASSATT, Five O'Clock Tea *(1880). Keen observation of accidental gestures gave Cassatt's paintings freshness and immediacy. In this depiction, two women gaze out to the right of the composition, as if they were looking at someone just beyond the limits of the canvas. Taking a sip of tea, the guest—still wearing her hat and gloves—blocks a full view of her face.*

MUSEUM OF FINE ARTS, BOSTON. OIL ON CANVAS (25½×36½ INCHES).

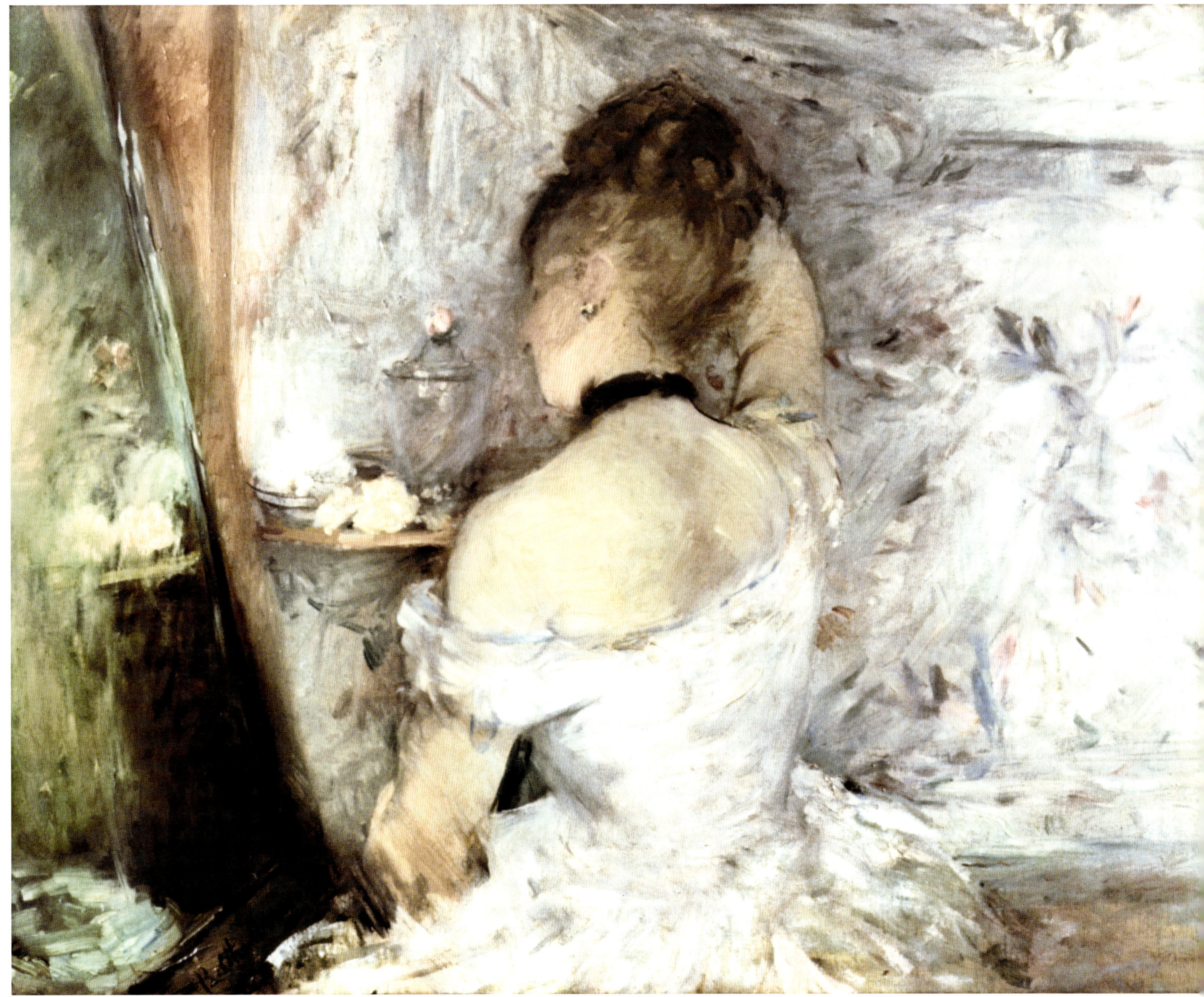

Berthe Morisot, Woman at her Toilette *(c. 1875). In a swirl of delicate strokes, Morisot evokes a fleeting and intimate glimpse of a woman arranging her hair at her dressing table mirror. The palette features a nuanced range of icy pale tones of pink, blue, white, and silver. This painting is an example of Morisot's ephemeral approach.*

The Art Institute of Chicago. Oil on canvas (23¾×31⅝ inches).

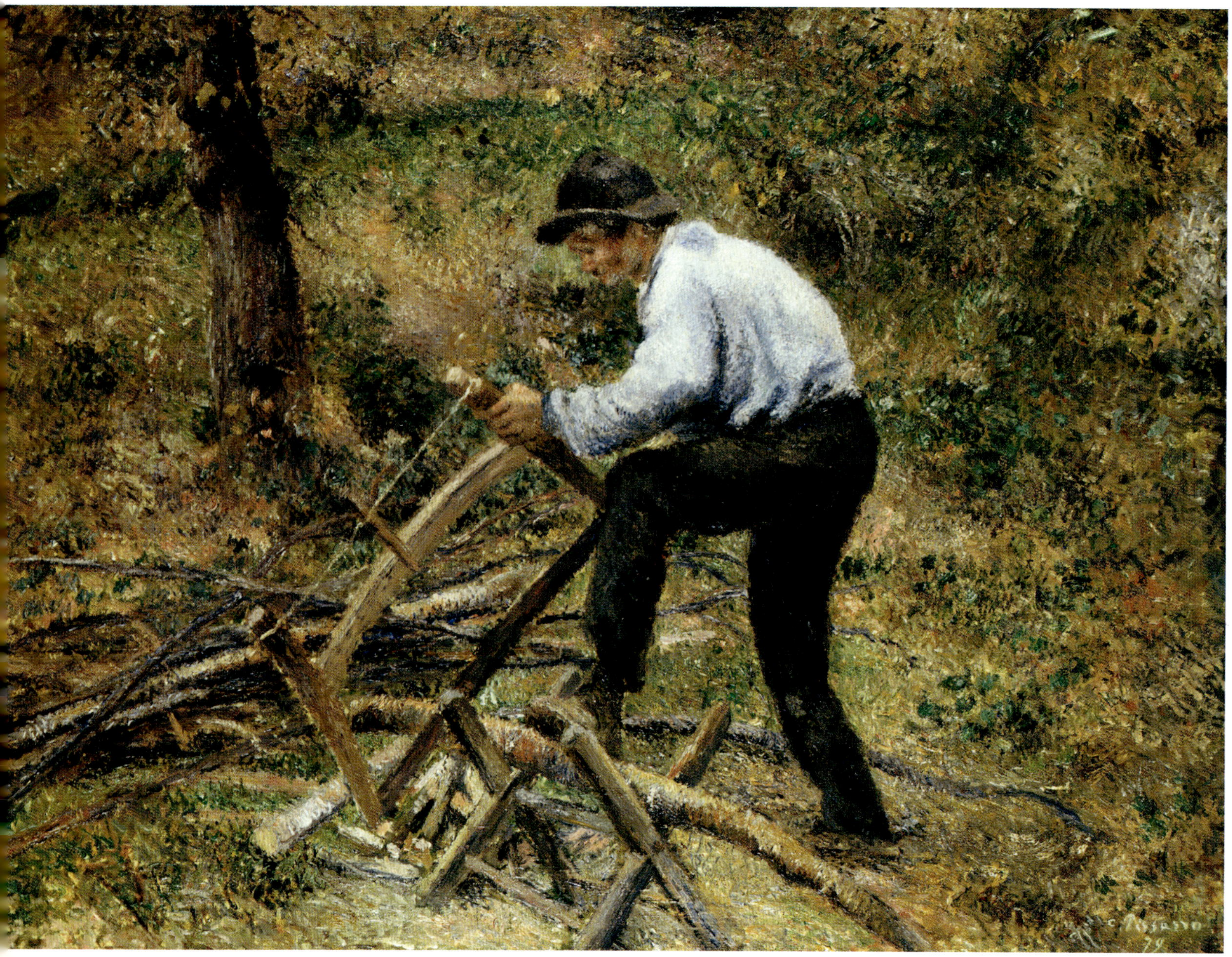

CAMILLE PISSARRO, The Woodcutter *(1879). The figure of Pissarro's woodcutter recalls the peasant laborers painted by Jean Francois Millet. With solid weight and strong contours, the woodcutter seems to have been shaped by his work, by the repetitive motion of dragging his saw back and forth through the wood. But the background has a vanishing quality, with light sparkling on the dense foliage.*

ROBERT HOLMES À COURT COLLECTION, PERTH, WESTERN AUSTRALIA. OIL ON CANVAS (35×45¾ INCHES).

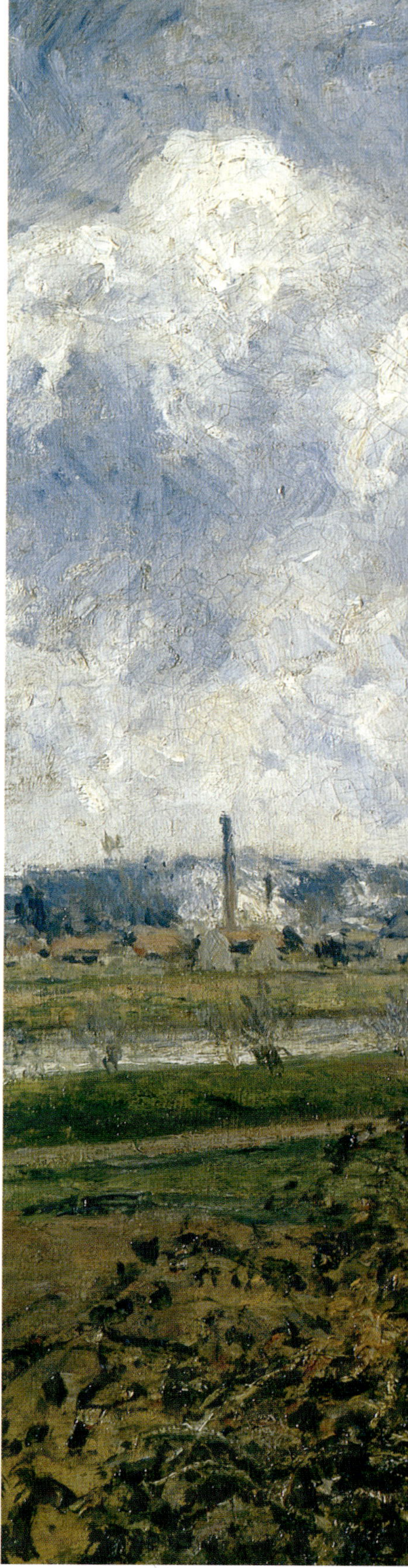

CAMILLE PISSARRO, Pathway at Chou in March *(1878). Pissarro was a dominant presence in the sixth exhibition, represented by 28 works. Notably, his mastery of plein air painting and observed sensation is in full play in* Pathway at Chou in March. *Under a volatile, cloudy sky, mist cloaks the distant trees in a blue haze. The glaze of icy color in the foreground evokes the still-hard ground in the early spring.*

MUSÉE DES BEAUX-ARTS, DOUAI, FRANCE. OIL ON CANVAS (19¾×36¼ INCHES).

The Sixth Exhibition 1881

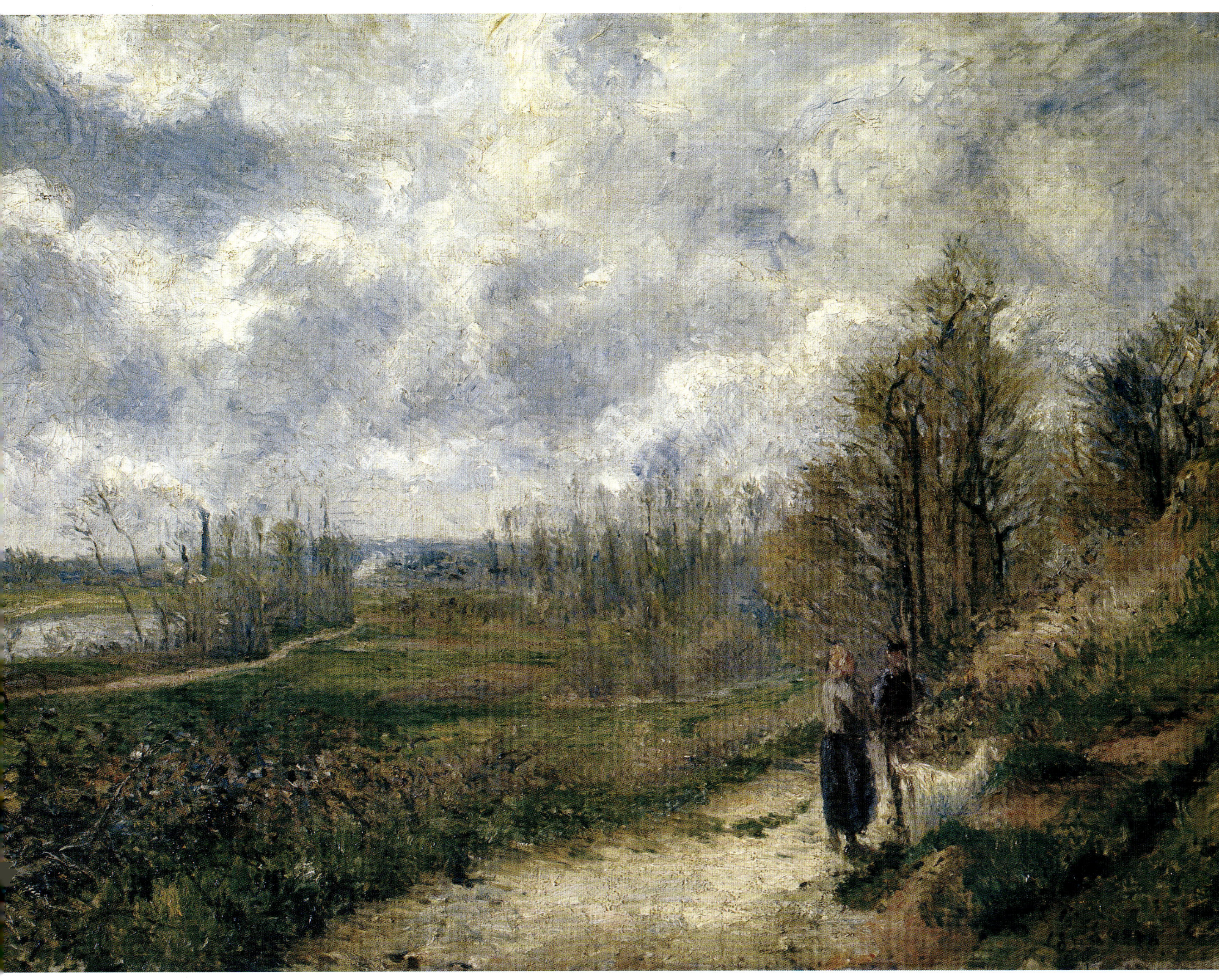

Mary Cassatt (American, 1844–1926), The Cup of Tea *(1879). While some critics were uncertain as to whether Cassatt was English or American, the writer Gustave Geffroy declared that she was "exquisitely Parisian." He singled this work out as his favorite in the exhibition for its nuance of color and delicate play of light on sumptuous surfaces. Joris-Karl Huysmans agreed, suggesting the work expressed "a flutter of feminine nerves."*

The Metropolitan Museum of Art, New York. Oil on canvas (36⅜×25¾ inches).

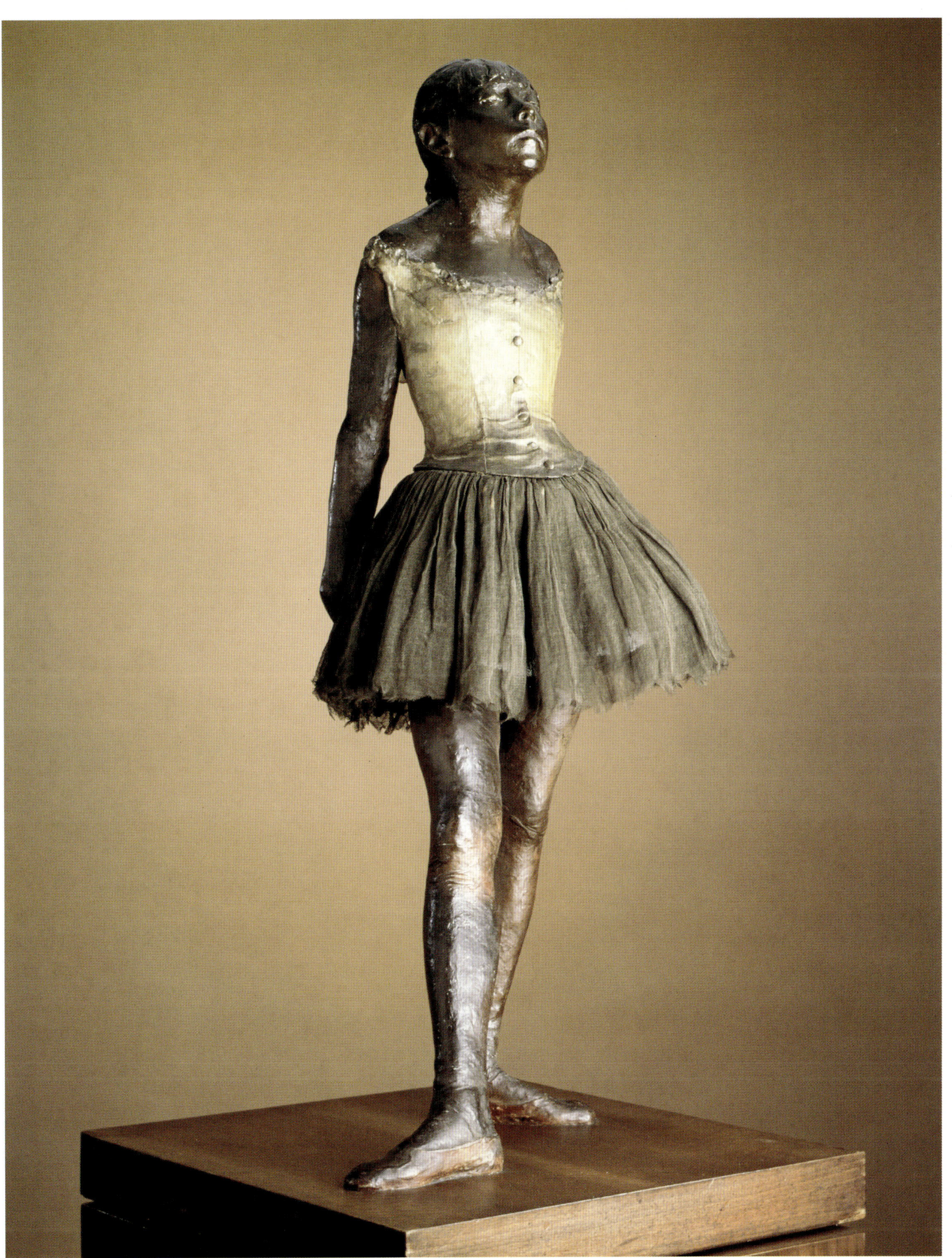

HILAIRE-GERMAIN-EDGAR DEGAS, Little Dancer of Fourteen Years *(1880; cast 1920). The taut contours of Degas's small bronze figure convey the nervous discipline of a young dancer. The position of her arms, drawn straight down and clasped behind her back, articulates the fragile bones of her chest and shoulders; the forward thrust of her head strains her facial features. Blurring the line between rendering and reality, Degas gave this dancer a real costume made of gauze and tied her braid with a satin ribbon.*

THE SAINT LOUIS ART MUSEUM. BRONZE, GAUZE, AND SATIN (38 7/16 INCHES HIGH).

THE SEVENTH EXHIBITION 1882

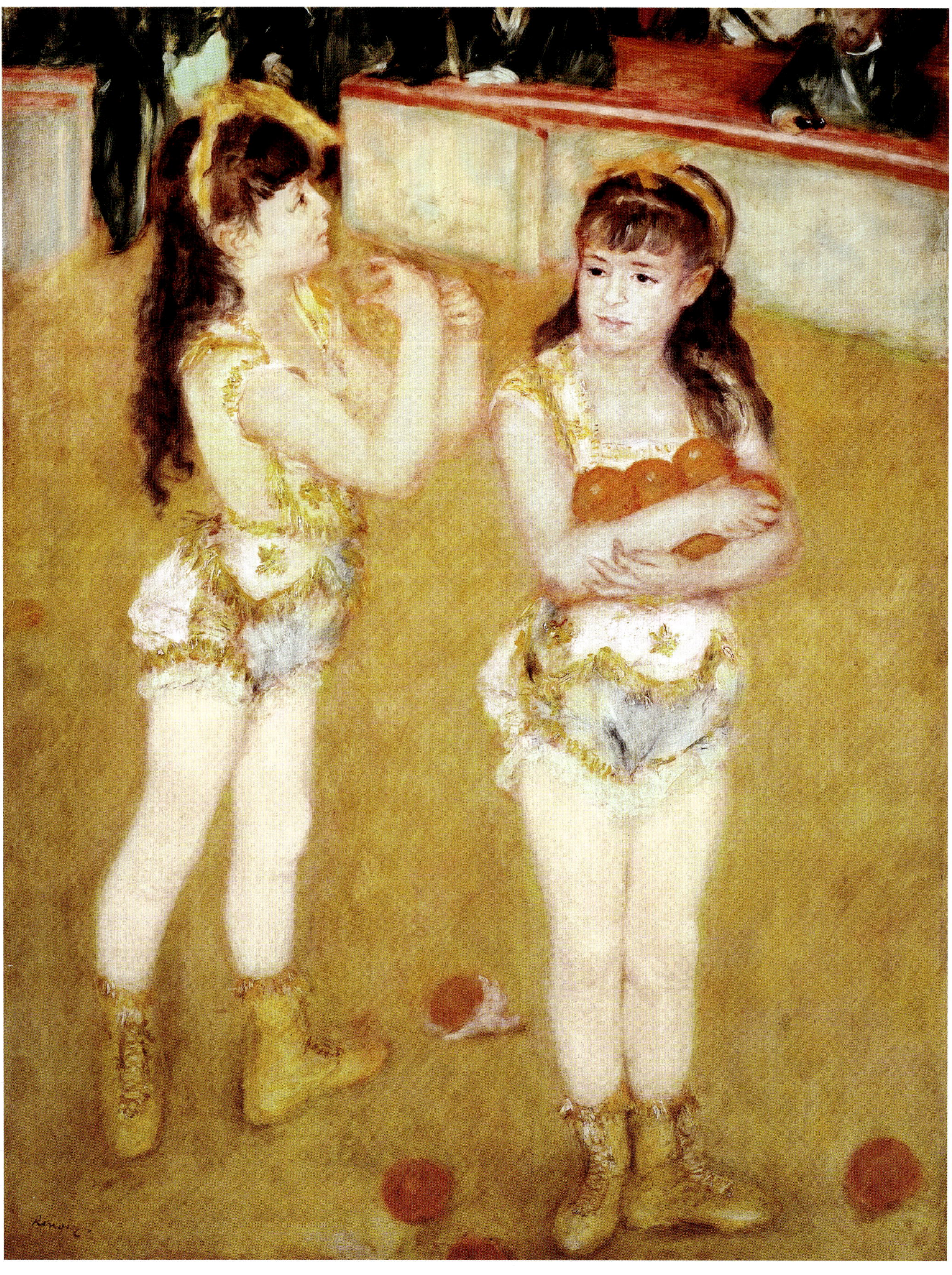

PIERRE-AUGUSTE RENOIR, Acrobats at the Cirque Fernando (Francisca and Angelina Wartenberg) *(1879). After withholding his works from the Impressionist exhibitions since the third exhibition of 1877, Renoir submitted 27 works to the seventh exhibition. In this painting, Renoir presents a sentimental anecdote as well as a subject from modern life. The girls have been identified as Francesca and Angelina Wartenberg, who juggled and performed gymnastics in their father's circus.*

THE ART INSTITUTE OF CHICAGO. OIL ON CANVAS (51¾×39⅛ INCHES).

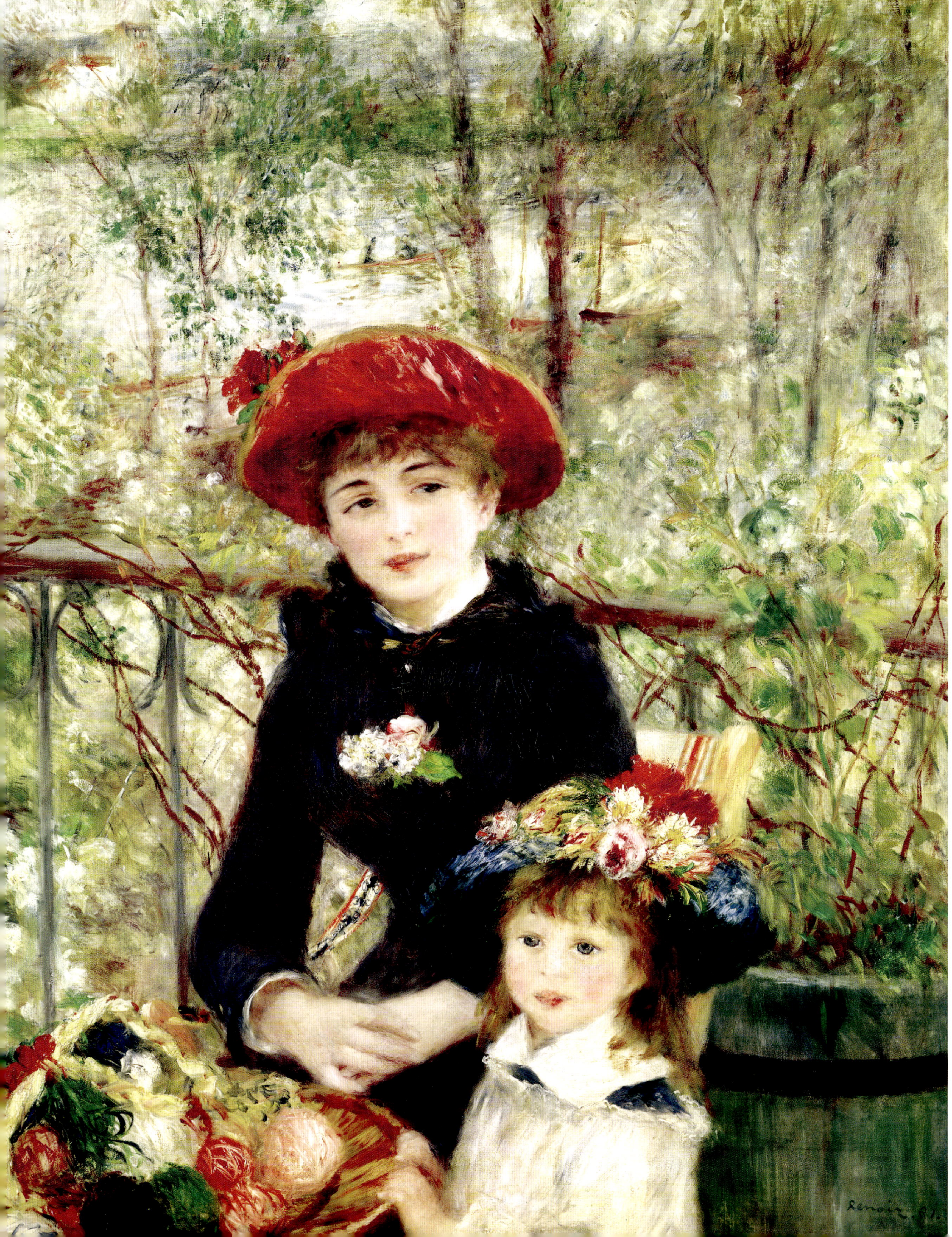

Pierre-Auguste Renoir, Two Sisters (On the Terrace) *(1881). Like* The Luncheon of the Boating Party *(1880–81), this painting is set on the upper terrace of the Restaurant Fournaise. However, the time of the year is spring. The flowering plants and vines behind the terrace rail have just come into bloom, and in the distance the full cumulus clouds appear as bluish, glistening reflections on the river. The sitters, who in fact were not related, wear bright, strong colors in front of the more delicate palette of foliage and flowers.*

The Art Institute of Chicago. Oil on canvas (39⁹⁄₁₆×37⅞ inches).

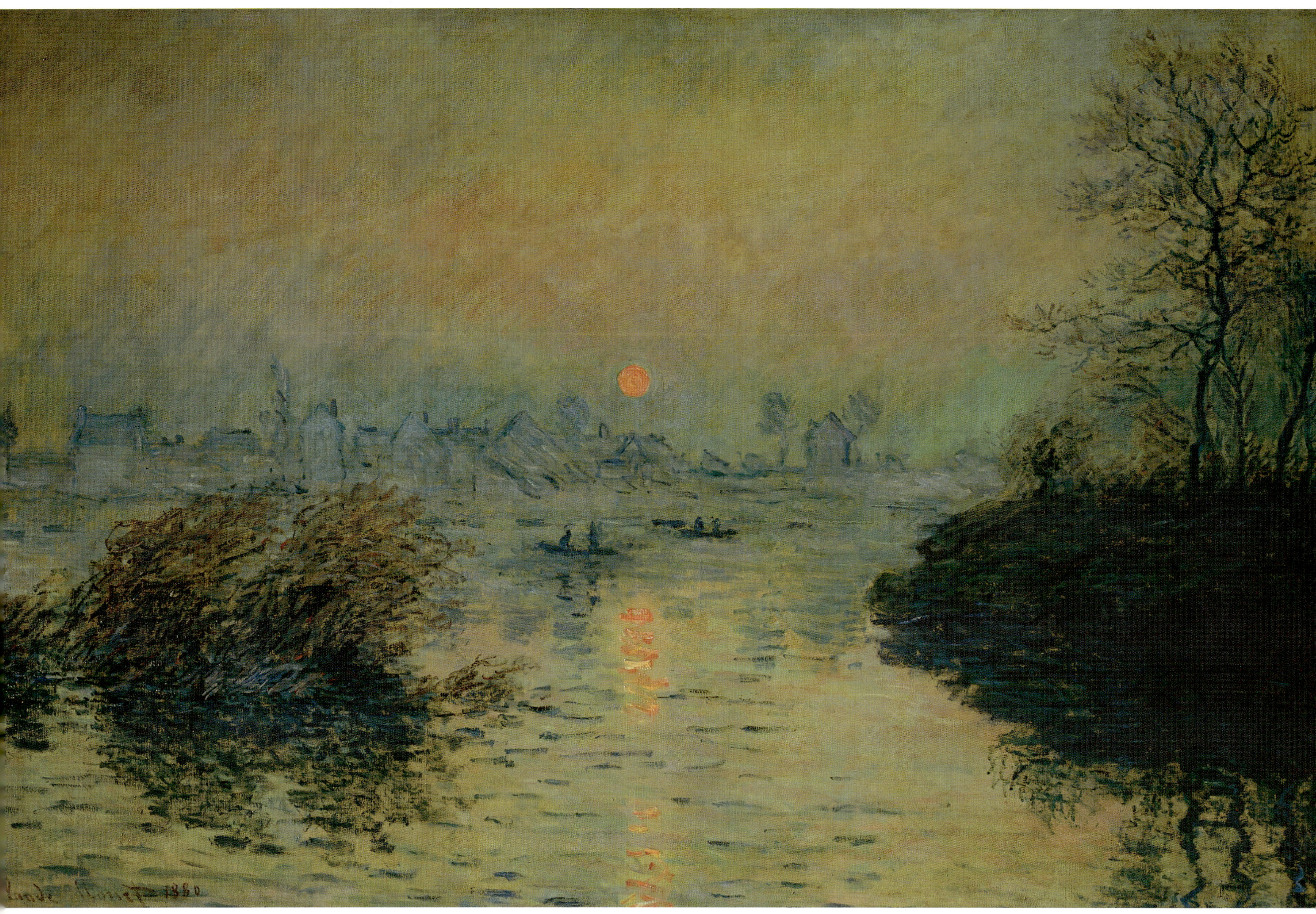

CLAUDE MONET, Setting Sun over the Seine at Lavacourt, Winter Effect *(1880). In his last Impressionist exhibition, Monet revisited the type of subject that prompted so much notoriety at the initial exhibition of the Société Anonyme. Although the location has changed from Le Havre to Lavacourt and the time of the day from sunrise to sunset, Monet again captured the dazzling effect of light on water, with boats appearing as ephemeral silhouettes.*

MUSÉE DU PETIT PALAIS, PARIS. OIL ON CANVAS (39⅜×59⅞ INCHES).

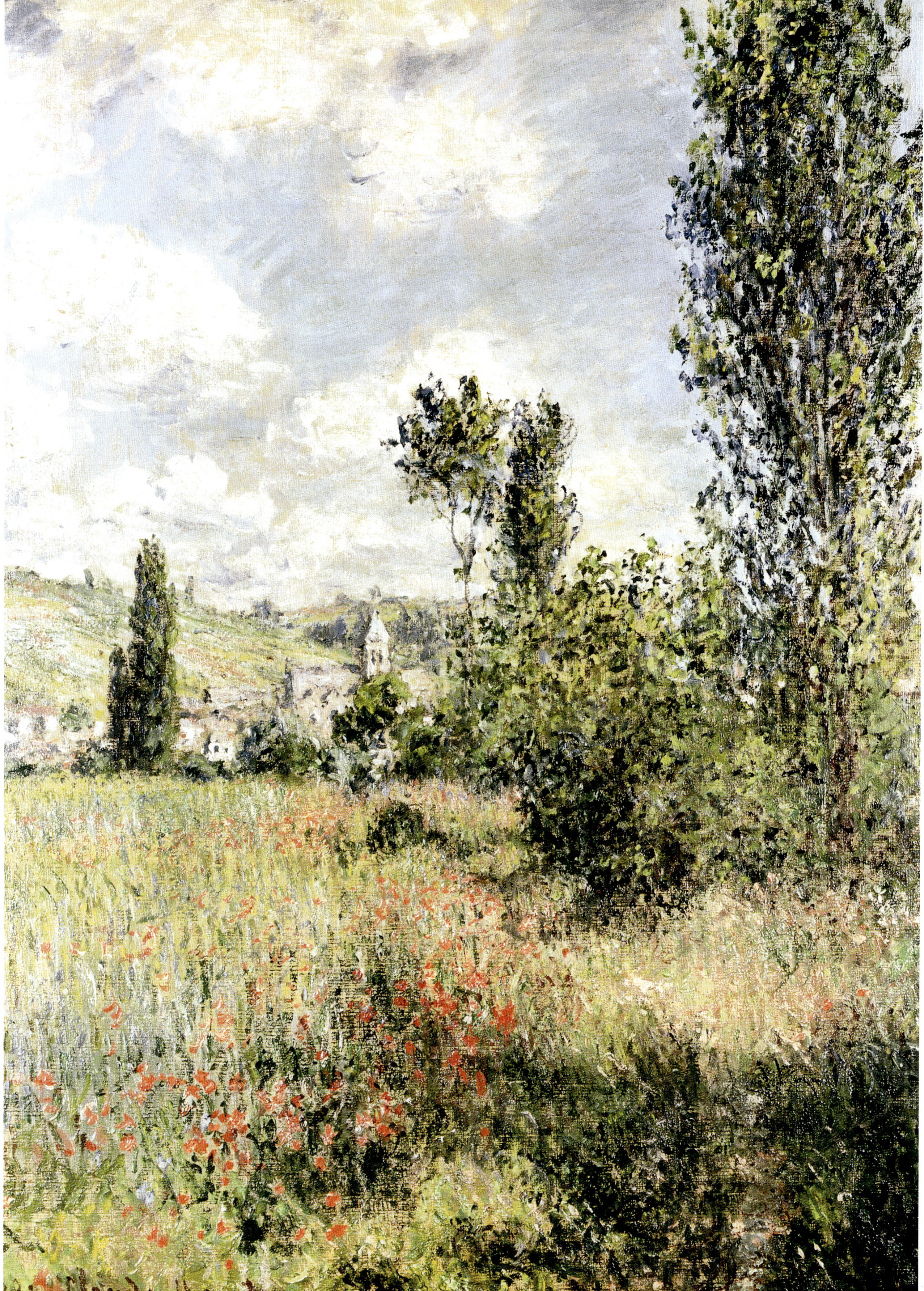

CLAUDE MONET, View of the Vétheuil *(1880). Monet dominated the seventh exhibition with 35 works. This view of a meadow in bloom on the outskirts of the rural village Vétheuil features pure, bright pigment applied to the surface of the canvas with a light touch and a sure hand. Monet's supremacy in the landscape genre was now undisputed, but the conservative critic Alfred Wolff grudgingly said that among the large display of Monet's paintings there were only "two or three pretty things."*

THE METROPOLITAN MUSEUM OF ART, NEW YORK. OIL ON CANVAS (31½×23¾ INCHES).

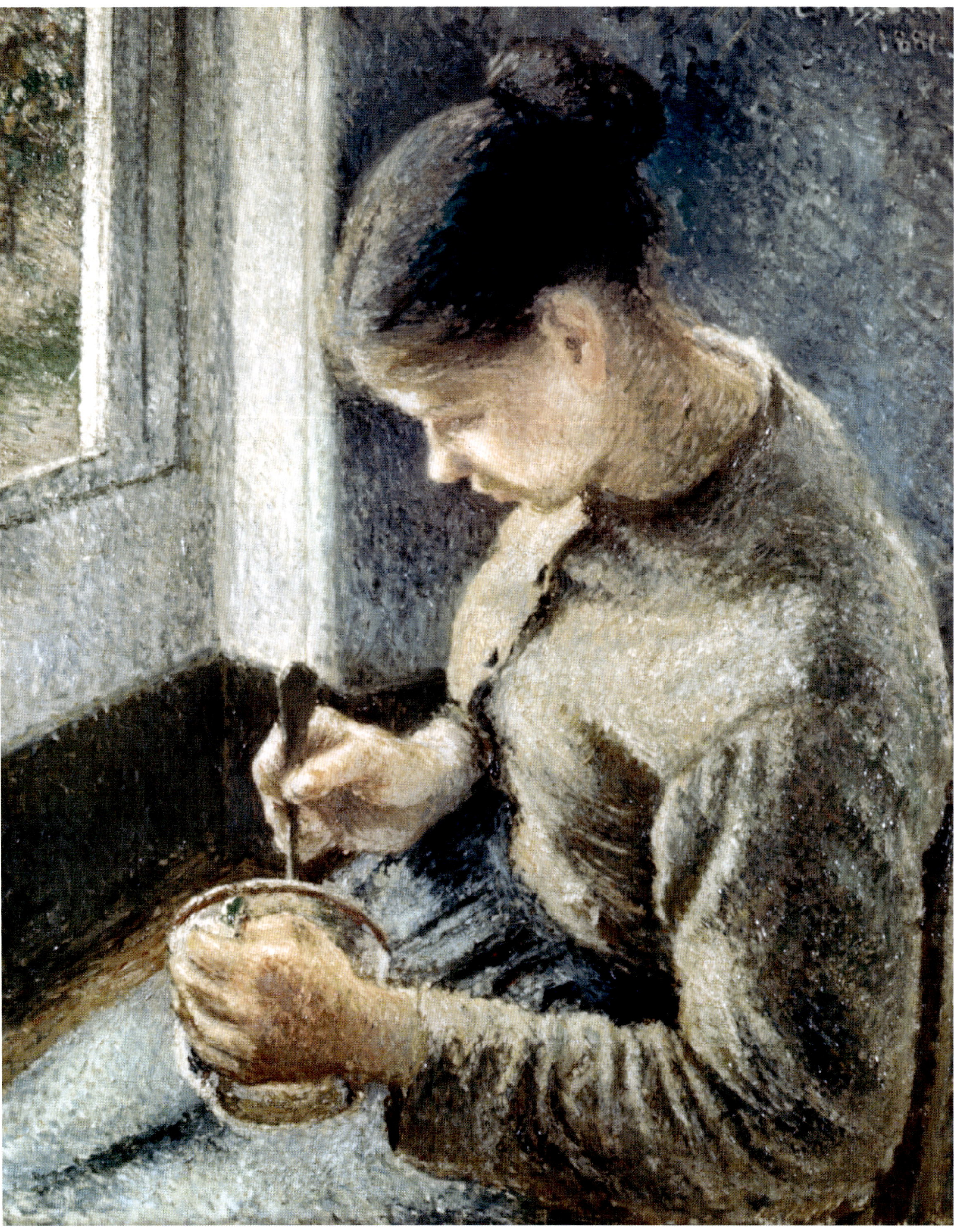

CAMILLE PISSARRO, Café Au Lait *(1881). The oblique view adds an element of intimacy to Pissarro's portrait of a young woman stirring her cup of café au lait. He seems to have gazed at her from a close range from above, as if he was standing beside her. With a limited palette of blue and brown, Pissarro conveys a simple atmosphere of the rustic kitchen, enforced by his rough brush stroke and solid composition.*

THE ART INSTITUTE OF CHICAGO. OIL ON CANVAS ($25\frac{11}{16} \times 29\frac{9}{16}$ INCHES).

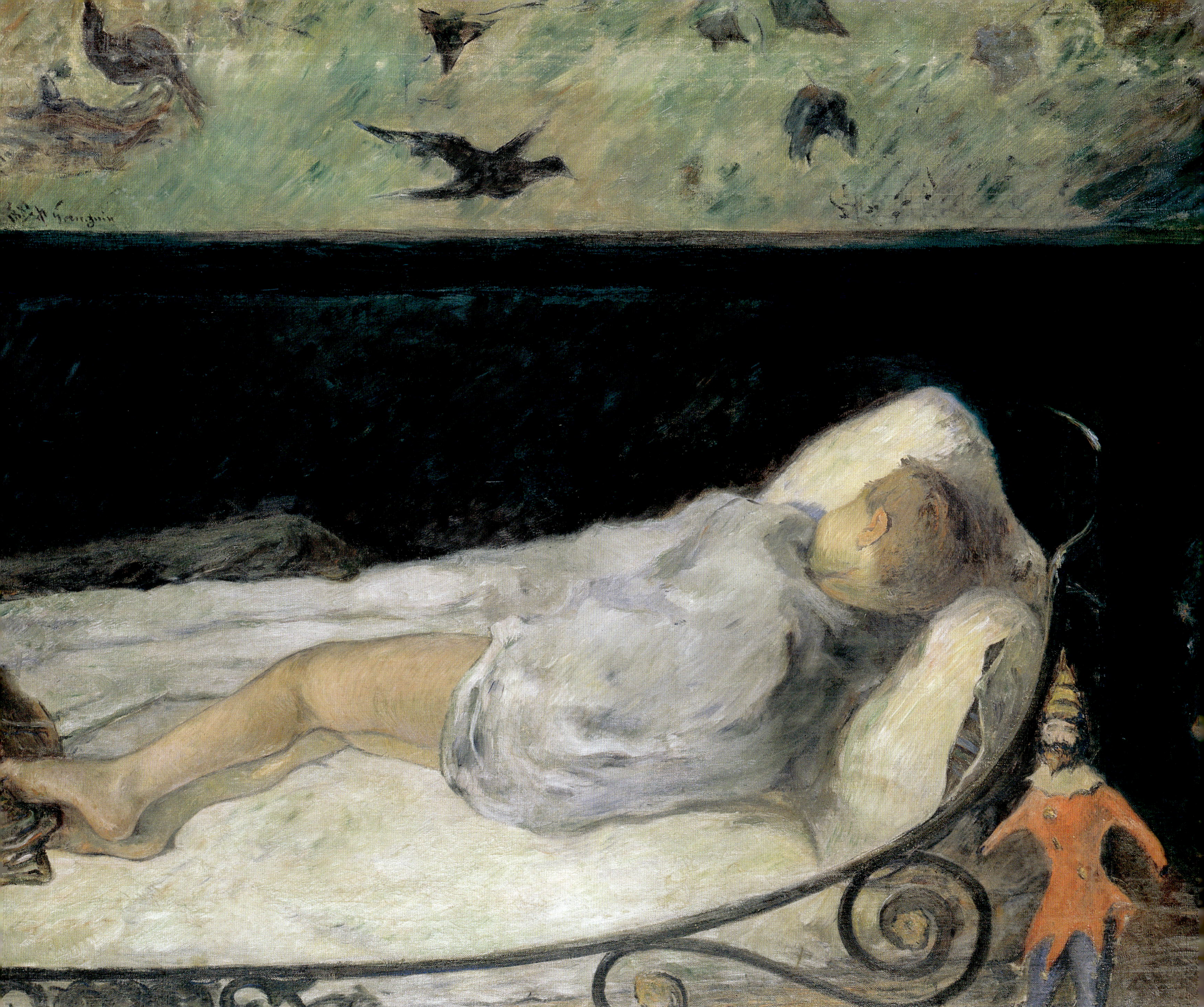

Paul Gauguin, The Little One is Dreaming, Etude *(1881). With more than a dozen works, Gauguin was a stronger presence at the seventh exhibition than in the previous ones. He labeled his work* etude, *or study, suggesting that the work was observed and swiftly painted to capture the momentary effect. The subject is one of Gauguin's children, asleep in a cradle with her back to the viewer, an intimate glimpse into his family life.*

Ordrupgaard, Copenhagen, Denmark. Oil on canvas (23⅝×29⅛ inches).

THE FINAL EXHIBITION

It is as if the artists have different pairs of glasses that they anchor on their noses when they want, with lenses made to give the tones they seek. This is the only way to explain categorically the orgy of tones that can at times be found in a single painting.

JEAN DE NIVELLE, *LE SOLEIL,* MARCH 4, 1882

IN FEBRUARY 1882, the collapse of the Union Générale bank generated a crisis in the French economy. Widespread panic deflated the stock market, and to escape rising debt, many in the newly affluent business class declared bankruptcy. Throughout the country, financial institutions called in their loans, and Durand-Ruel, who had funded his galleries through the Union Générale, found himself in difficult financial straits. The economic crisis had a surprising effect on the public reception of Impressionism. Although art sales plummeted, Durand-Ruel mounted a vigorous promotional campaign in an attempt to recover his business. In 1883 he initiated a program of solo exhibitions in his Paris gallery to feature the works of Claude Monet, Pierre-Auguste Renoir, and Alfred Sisley. He also arranged small group exhibitions in London, Berlin, and Boston, where the works sparked interest and controversy.

Despite a second London exhibition in April 1884, Durand-Ruel was nearly bankrupt by May. To protect his own interests, Monet accepted an invitation from rival art dealer Georges Petit to display paintings at Petit's annual Exposition International. However, he also continued his association with Durand-Ruel, and his work dominated the influential exhibition The Impressionists of Paris that Durand-Ruel organized for the American Art Association in New York City in April 1886. The exhibition drew tremendous crowds and wide press coverage, igniting a passion for Impressionist painting among American collectors. In the course of reviving his business, Durand-Ruel built an international reputation

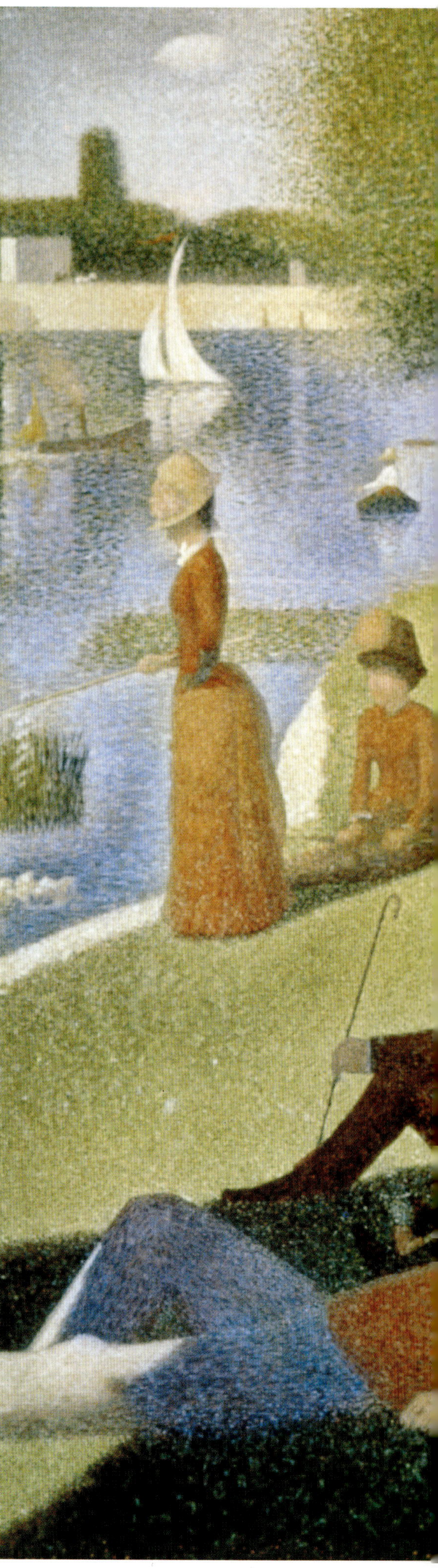

GEORGES SEURAT, Sunday Afternoon on the Island of the Grande-Jatte *(1884–86). Epic in scale and revolutionary in technique, Seurat's depiction of a middle-class crowd enjoying a leisurely afternoon in a public park dominated the final exhibition. Seurat had chosen a subject associated with "classic" Impressionism as seen in the work of Claude Monet and Pierre-Auguste Renoir. But he conceived his composition through an extensive series of pencil, chalk, and oil sketches that replaced the impression of spontaneity with a deliberate and formalist approach to spatial organization.*

THE ART INSTITUTE OF CHICAGO. OIL ON CANVAS (81×120⅜ INCHES).

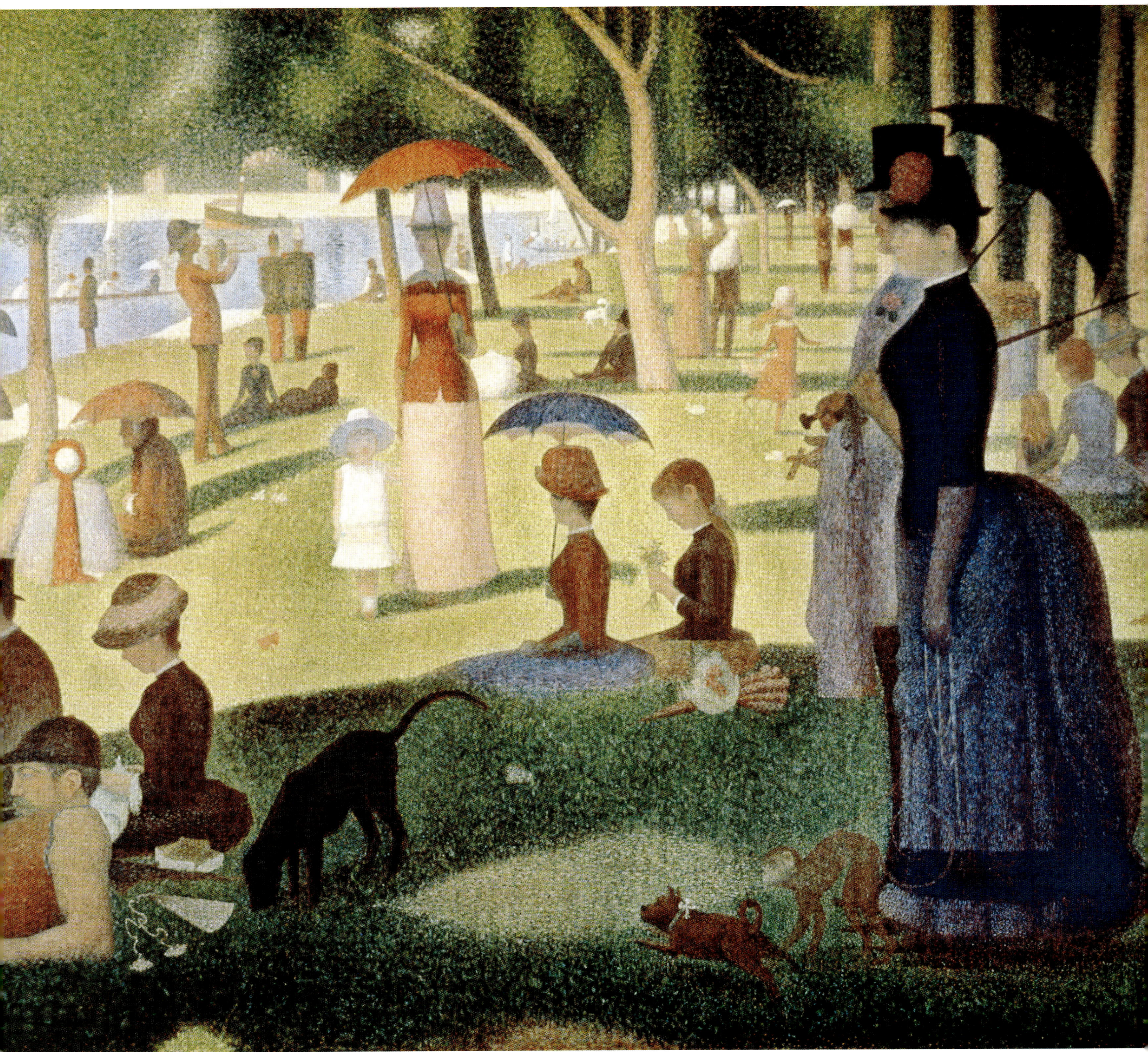

The Final Exhibition

for Impressionism, with Monet and his signature spontaneous approach forging the definitive expression of the movement.

The years between the seventh and eighth Impressionist exhibitions also saw the rise of new and independent exhibition societies. In 1883 Les Vingt (The Twenty) was founded in Brussels by journalist Octave Maus. Organized to promote advanced ideas in art and literature, that annual exhibition served as a showcase for Symbolist art but also featured the works of key Impressionists. Renoir proposed his own organization, the Société des Irregularistes, which never advanced beyond the planning stage. Another society, the Groupe des Artistes Indépendents, held its first exhibition in a post office building in the Tuileries in May 1884. Works by more than 400 artists were featured, including Georges Seurat's *Bathers at Asnières* (1884), which had been rejected by the Salon. At the opening, disputes broke out between members of the executive committee, and the police were summoned to intervene. Later that year, under the direction of the Symbolist writer and artist Odilon Redon, they reorganized as the Société des Artistes Indépendents and pledged to hold regularly scheduled exhibitions. They presented the first real challenge to the Impressionists as an alternative venue for progressive art.

In December 1884, after the first exhibition of the Société des Artistes Indépendents, Monet suggested that the core circle of the Impressionists hold monthly meetings. After much debate, a new exhibition was planned for 1886, and despite their growing differences, all the members gave the idea their initial endorsement. Degas's adamant refusal to accept the assistance of dealers prompted Monet, Caillebotte, Renoir, and Sisley to withdraw. Pissarro, who shared responsibility with Degas for organizing the exhibition, was a strong advocate of the new generation of progressive artists. He was concerned about Gauguin's future; in 1883, with the financial crisis unresolved, Gauguin had quit his work as a stock

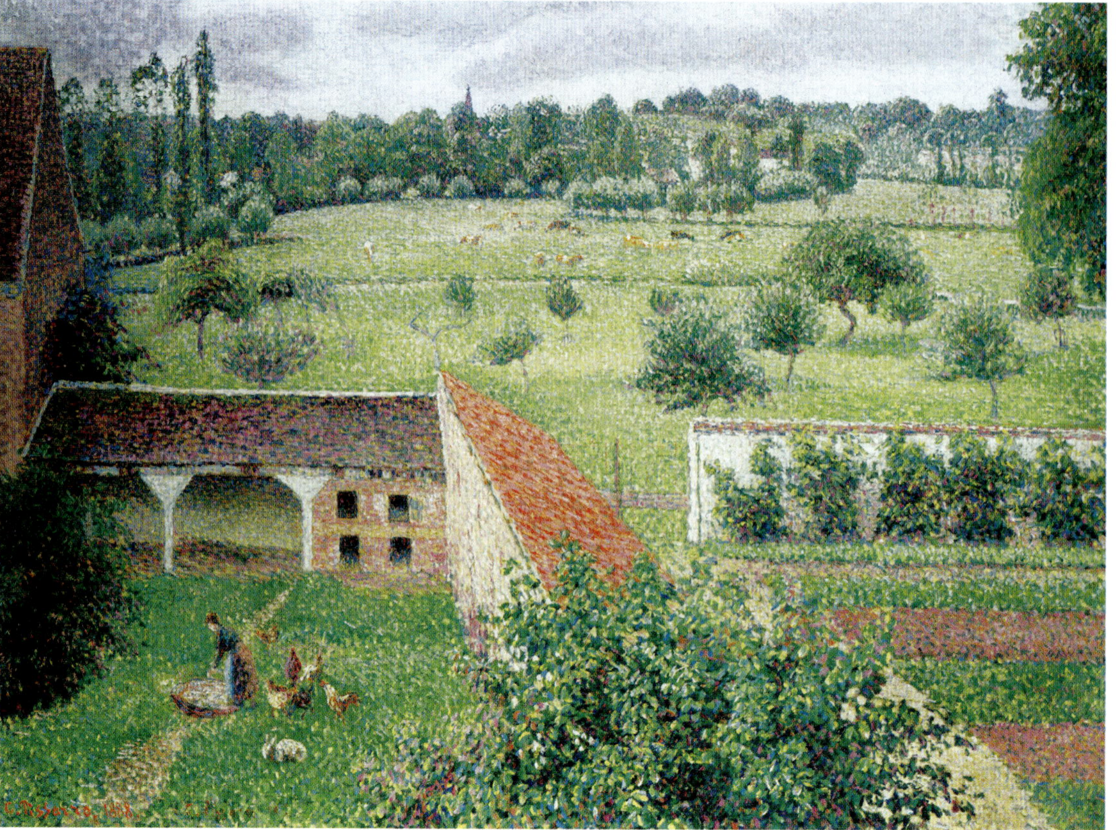

Camille Pissarro, View from My Window, Eragny *(1886–88). Pissarro began to experiment with applying dots of pure pigment on the canvas, as seen in this painting. This method was developed by Georges Seurat and later would be referred to as Neo-Impressionism.*

The Ashmolean Museum, Oxford, England. Oil on canvas (25⅝×31½ inches).

agent to devote his time to painting. Pissarro may have desired as well to promote the work of his son Lucien, a promising printmaker, but he was also intrigued by the work of the young painter Georges Seurat. Informed by recent discoveries in optical theory, Seurat had developed a method of applying dots of pure pigment on his canvas in close juxtaposition, simulating the action of individual rays of light. Seurat proposed that the viewer's retina—rather than the painter's brush—would blend the colors, recreating in paint the luminous and vibrant effect of looking at nature. Seurat's friend Paul Signac had also adopted this technique, which the young painters regarded as based in science rather than sensation.

The eighth exhibition boasted a fashionable location on the rue Lafitte among chic shops, galleries, and cafés. It ran concurrent with the Salon, which Pissarro felt was a bad decision. He wrote to his son Lucien, "To pay for an exhibition at the same time as the Salon is to run the risk of selling nothing. Miss Cassatt and Degas say that's not the purpose of the exhibition, but that's easy to say when your bread's assured." Seventeen artists were represented by more than 240 works. Again, the exhibition was notable for its variety: Prints, drawings, and painted fans were featured along with paintings. From the outset, Degas objected to the work of Seurat and Signac, but Pissarro had already begun to experiment with the new technique. To appease Degas, their works were placed in a separate room at the back of the gallery suite. Degas chose this strategy to allow the critics to view the more conventional works before confronting the radical paintings, but his own images of women bathing received the harshest attacks. The writer Gustave Geffroy compared the experience of viewing Degas's bathers to peeping through a keyhole.

Seurat's *Sunday Afternoon on the Island of the Grande-Jatte* (1884–86) was the centerpiece of the final room of the exhibition. Epic in scale, Seurat's painting addressed a subject long associated with Impressionist painting: people in a public park on a sunny afternoon. But in contrast to the fleeting sense of momentary observation that had become the hallmark of Impressionist plein air painting, the most striking feature of Seurat's painting was its rigorous formal organization. Along with Signac and Pissarro, Seurat presented an alternative to the prevailing definition of Impressionist painting. The critic Félix Fénéon, the first to attempt to explain the new approach to the public in his review "Les Impressionistes," named the style Neo-Impressionism. Although it shattered the now-conventional perception of Impressionism as an unmediated rendering of fleeting visual sensations, *Sunday Afternoon on the Island of the Grande-Jatte* embodied the independent and progressive spirit of the initial Impressionist experiment.

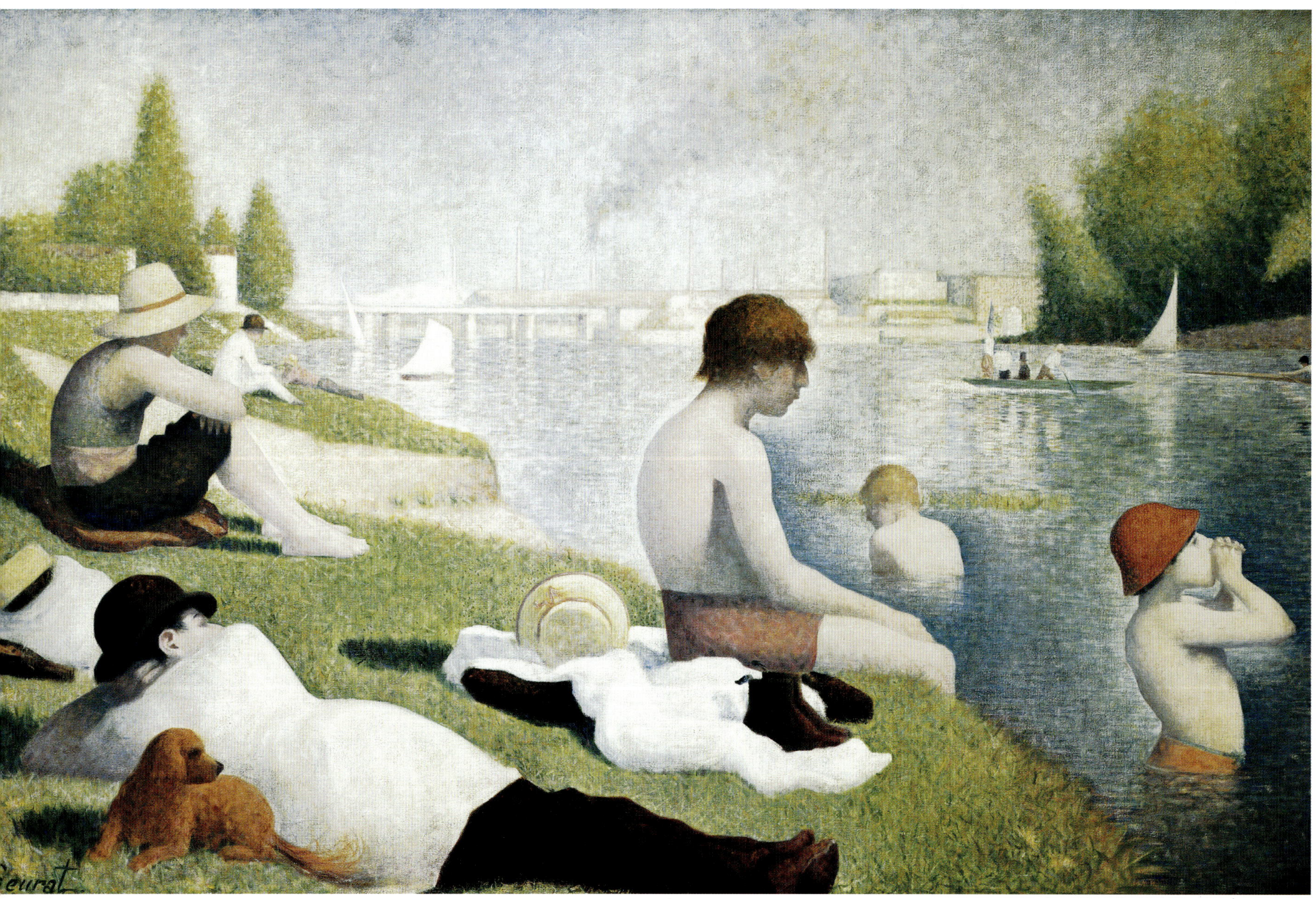

GEORGES SEURAT, Bathers at Asnières *(1884). Part of a new generation that watched as Impressionism rose from notoriety to acceptance, Seurat sought what he believed to be a more rigorous approach through structure and color theory. This painting, rejected by the Salon of 1884, offers a counterpoint to Renoir's vision of middle-class leisure that is epic rather than intimate and formal rather than spontaneous.*

THE NATIONAL GALLERY, LONDON. OIL ON CANVAS (79⅛×118⅛ INCHES).

GEORGES SEURAT, Le Bec du Hoc, Grandcamp *(1885). Seurat sought a scientific approach to the visual sensations associated with Impressionism. He developed a method of applying pure pigment to his canvas in individual dots asserting that, when placed in close proximity, the colors would be perceived as a luminous mixture. His method became known as Neo-Impressionism because it advanced ideas concerning visual perceptions.*

TATE GALLERY, LONDON. OIL ON CANVAS (25½×32⅛ INCHES).

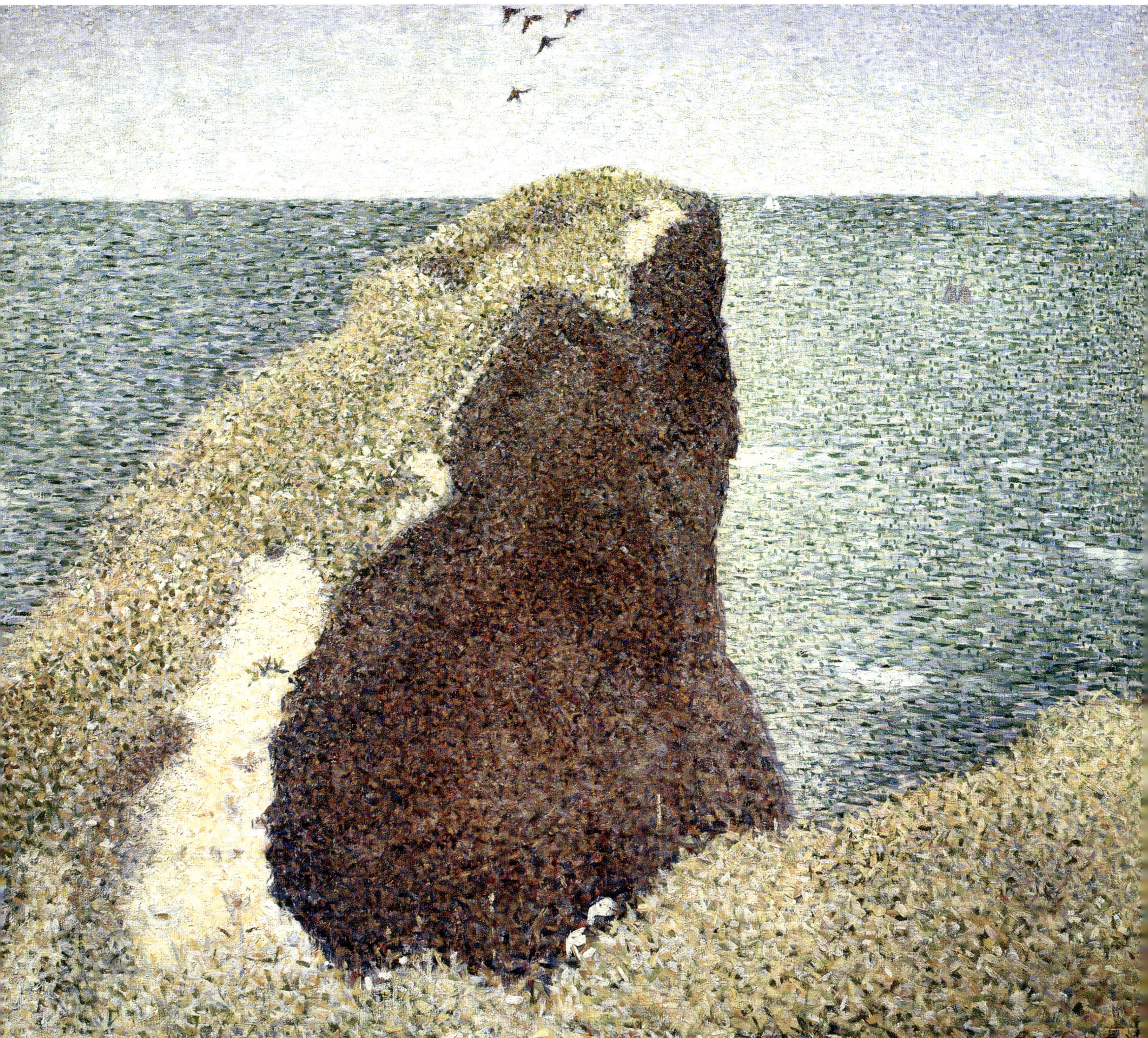

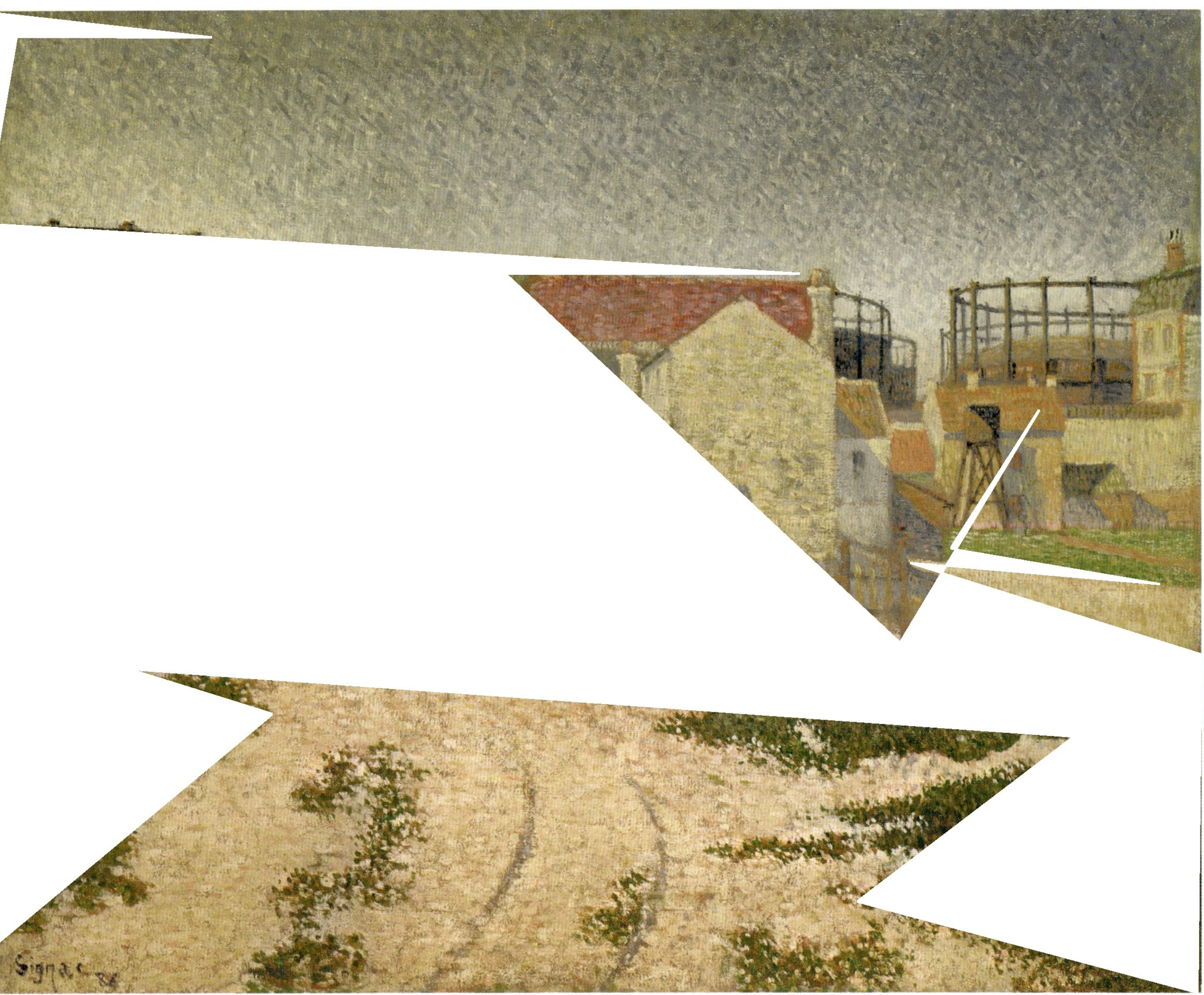

PAUL SIGNAC, The Gas Tanks at Clichy *(1886). After meeting Seurat in 1884, Signac began his own experiments in Neo-Impressionism. He chose an industrial site, a group of gas tanks, as his subject but used luminous color to transform them with a scintillating interplay of vibrant tones. Signac used the method to his own ends by employing a subtle gradation of hue and strongly anchored forms.*

NATIONAL GALLERY OF VICTORIA, MELBOURNE, AUSTRALIA. OIL ON CANVAS (25⅝×31⅞ INCHES).

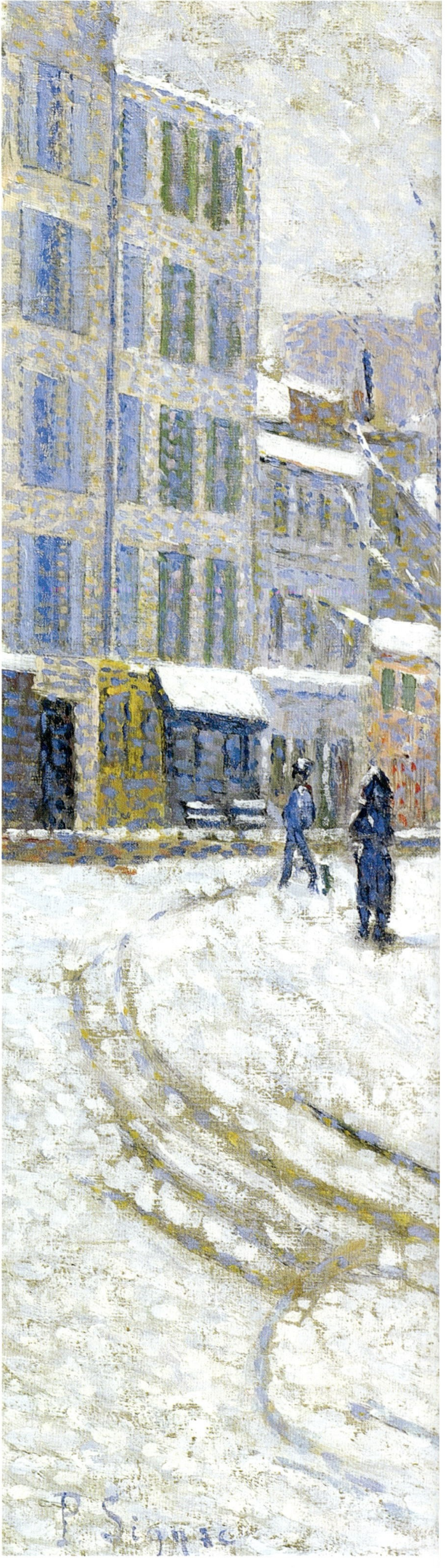

PAUL SIGNAC, Snow, Boulevard de Clichy, Paris *(1886). Signac drew from both classic Impressionism and the scientific formulation of Neo-Impressionism in his view of an urban street cloaked with snow. His pale, shimmering palette, with delicate tones of pink and violet, reveals his early admiration for the work of Monet, but he applied his pigment in the characteristic dots meant to excite the viewer's optical perceptions.*

THE MINNEAPOLIS INSTITUTE OF ARTS. OIL ON CANVAS (18¼×25⅞ INCHES).

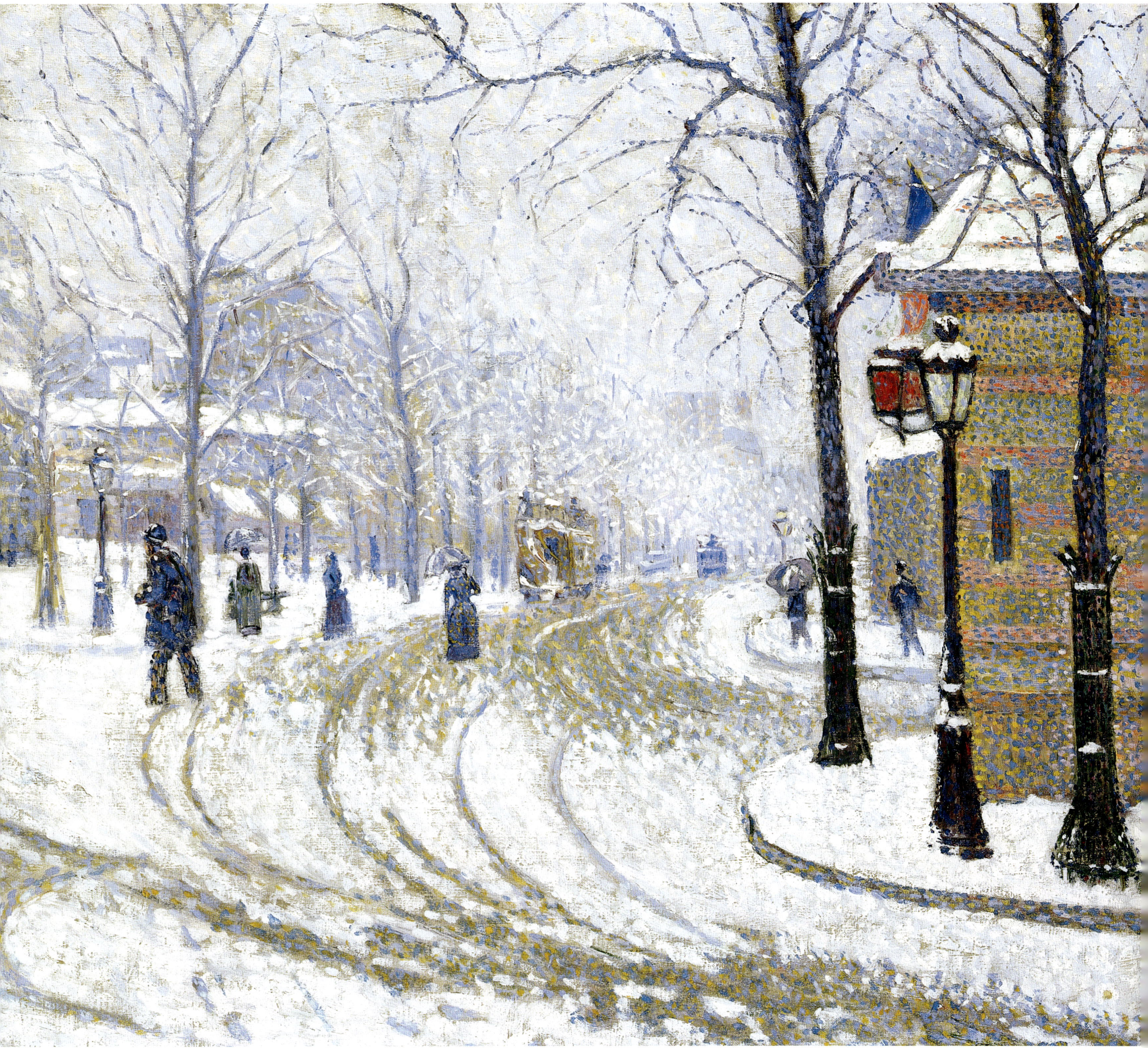

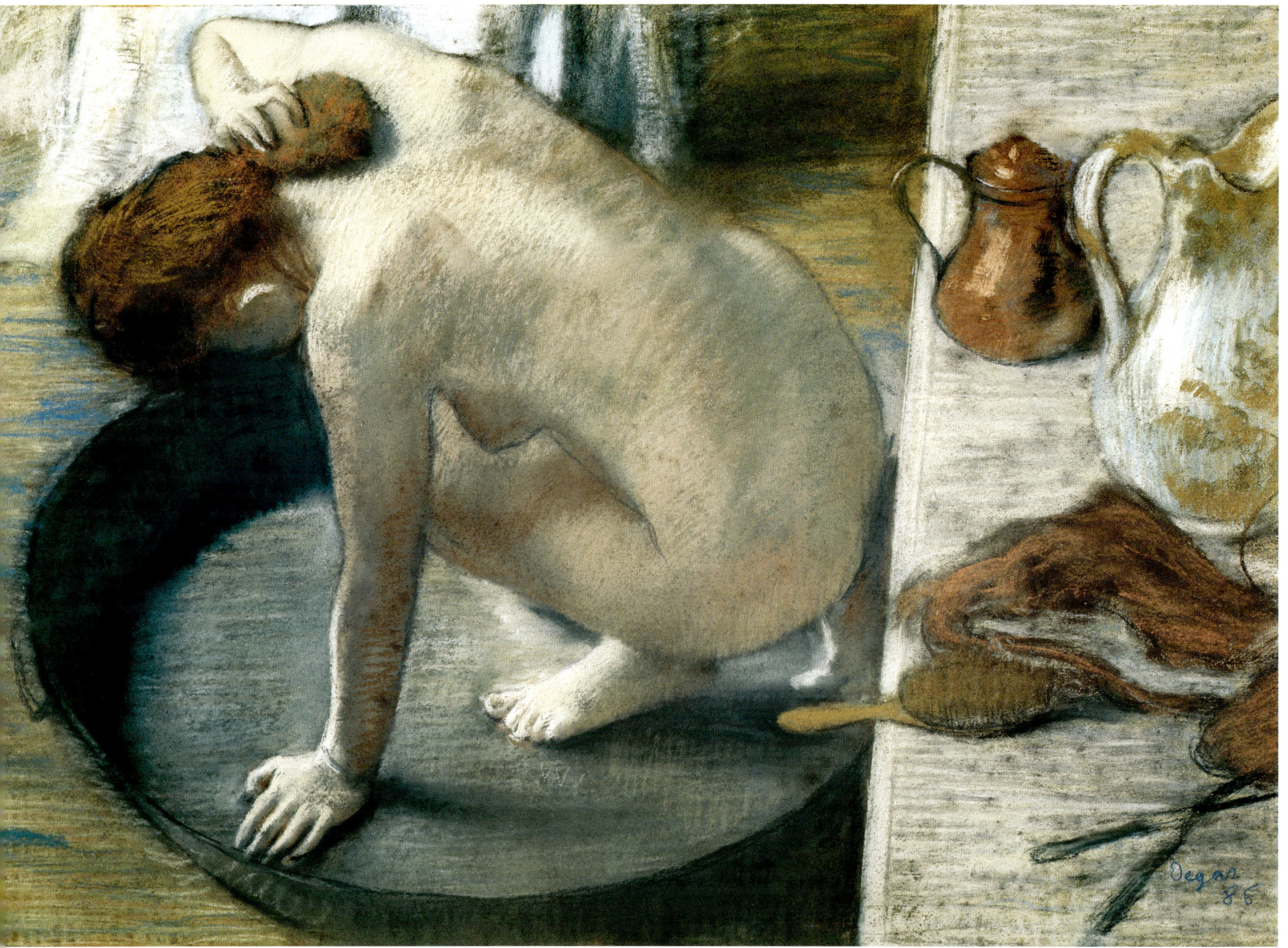

HILAIRE-GERMAIN-EDGAR DEGAS, The Tub *(1886). In his series of women bathing and dressing, Degas pioneered a new approach to the nude. The academic formulation of the nude was based on beauty, and the figure was composed in a way that celebrated the regularity of proportion and the grace of movement. Degas preferred to portray the accidental gesture, as if the figure was caught unawares. Degas heightened this sense of voyeurism with a high point of view, looking down at the figure and into the tub.*

MUSÉE D'ORSAY, PARIS. PASTEL (23⅝×32⅝ INCHES).

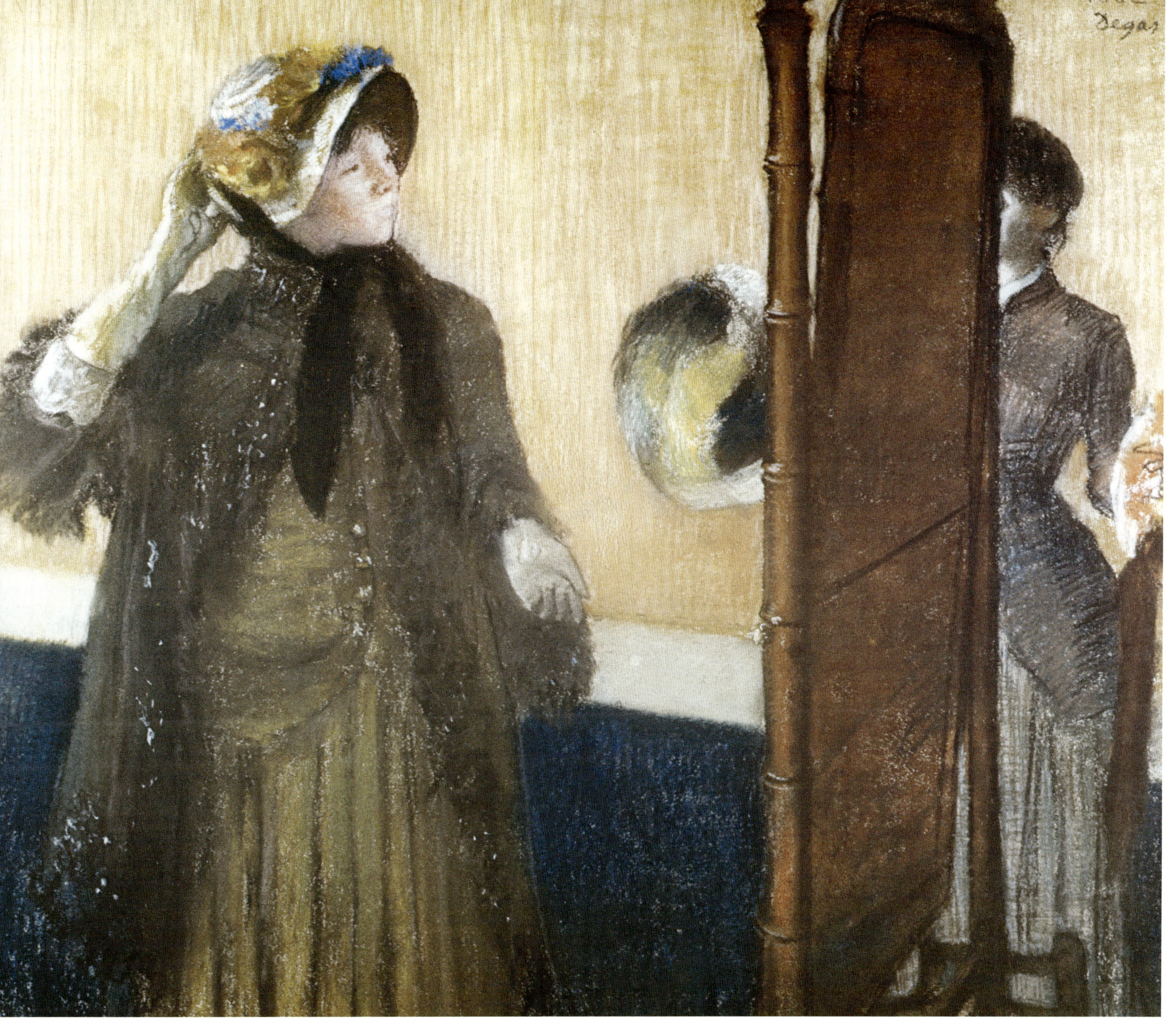

HILAIRE-GERMAIN-EDGAR DEGAS, At the Milliner's *(1882). Degas's own approach to spontaneous observation involved a daring spatial organization characterized by cut-off figures, acute lines of vision, and asymmetrical composition. Here, in a pastel of a woman trying on a bonnet in front of a mirror, the mirror frame is set at an oblique angle to the right side of the composition, bisecting the form of the attending saleswoman who holds out another hat.*

THE METROPOLITAN MUSEUM OF ART, NEW YORK. PASTEL ON PALE GRAY WOVEN PAPER, LAID DOWN ON SILK BOLTING (30×34 INCHES).

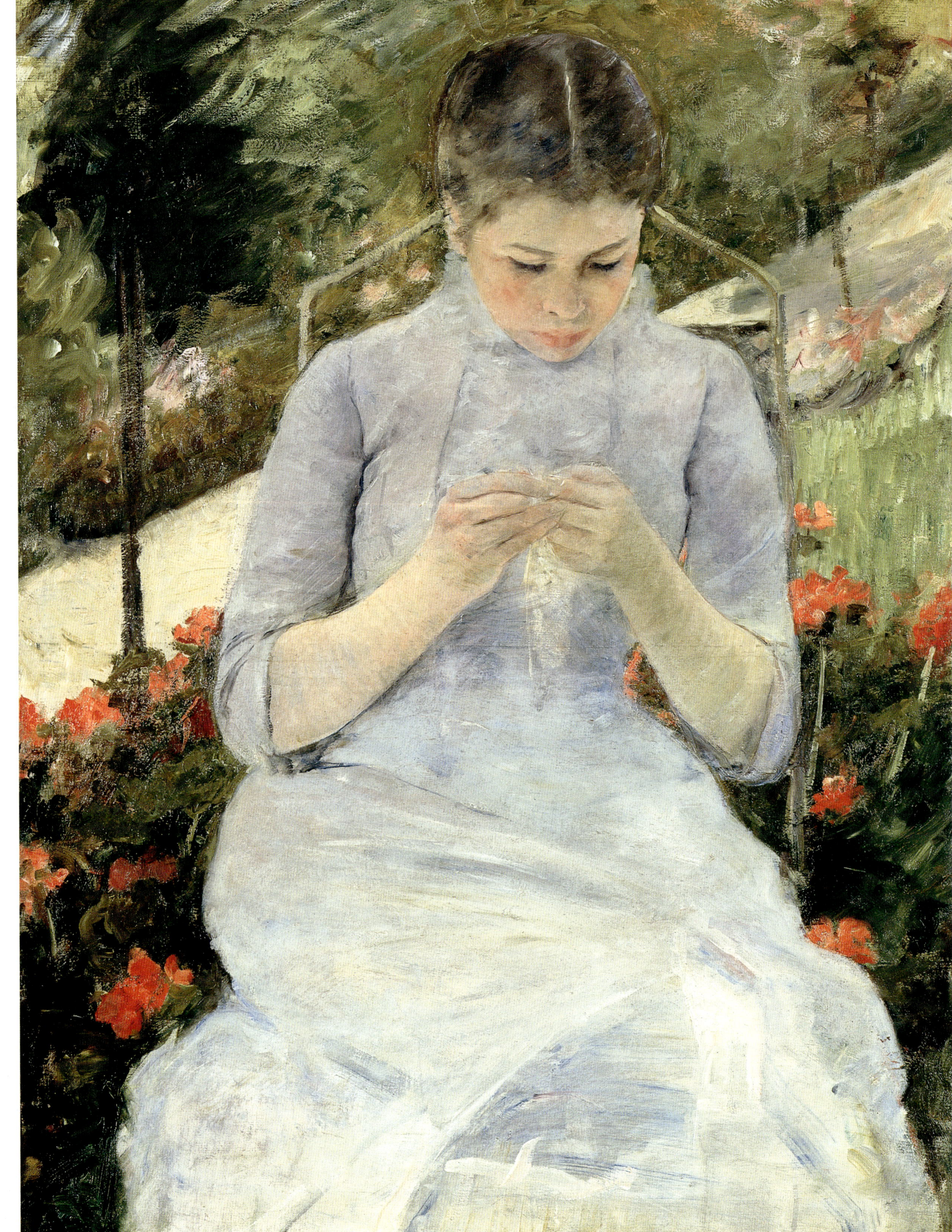

Mary Cassatt, Young Woman Sewing in a Garden *(1880–82). Like Degas, Cassatt experimented with bold compositions. In this painting, the figure is pushed up to the very surface of the picture plane, while the garden path behind her cuts across the back of the canvas in a diagonal axis. But in contrast to Degas's tight drawing style, Cassatt handled her paint with a loose and confident stroke.*

Musée d'Orsay, Paris. Oil on canvas (36¼×24⅜ inches).

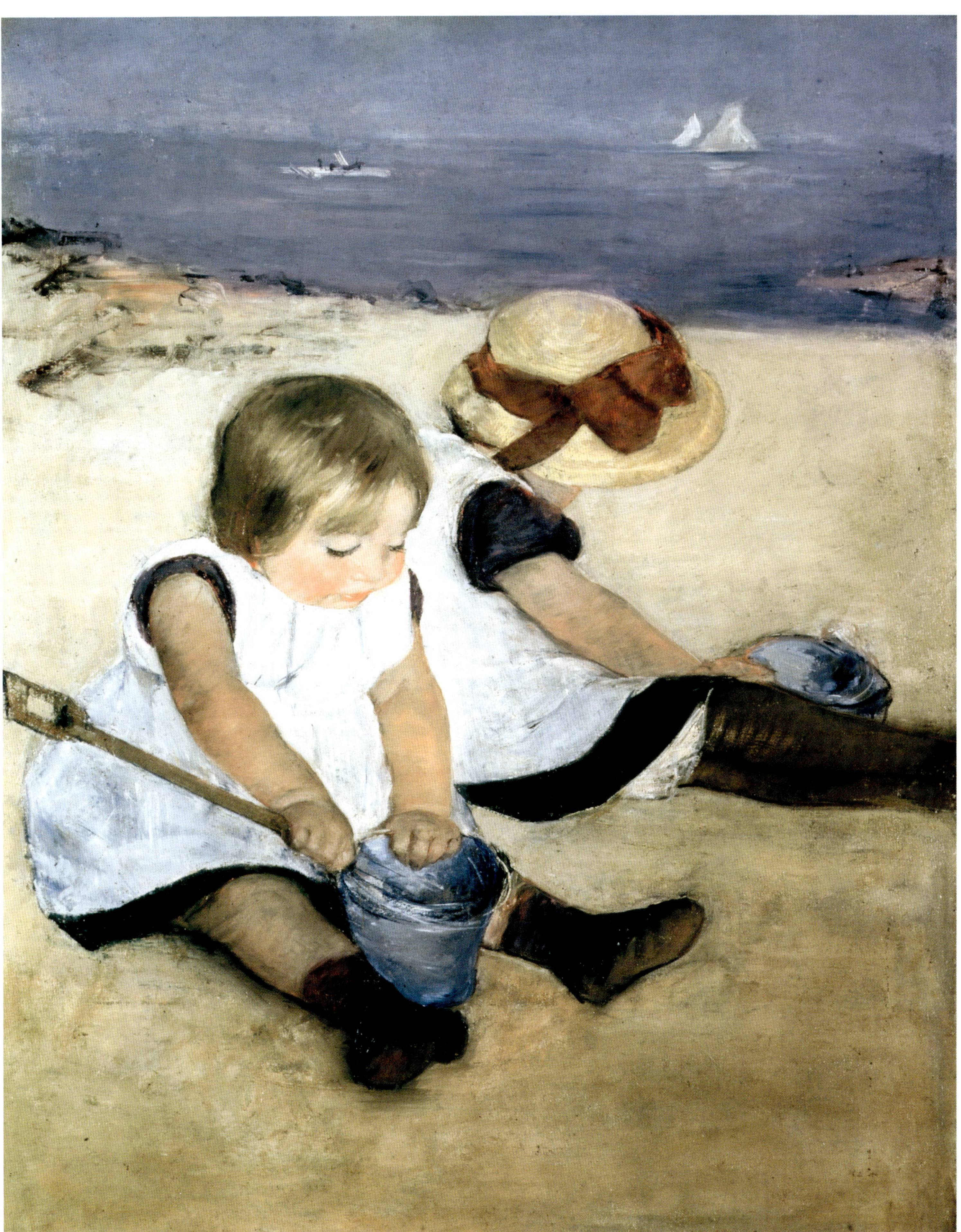

MARY CASSATT, Children Playing on the Beach *(1884). Cassatt looked at children with an honest eye. She captured their clumsy and often random motions and gave them a real rather than a cherubic aspect. With legs sprawled out for balance and a shovel gripped awkwardly in a little fist, the child in the foreground is intent on the act of filling a bucket, fully unaware of the viewer's gaze.*

NATIONAL GALLERY OF ART, WASHINGTON, D.C. OIL ON CANVAS (38⅜×29¼ INCHES).

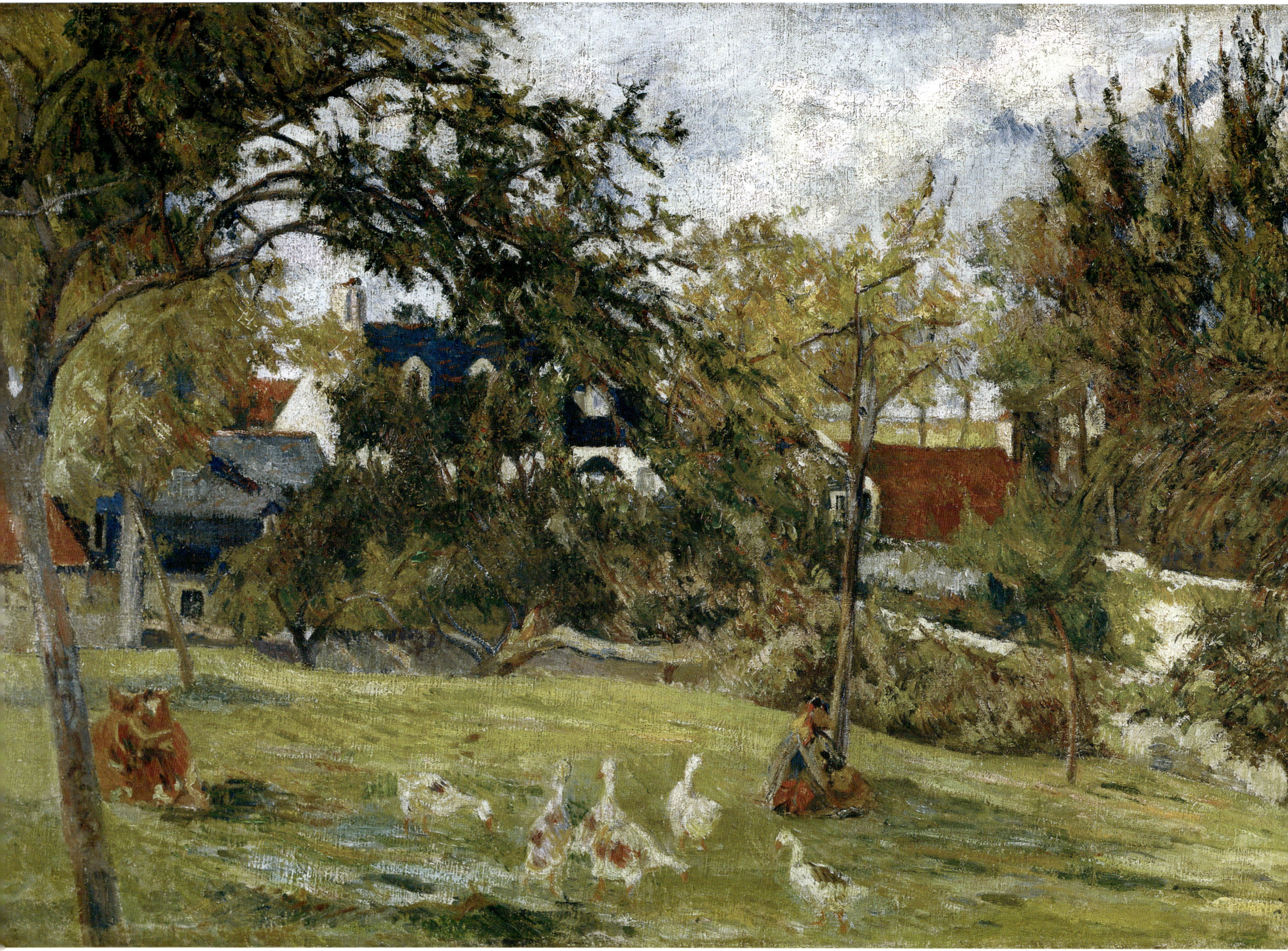

PAUL GAUGUIN, Paysage à Saint-Cloud *(1885). Gauguin did not fare well with the critics at the eighth exhibition. When compared to Seurat's scientific formulations, Gauguin's naturalist landscapes were dismissed as classic Impressionism: competent, well-painted, but nothing new and pale next to the "old masters" such as Pissarro and Monet. He soon rejected the naturalist approach for an art based on memory and imagination.*

THE JOAN WHITNEY PAYSON COLLECTION AT THE PORTLAND MUSEUM OF ART, MAINE. OIL ON CANVAS (22×39⅜ INCHES).

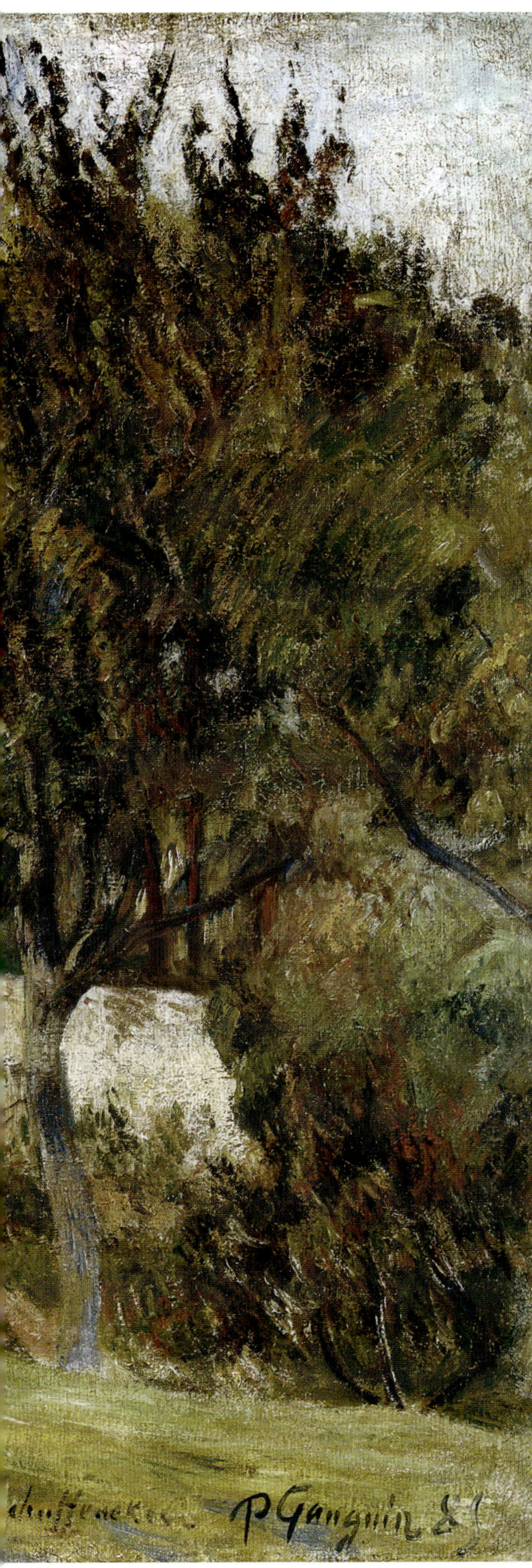

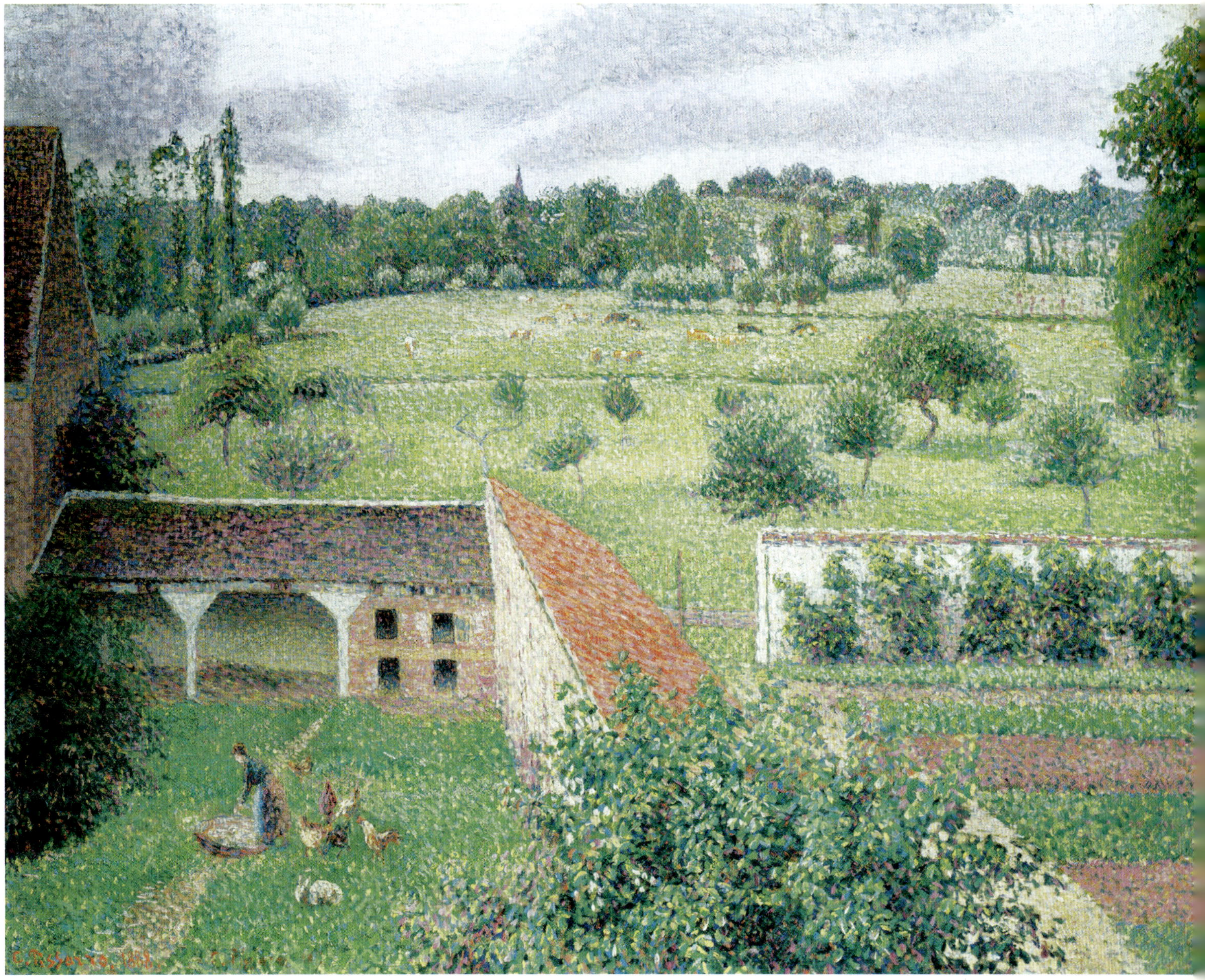

Camille Pissarro, View from My Window, Eragny *(1886–88). Always open to new ideas, Pissarro experimented with Neo-Impressionism. His composition is organized into planes, reflecting the orderly garden plots and fields that he observed from his window. His color, applied in dots and dabs, is fresh and bright, with pure high hues in the foreground and a subtle and muted mix in the sky. Tone conveys the atmospheric effect, seen in the shades of pale blue, pink, and violet in the distant clouds.*

The Ashmolean Museum, Oxford, England. Oil on canvas (25⅝×31½ inches).

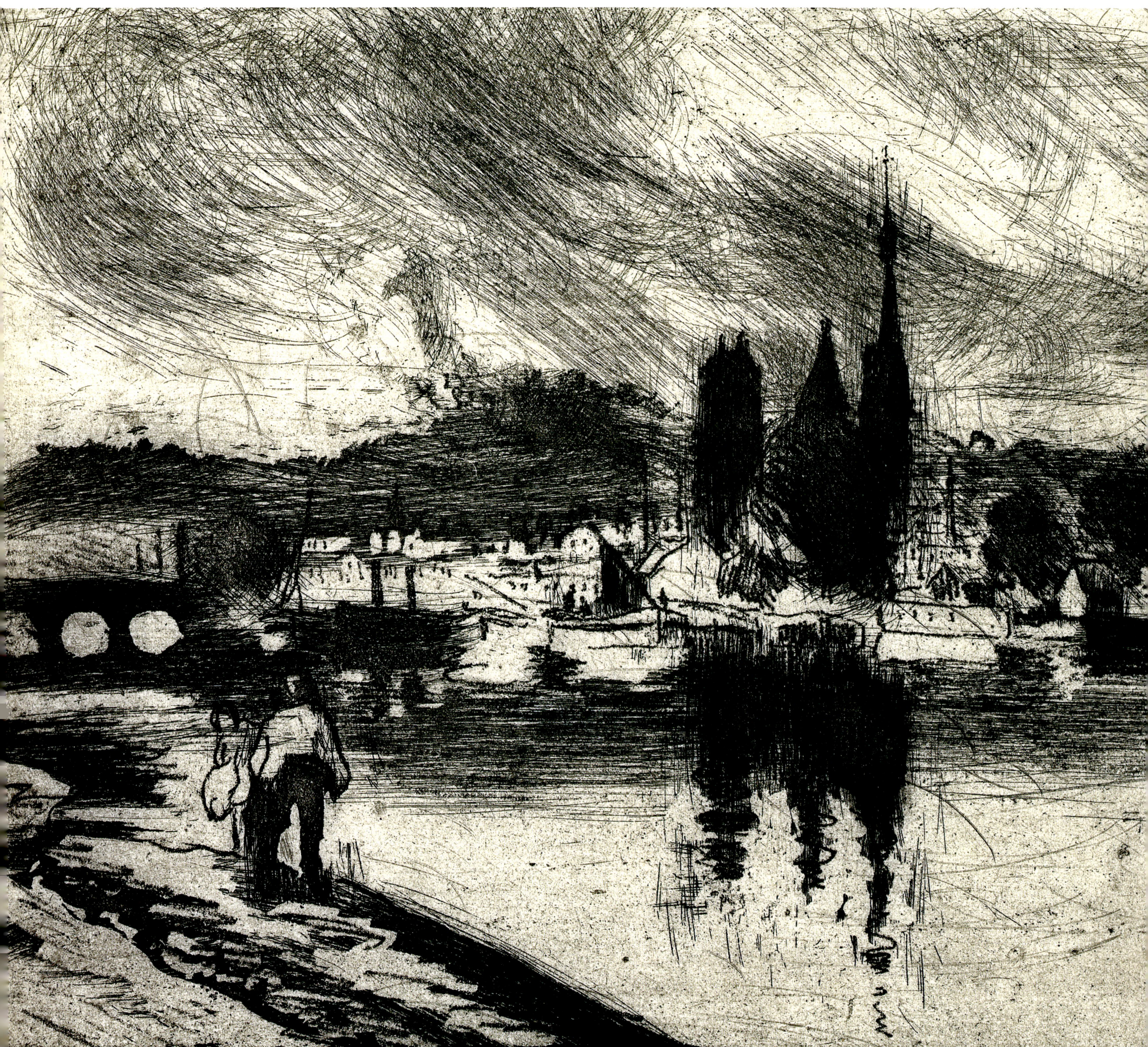

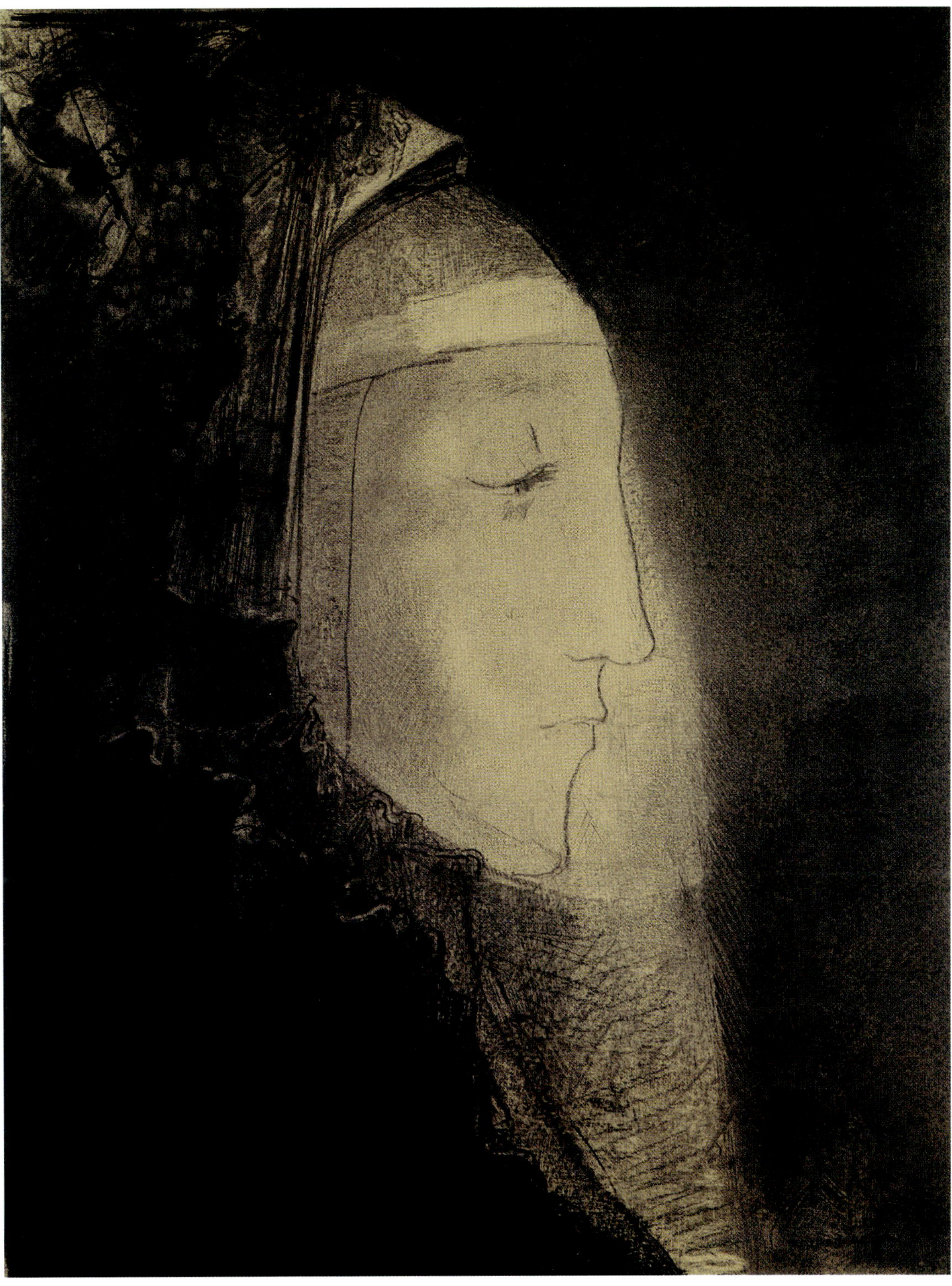

ODILON REDON, Profil de Lumiere *(1886). Redon joined the Impressionists for the last exhibition. He exhibited 14 works, most in charcoal on paper. Like Seurat and Signac, he embodied the spirit of a new generation of independent innovation. His work was evocative, fantastic, and mysterious rather than rigorous and scientific, and he drew upon freedom of imagination rather than disciplined theoretical investigations. Critics found his departure of vision startling, prompting comparisons to the poetry of Charles Baudelaire and Edgar Allan Poe.*

MUSÉE DU LOUVRE, PARIS. CHARCOAL (15¼×11⅜ INCHES).

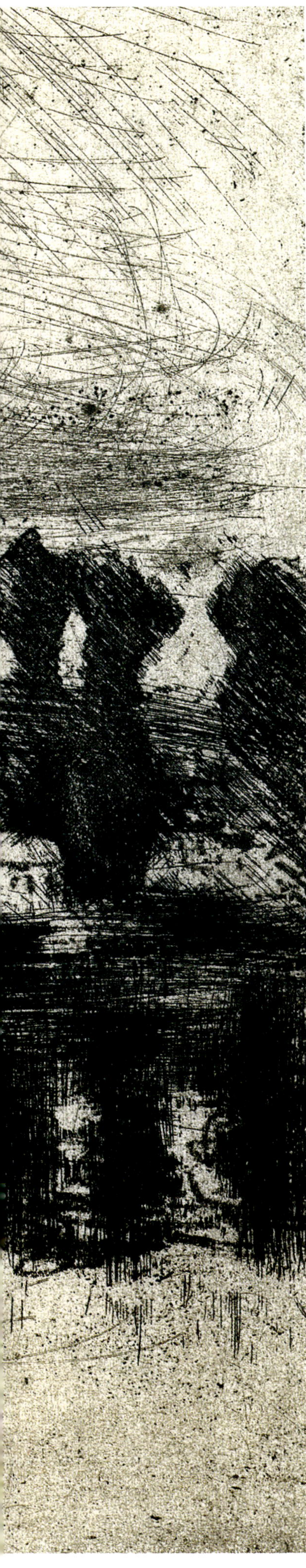

CAMILLE PISSARRO, View of Rouen (Cours-la reine) *(1884). Pissarro exhibited works in a wide variety of media in the eighth Impressionist exhibition, including oil paintings, painted fans, pastels, and etchings. In this etching of a view across the water looking at the cathedral, Pissarro replaced color with tone to express atmospheric effects, including the reflections on the water and the heavy, wintry sky.*

PRINT COLLECTION, THE MIRIAM AND IRA D. WALLACH DIVISION OF ART, PRINTS, AND PHOTOGRAPHS, THE NEW YORK PUBLIC LIBRARY, ASTOR, LENOX, AND TILDEN FOUNDATIONS, NEW YORK. ETCHING AND AQUATINT (5⅞×7¾ INCHES).

A Legacy of Independence

Because Impressionism was associated with the presumed uniqueness of the depicted moment and the singularity of a supposedly spontaneous technique, the artist had to make the execution of each painting outdo the performance of the last. The expression of individual experience that should have been the most self-fulfilling aspect of Impressionism might in the end be a self-defeating process.

Félix Fénéon, "Les impressionnistes," *La Vogue,* June 1886

Manet earned his long-sought-after recognition during the same years that the Impressionist experiment drew to a close. From 1879 through 1882, his works were accepted for exhibition at the Salon. In 1881 he won a second-class medal for one of his portraits, and later that year, the French government made him a Chevalier of the Legion of Honor for his contribution to national culture. *A Bar at the Folies Bergere* (c. 1882), which appeared at the Salon of 1882, represented the changes that Manet had generated in the course of his career. Set in a popular café, alive with social activity, the painting reveals that Manet had truly become Baudelaire's passionate observer. The frank stare of the barmaid bridged the gulf between the ideal world of art and the real world of the viewer. But Manet's light touch and shimmering palette is marked by the influence of the group of artists he had initially inspired. Intent on changing the system rather than challenging it, Manet had never been willing to stake his reputation with the Impressionists, but he had provided both the impetus and a strong endorsement for their endeavor.

Well before the final exhibition, the core members of the Impressionist circle had dispersed to seek their individual artistic objectives and build independent careers. Renoir enjoyed continued success with the Salon juries but no longer felt compelled to place his work before their judgment. He last exhibited at the Salon in 1890. His portraits brought him a steady and substantial income, allowing him to pursue his rising interest in painting the female figure in contemporary

Paul Cézanne, The Card Players *(1890–92). Cézanne painted at least five variations of men playing cards in a café. In this version, the bottle on the table, with its gleaming white highlight, divides the composition in two, calling attention to the light and dark tonalities of the dress of the two figures. It is not so much a portrait of the two men as it is an exploration of the potential nuance of volume and color.*

Musée d'Orsay, Paris. Oil on canvas (18¾×22½ inches).

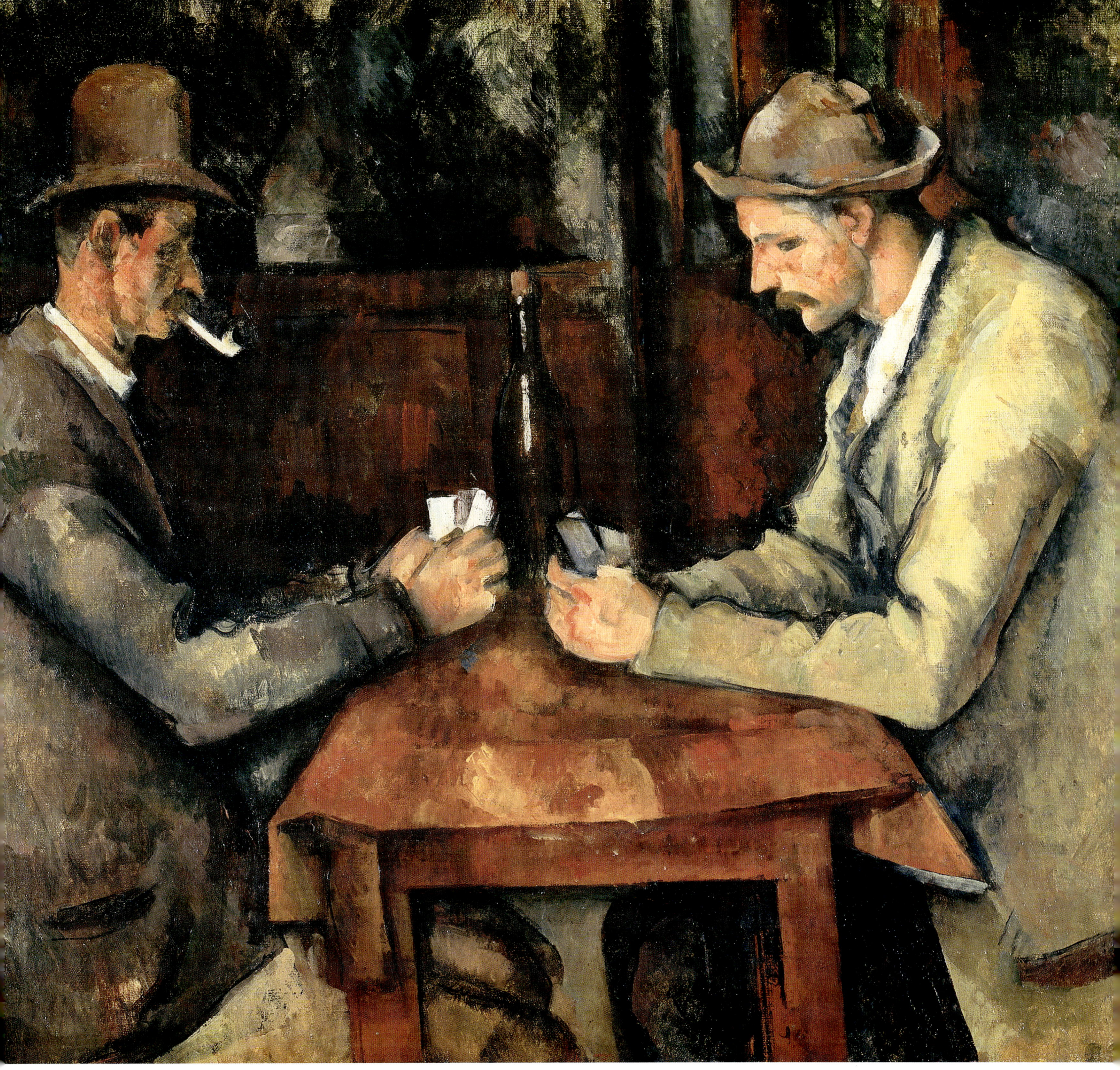

A Legacy of Independence

guise as seen in *Young Girls at the Piano* (1892) or as a classical ideal as seen in his pastoral nudes.

Monet traveled throughout the 1880s, seeking challenging vistas for his plein air painting. By 1890 he returned home and spent more than a year painting stacks of wheat in a nearby farmer's field. His repeated observations, recorded on more than 25 canvases, chart the subtle change of light over hours of the day and the course of seasons. His fascination with nature's mutability endured to the end of his life, and nature's most evanescent effects—the gentle motion of water, reflections trembling on the surface of a pond—inspired his last set of series paintings of the water lilies in his own garden.

Degas remained a staunch realist and never lost his bold approach to composition. However, his failing sight forced him to rely increasingly on gesture, memory, and touch as he worked in the media of pastel and sculpture.

To the end, Pissarro remained the most experimental, always open to new influences and always supportive of young, struggling artists. However, he never fully abandoned his attachment to plein air painting, as seen in the fresh color and tangible atmosphere of his late painting *The Rooftops of Old Rouen, Grey Weather* (1896).

With Seurat's early death, Signac became the standard-bearer for Seurat's Neo-Impressionist theories. Many young artists briefly adopted the style in the course of finding their own mode of expression.

When Vincent van Gogh arrived in Paris in March 1886, he attended the final Impressionist exhibition and experimented with all the new methods, including his own interpretation of Seurat's theory. As a result, he added color to the dark palette he had developed on his own in Holland. When he left Paris for Arles in 1888, he hoped other artists would join him to live and work together as a community dedicated to advancing modern art. His desire to create a Studio of the South never became a reality, but his forceful and sometimes arbitrary use of color had a profound influence on a new generation of artists.

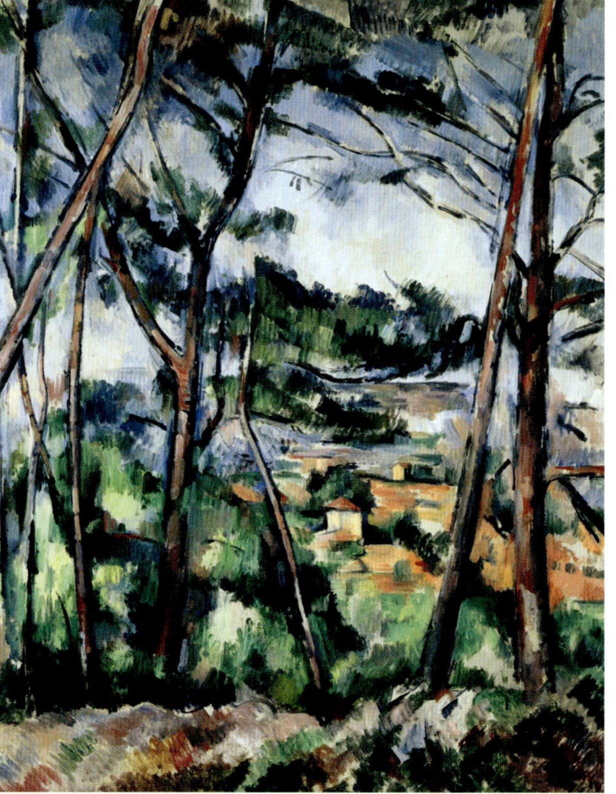

Paul Cézanne (French, 1839–1906), Landscape near Aix, the Plain of the Arc River *(1892–95). Cézanne participated in only two Impressionist exhibitions, the first in 1874 and the third in 1877. Fiercely independent, he followed his own path, seeking to turn his observations of nature into a painted structure of squarely brushed color and interlocking planes and volumes. He believed that painting reflected the interaction of the eye and the mind, the former taking in the image of nature and the latter translating it into color and form that suggest rather than mirror the perceptions of the surrounding world.*

Carnegie Museum of Art, Pittsburgh. Oil on canvas ($32\frac{1}{4} \times 26$ inches).

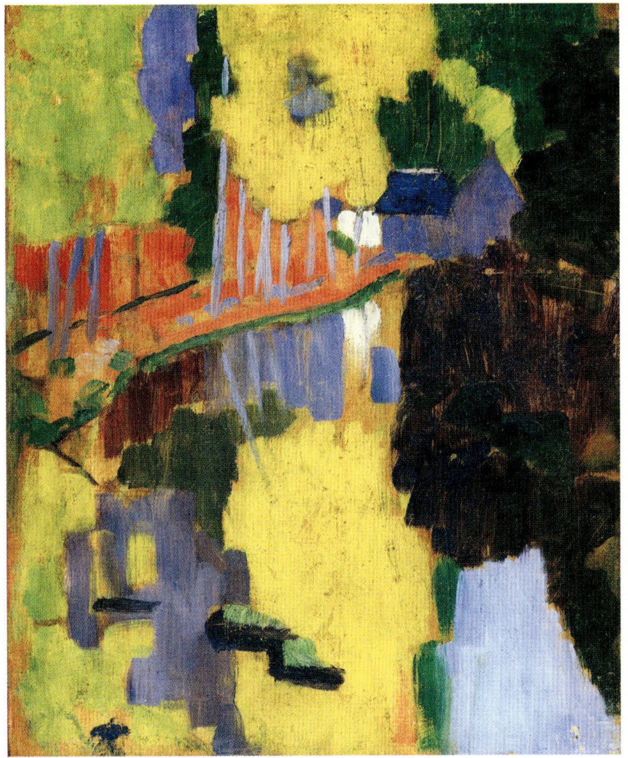

Paul Sérusier, The Talisman *(1888). Set in the same wood as Bernard's portrait of his sister, Sérusier's small painting suspends all links to naturalistic representation. Sérusier was introduced to Gauguin in the summer of 1888, and he painted* The Talisman *in response to the older painter's influence. Gauguin encouraged him to use color in an imaginative way and to work with the most intense hues to express the essence rather than the appearance of each form. More than a landscape,* The Talisman *is a suggestive arrangement of colors on a two-dimensional surface.*

Musée d'Orsay, Paris. Oil on wood ($106\frac{1}{4} \times 84\frac{5}{8}$ inches).

Gauguin briefly joined van Gogh in Arles, but Gauguin had already moved far from his association with the Impressionists. In reviews of the final exhibition, critics had dismissed his work as classic Impressionism, and in reaction, Gauguin chose imagination and memory as central forces in his art. Always charismatic, Gauguin attracted a circle of young artists, including Paul Sérusier, who painted the enigmatic *The Talisman* (1888) in response to Gauguin's advice to take an imaginative approach to color. In Paris, Henri de Toulouse-Lautrec created a new type of passionate observer in his blunt and sometimes shocking images of nightlife and prostitutes.

Cézanne's deep desire to pursue his independent vision had prompted him to move away from Paris and withhold his works from the Impressionist exhibitions. However, he maintained a strong relationship with many of the core members, who always welcomed his support and his opinions. Cézanne never rejected his public identity as an Impressionist, but from the outset he had pursued a different path. Rather than capture the fleeting sensations of nature, Cézanne sought to develop a pictorial language that would parallel nature's underlying structural order. In his late career he limited his work to a select range of motifs: still life, the landscapes that surrounded his home in Aix-en-Provence, and a few figure compositions such as *The Card Players* (1890–92). But unlike Monet, who also chose a narrow repertoire to observe the changes in nature, Cézanne sought what was most enduring.

While each member of the Impressionist circle continued to seek an independent path, Caillebotte tried to preserve their united legacy. He was a wealthy man with an annual income, and over the years he had purchased works from the exhibitions. Upon his death in 1894, he willed his collection of Impressionist paintings to the French nation with the stipulation that they be displayed together in Paris, suggesting an initial exhibition at the Luxembourg Palace (the current venue for living artists) and later at the Louvre. After much opposition mounted by a committee from the academy, the nation accepted 38 of the 69 works, the number reflecting the space limitations at the Luxembourg Palace. Through his generous bequest, Caillebotte bestowed official sanction on the Impressionists without compromising their hard-won independence.

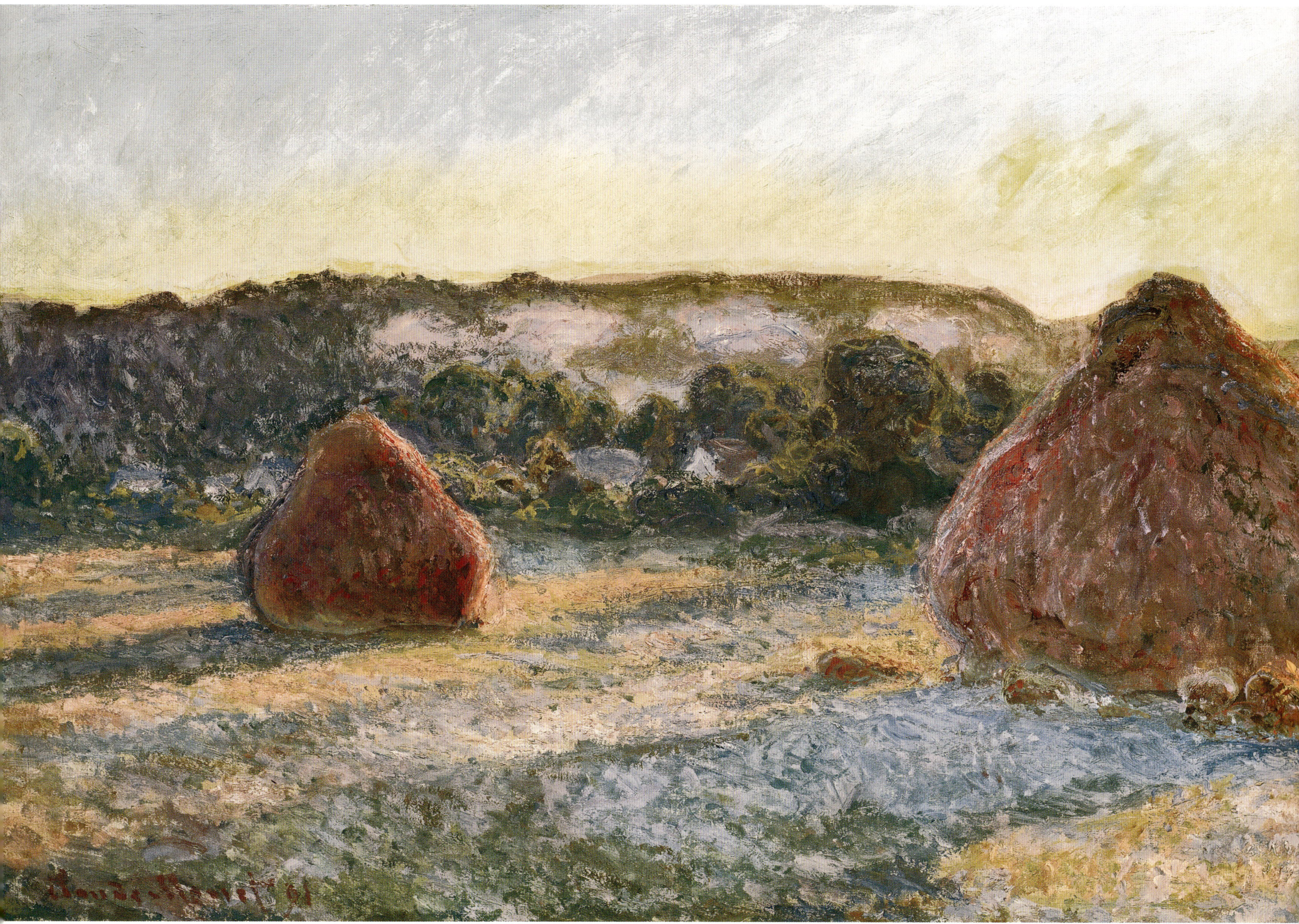

Claude Monet, Stacks of Wheat (End of Summer) *(1890–91). The idea of the series painting, which Monet debuted in the third Impressionist exhibition, continued to fascinate him. Over the course of more than a year, he painted at least 25 canvases of stacks of wheat in a farm field in Giverny. His observations record the shifting illumination through the diurnal and seasonal cycles, and working on different canvases through the day as the light changed, he expressed these effects as color sensations and subtle variations in tone.*

Gift of Arthur M. Wood, Sr., in memory of Pauline Palmer Wood, The Art Institute of Chicago. Oil on canvas ($23\frac{5}{8} \times 39\frac{3}{8}$ inches).

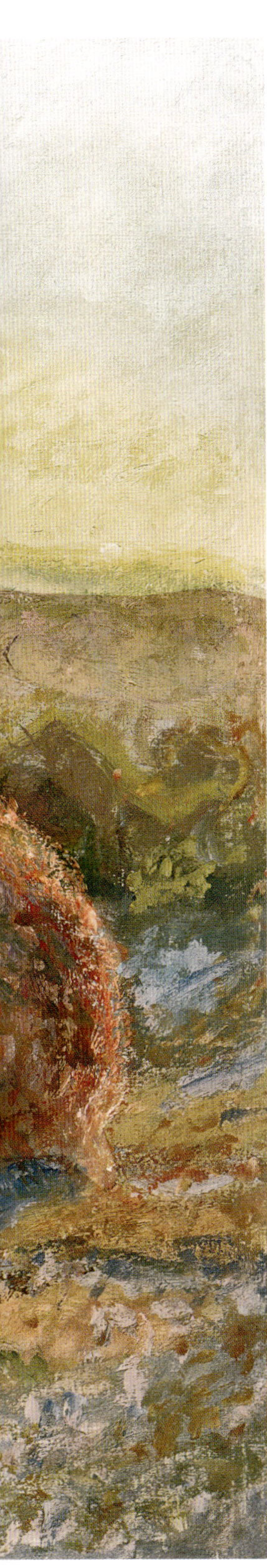

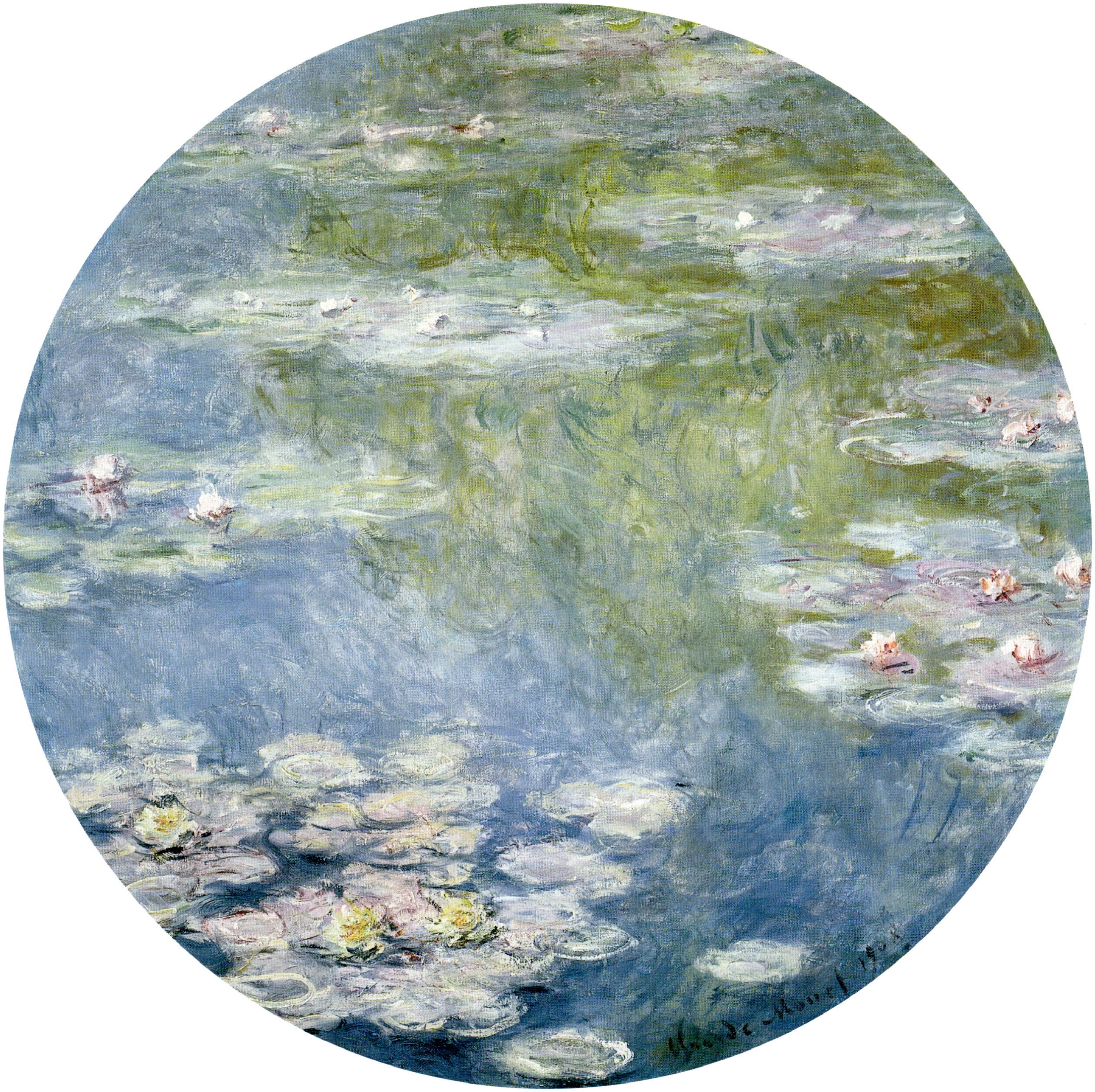

Claude Monet, Water Lilies *(1908). For six years Monet set his easel up next to his water garden and painted the random movements of the lilies and the volatile reflections on the glassy surface. It was the water, more than the lilies, that intrigued Monet; for Monet the flowers and the reflected images of the clouds indicated the endless visual potential of water in motion.*

Dallas Museum of Art. Oil on canvas (31½ inches in diameter).

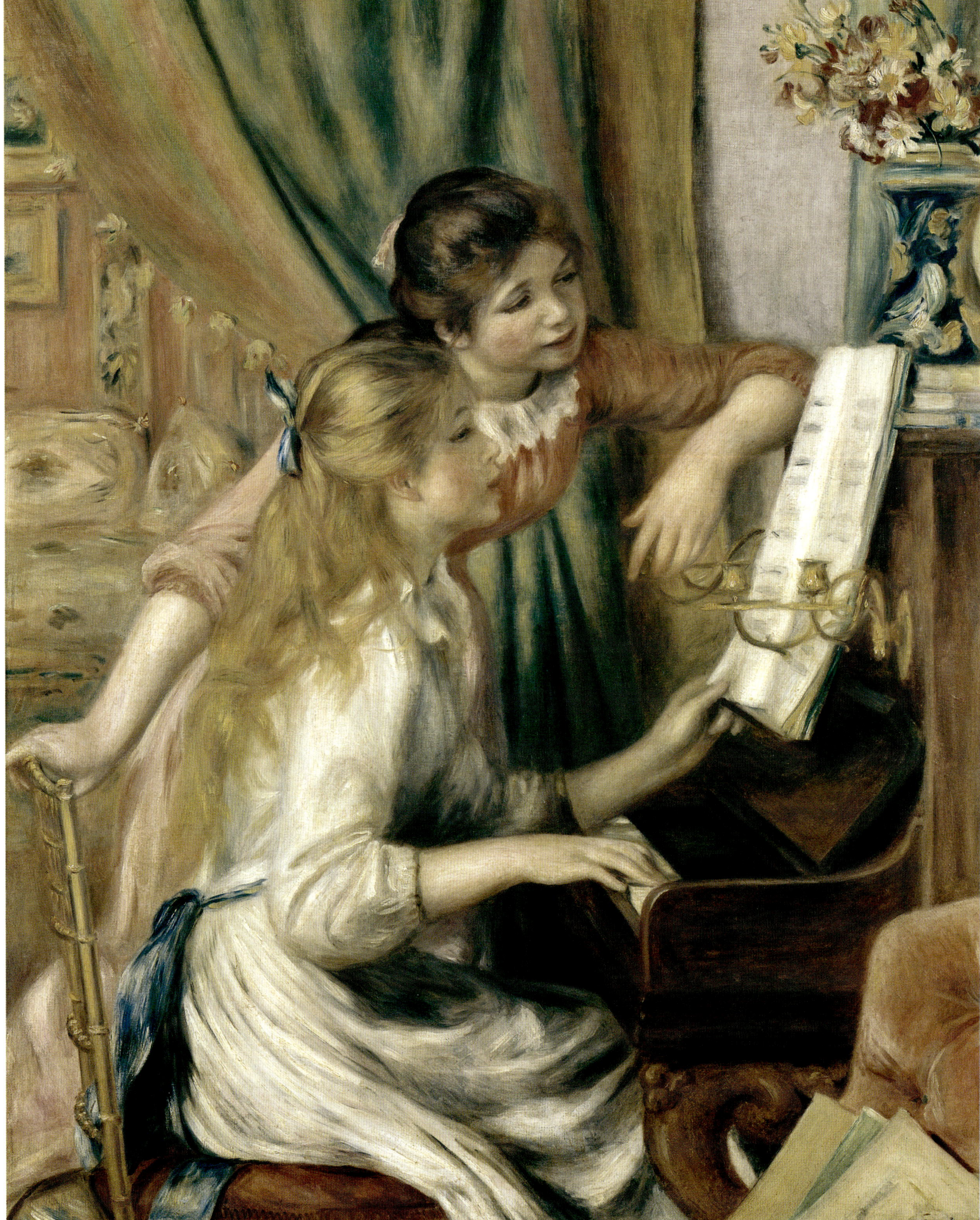

Pierre-Auguste Renoir, Young Girls at the Piano *(1892). The subject of middle-class entertainment continued to interest Renoir. Here, he has portrayed two young women involved in making music. This was a popular and highly respectable leisure activity for young women and, like the cozy, well-appointed interior, reflects a well-bred and comfortable bourgeois atmosphere.*

Musée d'Orsay, Paris. Oil on canvas (45⅝×35⅜ inches).

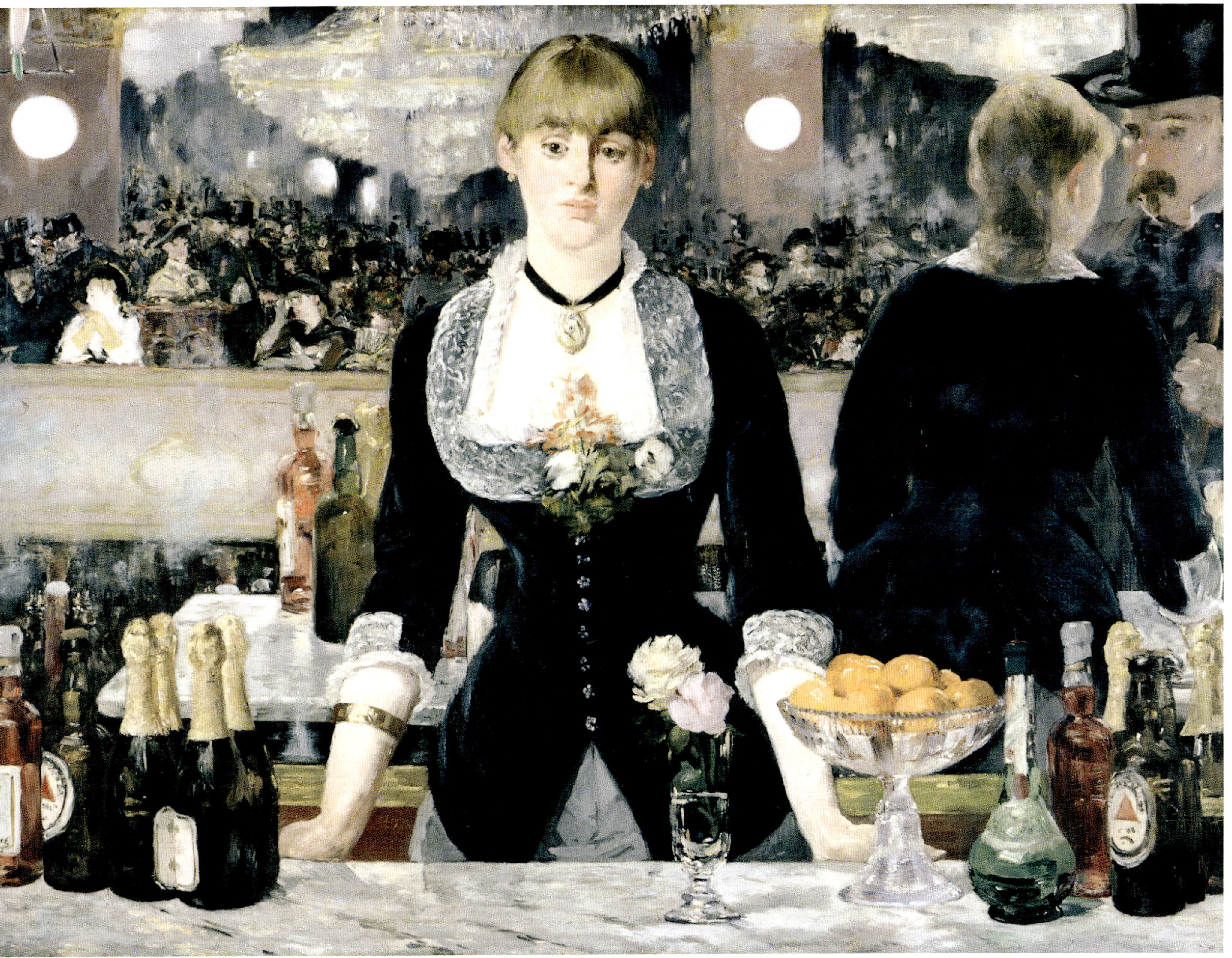

EDOUARD MANET, A Bar at the Folies Bergere *(c. 1882). Manet's painting of a barmaid in a cabaret intrigues the viewer with its spatial and psychological complexity. The mirror behind her transforms the shallow space in which she stands into a view of the entire room, where a lively and sophisticated crowd is enjoying the aerial act high above their heads. The barmaid appears lost in thought, but in the reflection, she is seen attending to a customer. To the end of his career Manet sought to portray the spirit of modern life.*

COURTAULD INSTITUTE GALLERY, LONDON. OIL ON CANVAS (37¾×51¼ INCHES).

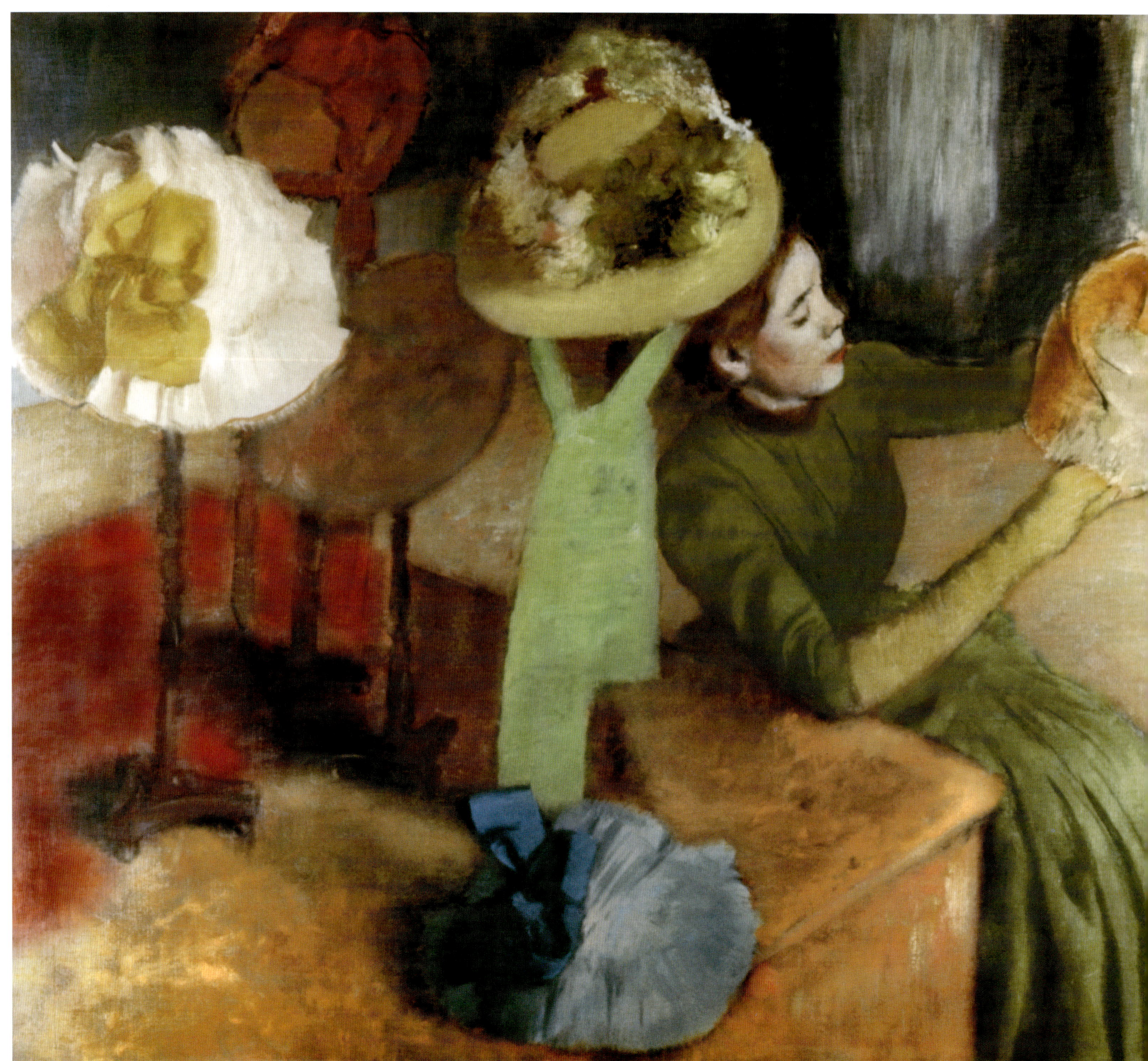

Hilaire-Germain-Edgar Degas, The Millinery Shop *(1884–90). Choosing a high point of view, Degas portrayed a milliner at work trimming a hat. The figure's absorption in her task, as well as her position deep in the composition, suggests that she is unaware of being observed. The hats, arranged on stands at random on her worktable, are more prominent in the composition than she is and, with their colorful ribbons and floral wreathes, have the decorative appearance of a fashionable modern still life.*

The Art Institute of Chicago. Oil on canvas (39⅛×43⁵⁄₁₆ inches).

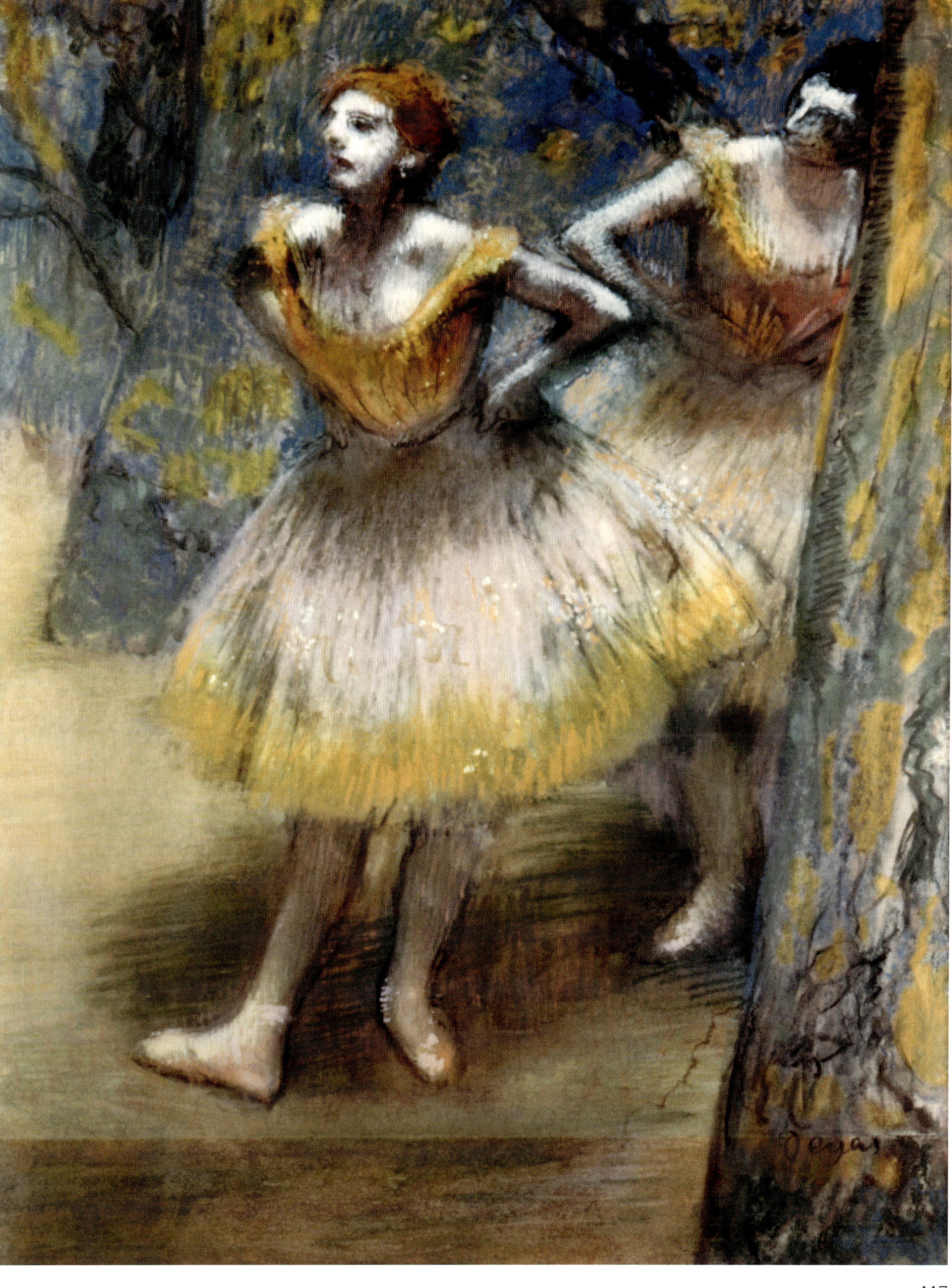

Hilaire-Germain-Edgar Degas, Two Dancers *(1890). Degas continued to portray dancers into his late career. As his eyesight began to fail, the strong, gestural activity of working pastel on paper gave him the effects that he desired as well as a medium he could control. The harsh color contrasts evoke the artificial stage lighting on the dancers' tulle skirts and the makeup powdered on their bare flesh as they wait in the wings.*

The Art Institute of Chicago. Pastel on cream woven paper, pieced and laid down on board (27¾×21⅛ inches).

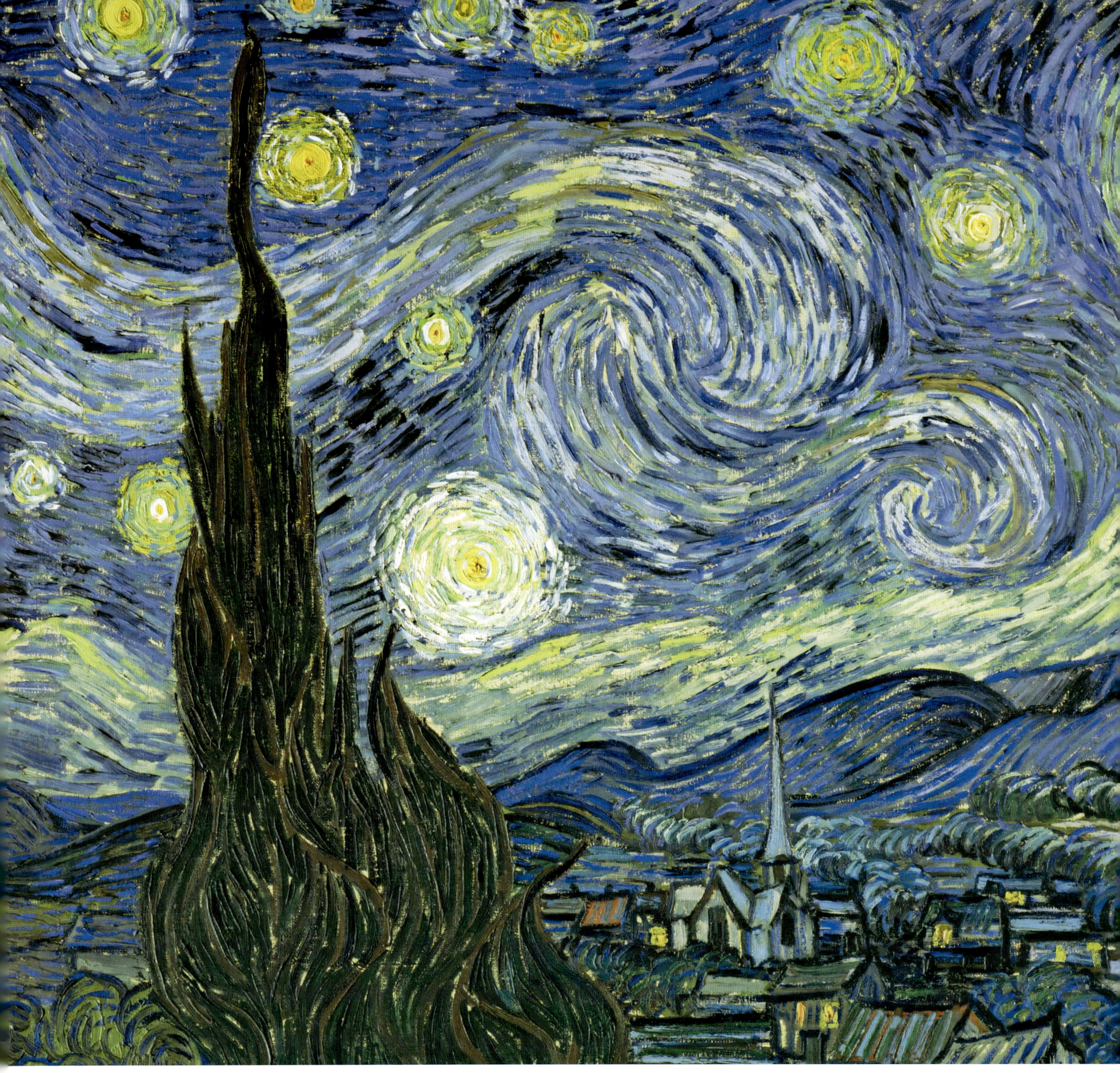

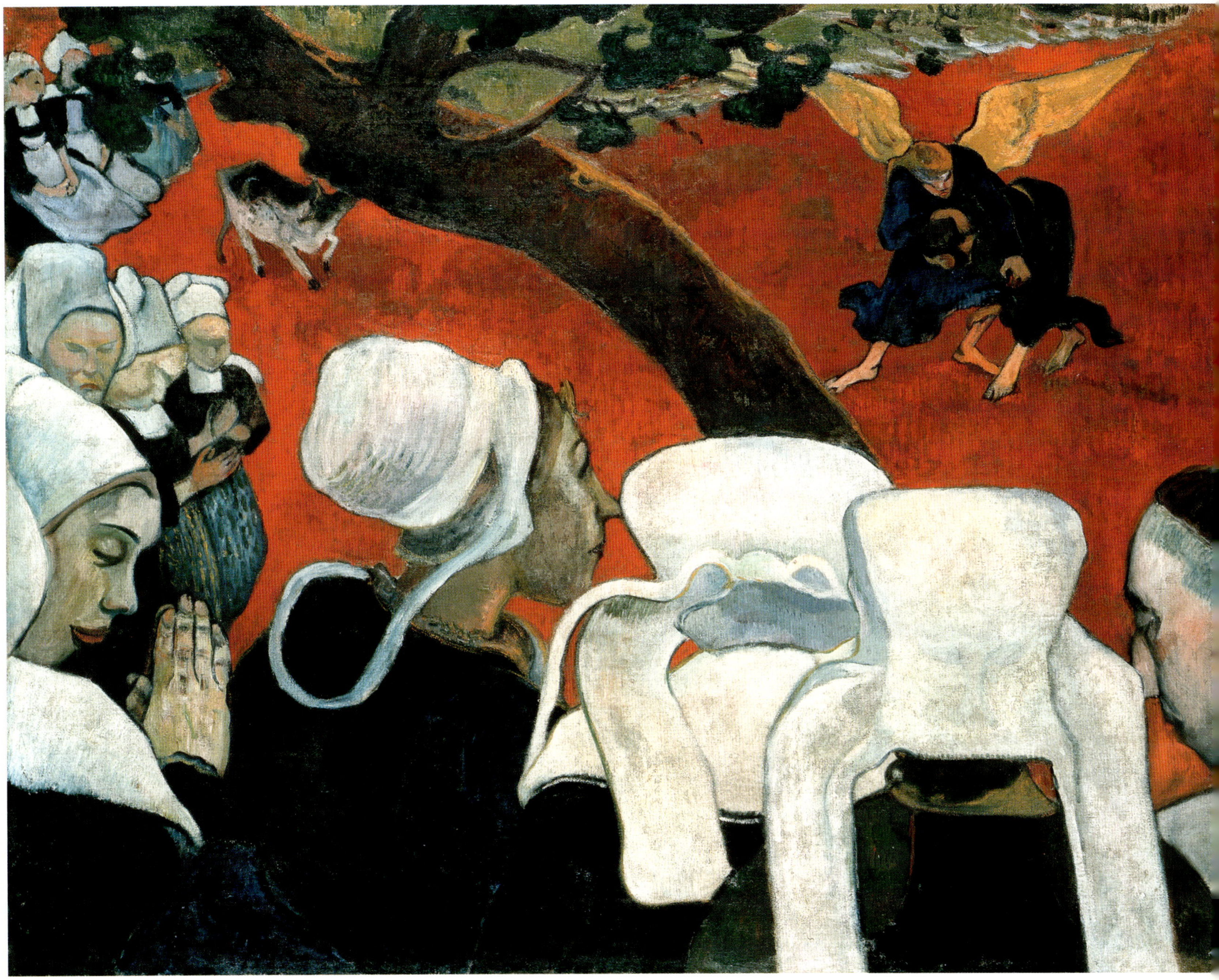

A Legacy of Independence

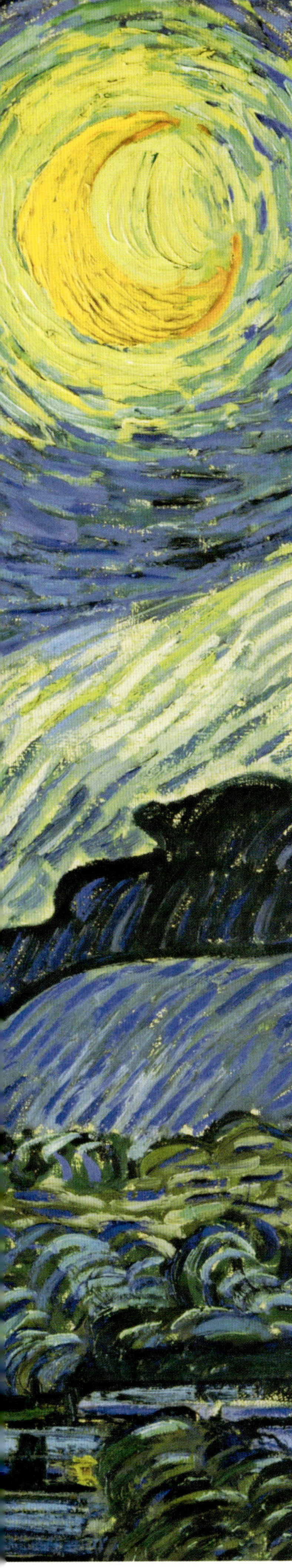

Paul Gauguin, Vision After the Sermon *(1888). After the eighth Impressionist exhibition, Gauguin struck out to find his own mode of expression. Searching for a more authentic environment than urban Paris, he made repeated visits to remote regions of Brittany. In a bold rejection of naturalism, he painted* Vision After the Sermon*—a depiction of Breton women and their priest who witness Jacob struggling with the angel—dissolving the barrier between the zones of religious belief and spiritual imagination.*

National Gallery of Scotland, Edinburgh. Oil on canvas (28¾×36¼ inches).

Vincent van Gogh, The Starry Night *(1889). Before he came to Paris in 1886, van Gogh had read about the Impressionists. He attended the eighth Impressionist exhibition and admired the work of Seurat, Pissarro, and Gauguin. He briefly experimented with their techniques but preferred to follow his own direction, using vibrant color contrasts and an expressive brush stroke. A dedicated plein air painter, van Gogh painted this image of a star-shot sky from a window in a hospital in Saint-Remy in Provence.*

The Museum of Modern Art, New York. Oil on canvas (29×36¼ inches).

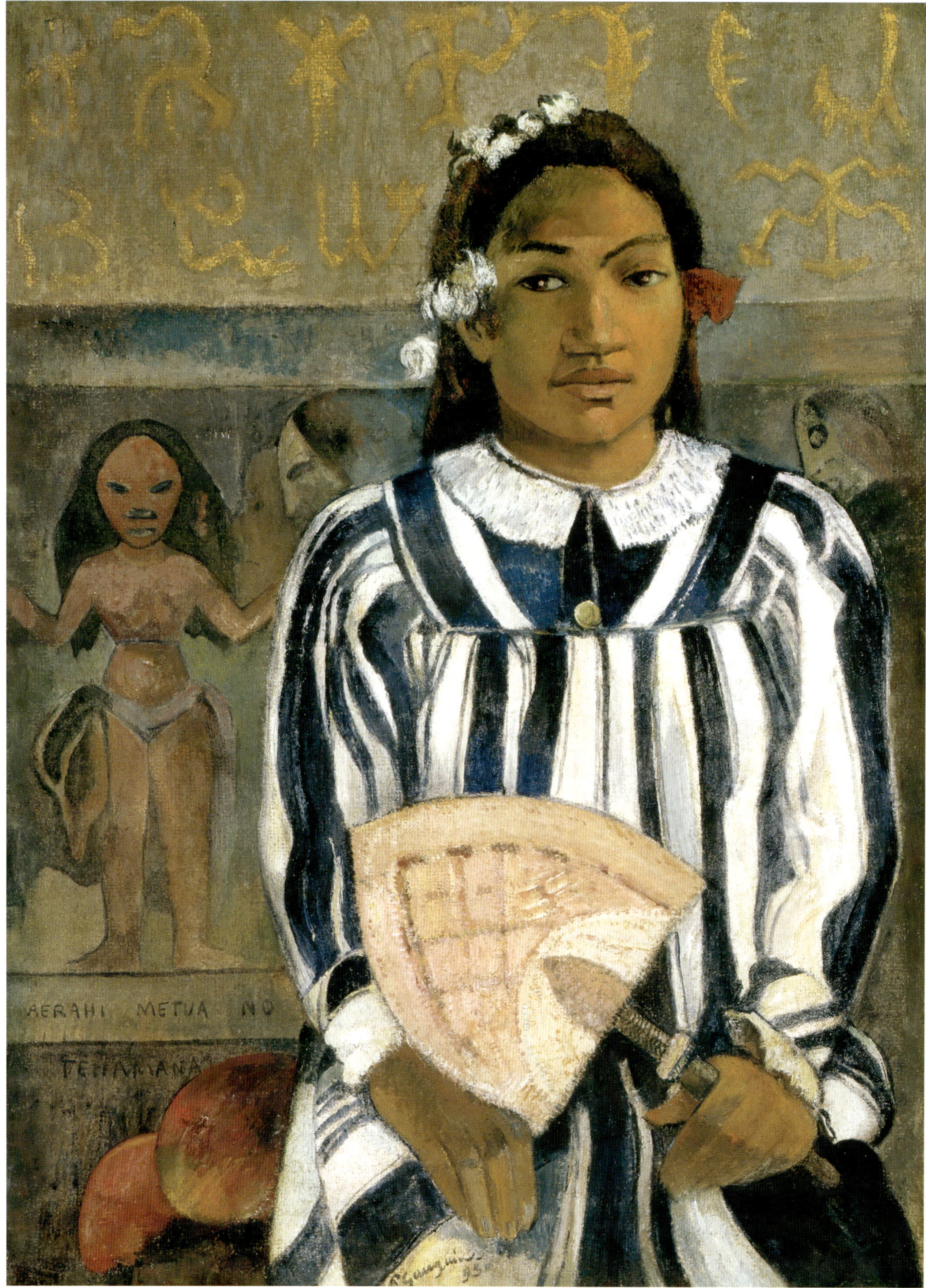

PAUL GAUGUIN, Tehamana Has Many Ancestors (Merahi metua no Tehamana) *(1893). Gauguin made his first journey to Tahiti in June 1891. He was disappointed that the primitive paradise that he sought was being subsumed by Western influence. The young woman in this portrait became his companion, and he painted Tehamana in the modest "Mother Hubbard" dress that was introduced to Tahitian women by missionaries. Nevertheless, the plaited fan and evocative images on the wall vividly portray the perseverance of Tehamana's ancient heritage.*

GIFT OF MR. AND MRS. CHARLES DEERING MCCORMICK, THE ART INSTITUTE OF CHICAGO. OIL ON CANVAS (30×21⅛ INCHES).

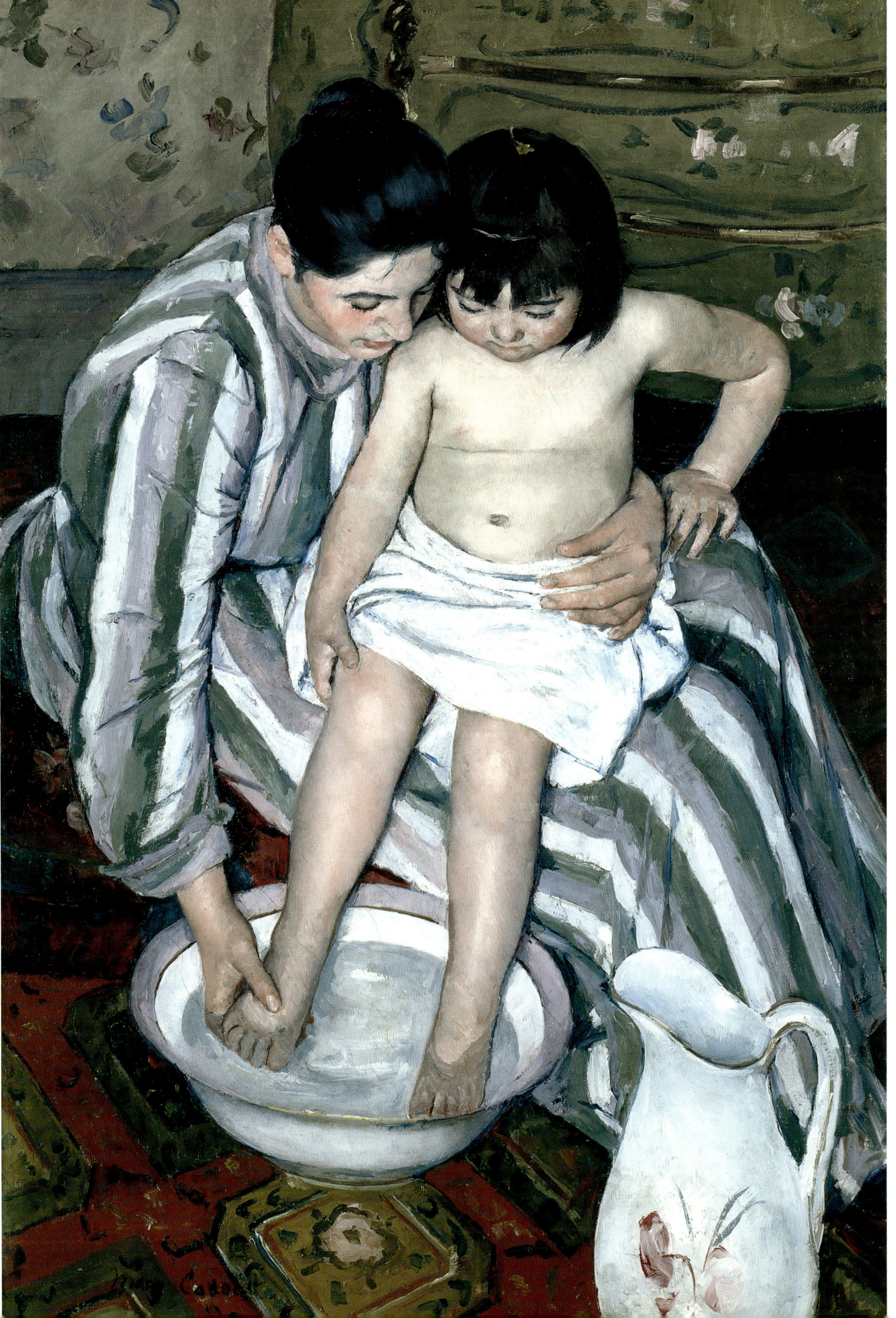

Mary Cassatt, The Child's Bath *(1893). In her later career Mary Cassatt's interest in Japanese art increased. She admired Utamaro, a late 18th-century ukiyo-e master who was renowned for his portrayal of the private lives of women going about their daily activities. In* The Child's Bath, *Cassatt adapted elements of the Japanese aesthetic—including asymmetrical composition, flattened space, areas of pattern, and steep perspective—to a Western image of maternal care.*

Robert A. Waller Fund, The Art Institute of Chicago. Oil on canvas (39½×26 inches).

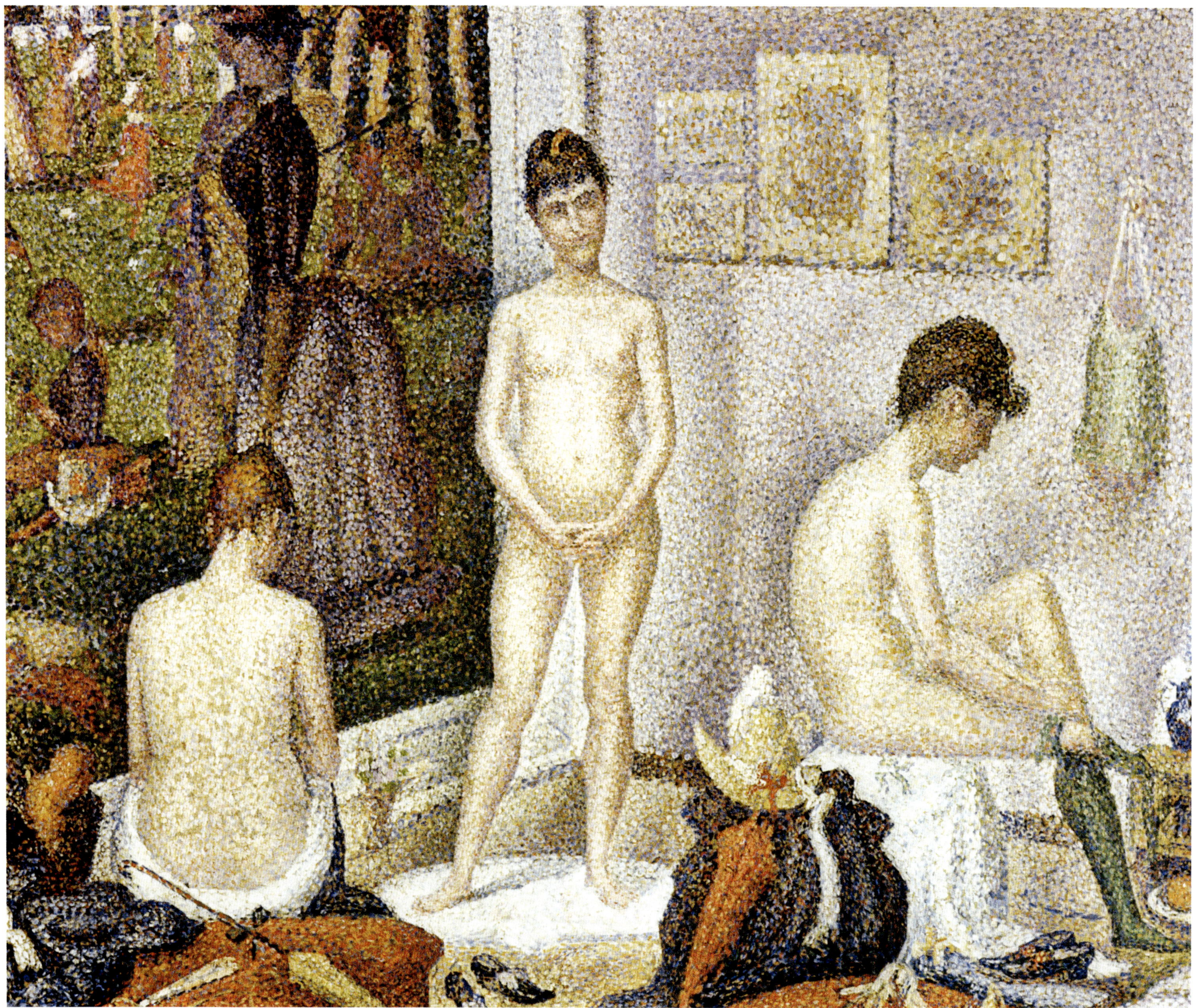

GEORGES SEURAT, The Models *(1886–87). Seurat continued to experiment with his optical color theories. In a small but luminous canvas depicting models in his studio, he varied his application of dabbed pigment from the loose spray of contrasting pinks and blues that color the walls to the more dense and nuanced treatment of the women's flesh. The canvas of* Sunday Afternoon on the Island of the Grande-Jatte *pinned to the wall behind them presents a contrast in tonality, which Seurat believed expressed differences in mood.*

THE BARNES FOUNDATION, MERION STATION, PENNSYLVANIA. OIL ON CANVAS (78¾×98⅜ INCHES).

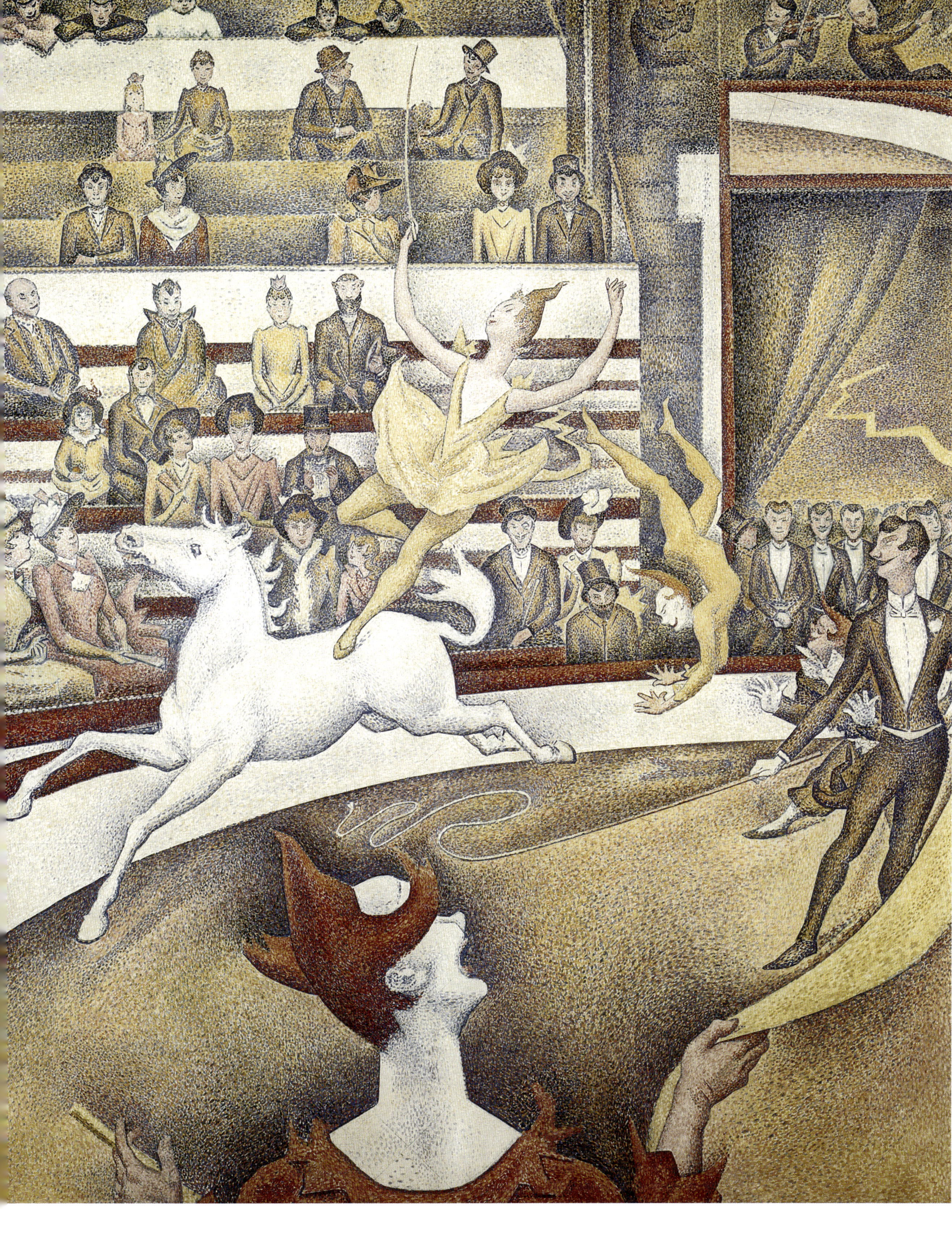

Georges Seurat, The Circus *(1890–91). In his last large-scale painting, Seurat selected a subject that had long been popular among the Impressionists: the lively public entertainment at the Circus Fernando. But unlike Degas's portrayal of a crowd holding their breath at an aerialist's dangerous performance, Seurat approached his subject in an intellectual rather than a responsive manner, using the image to explore his theories about color and line. The result is abstract and decorative, and the canvas was left unfinished at his death.*

Musée d'Orsay, Paris. Oil on canvas (73×59⅛ inches).

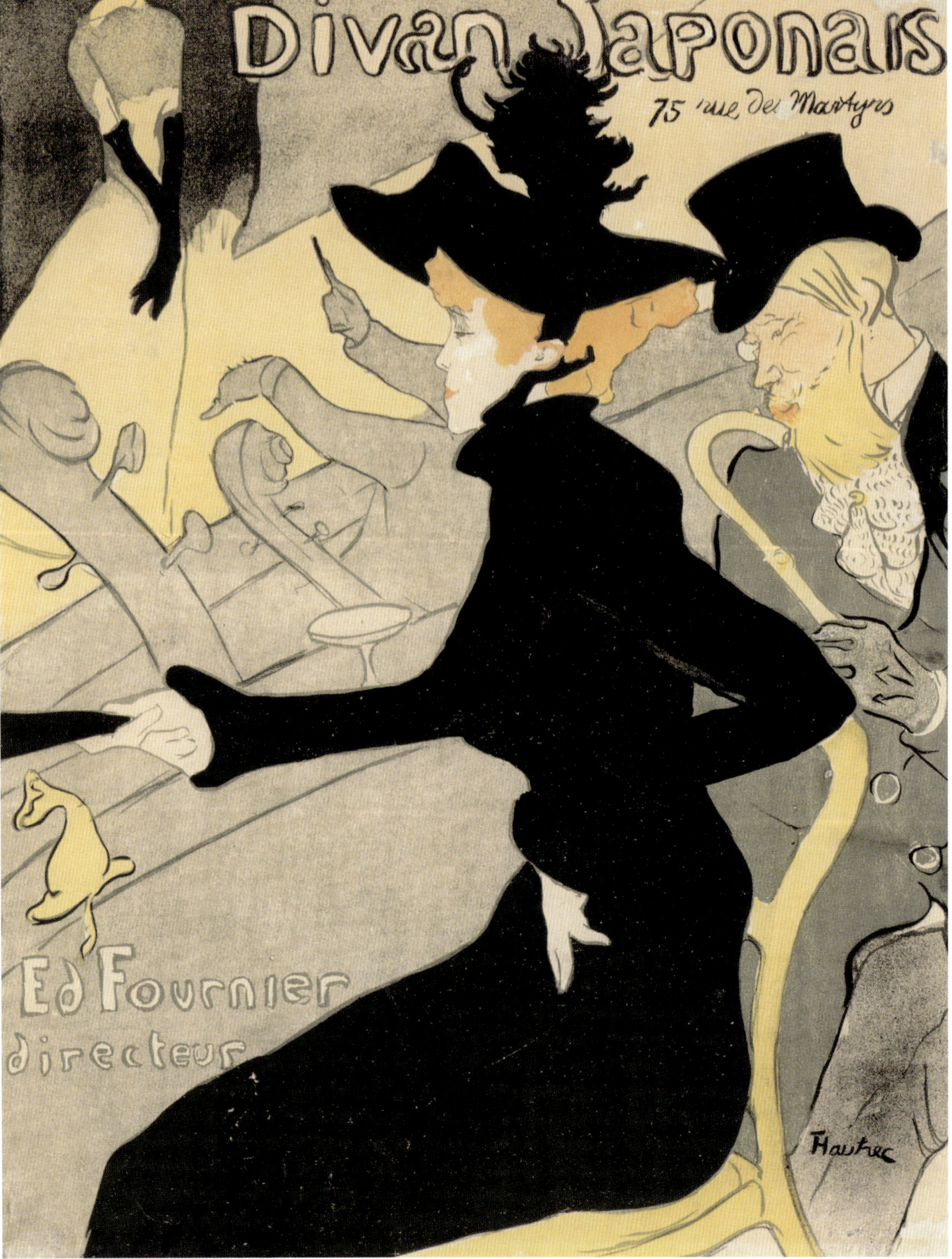

Henri de Toulouse-Lautrec, Divan Japonais *(1893). An ardent observer of the contemporary scene, Toulouse-Lautrec designed many lithographed posters advertising Parisian nightlife. The Café du Divan Japonais featured exotic touches such as bamboo furniture and paper lanterns. Toulouse-Lautrec responded to the fanciful atmosphere by incorporating Japanese visual elements in his design, such as asymmetrical composition and broad areas of color.*

Museum of Fine Arts, Boston. Oil on canvas (32×24½ inches).

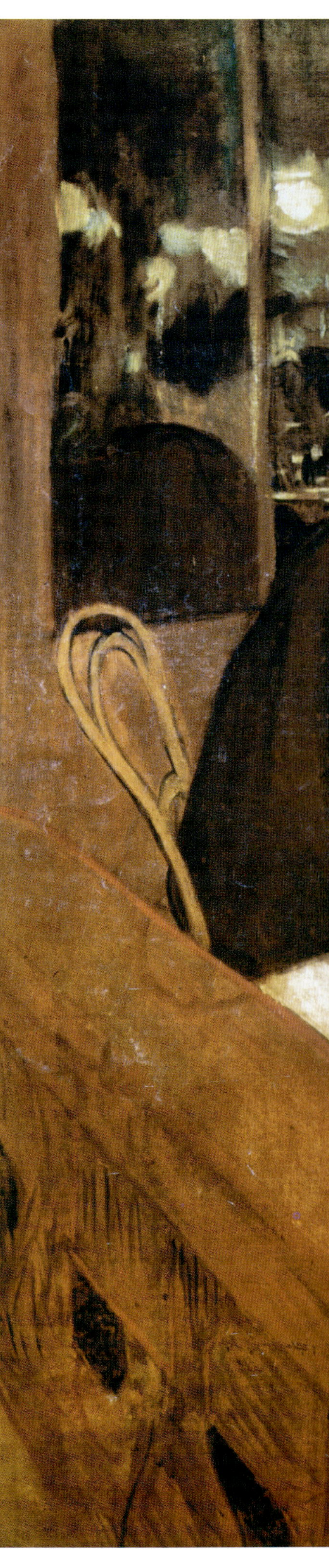

Henri de Toulouse-Lautrec, At the Moulin Rouge *(1892–95). Toulouse-Lautrec painted many of the subjects favored by the Impressionists, including the circus and the lively cabaret scene. Like Degas, he employed oblique axes and cut figures to express the sense of immediacy and action. The balcony rail in the left foreground of* At the Moulin Rouge *slices off the corner of the picture plane, and the figure at the right, whose white face powder gleams under the gaslight, appears to stride right out of the composition.*

The Art Institute of Chicago. Oil on canvas (48$\frac{7}{16}$×55½ inches).

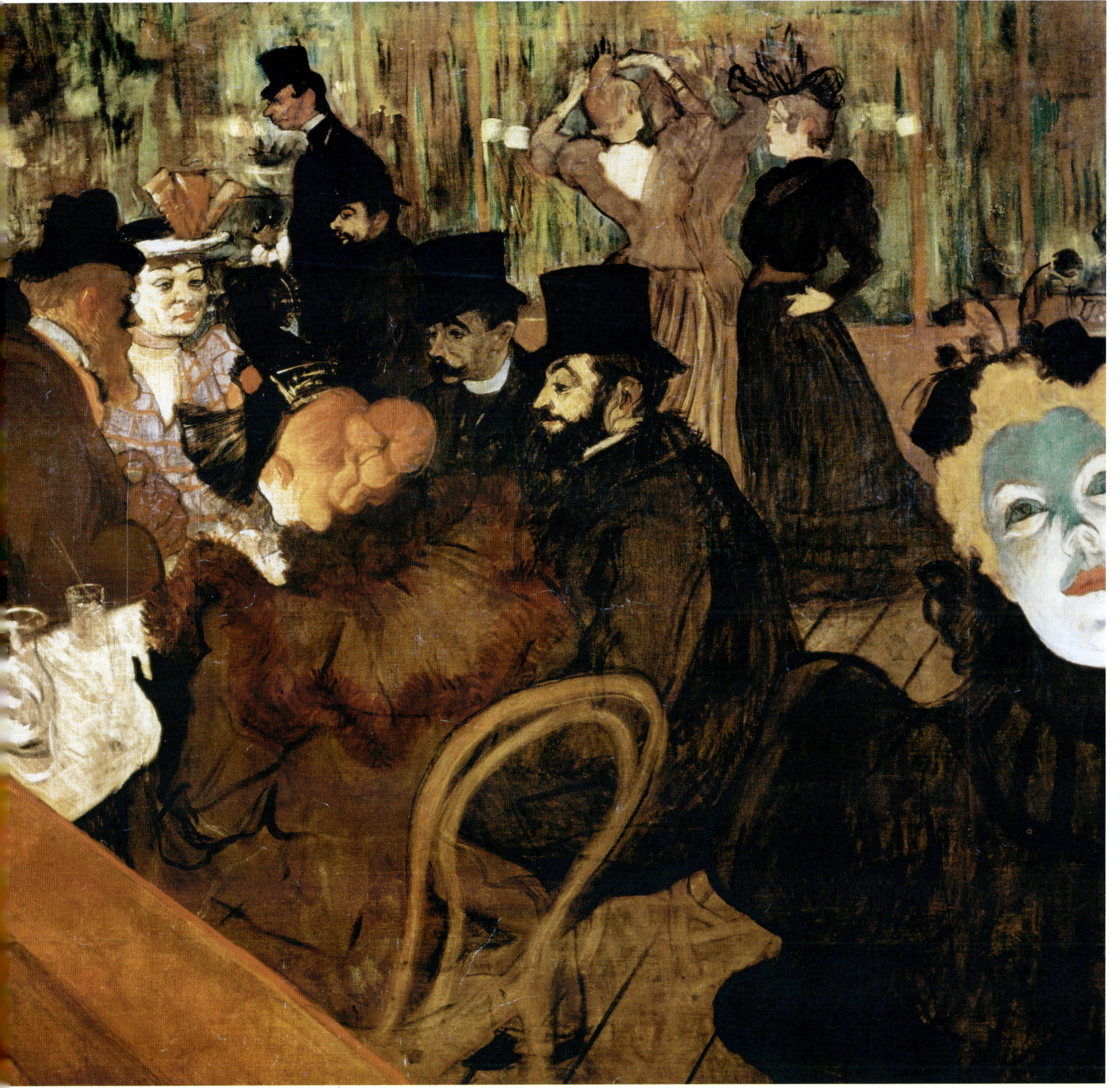

A Legacy of Independence

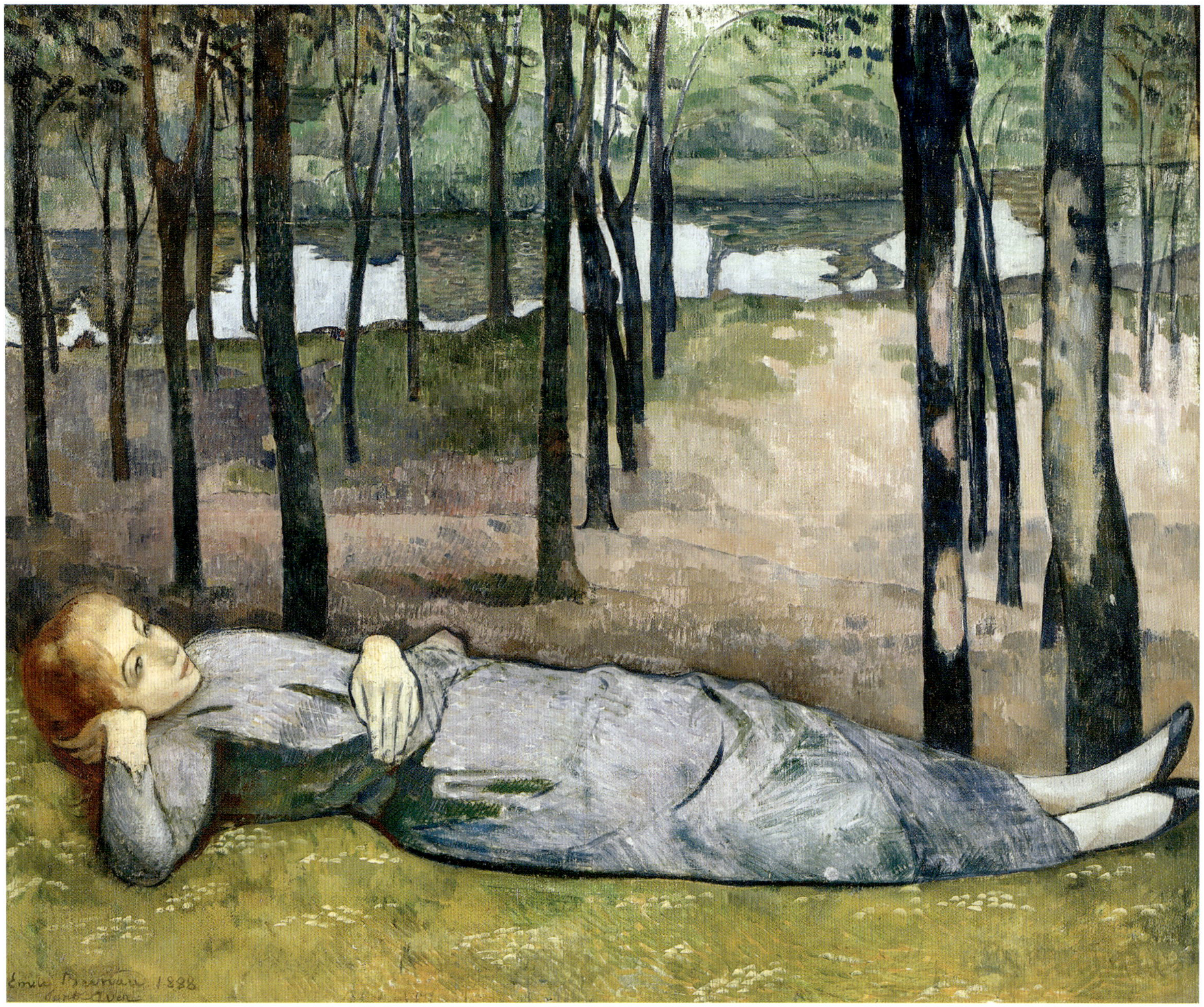

Emile Bernard, Madeleine in the Bois d'Amour *(1888). Bernard spent the summer in Pont Aven, Brittany, working with Gauguin. He painted his sister reclining on the ground near the bank of the Aven River. Her stiff posture and flattened form gives the work an iconic air, reinforced by the rigid arrangement of vertical trees and horizontal bands of land and water. Synthetism is the name Bernard and Gauguin gave this distinctive blend of natural elements, decorative composition, and evocative imagery.*

Musée d'Orsay, Paris. Oil on canvas (54¾×64⅛ inches).

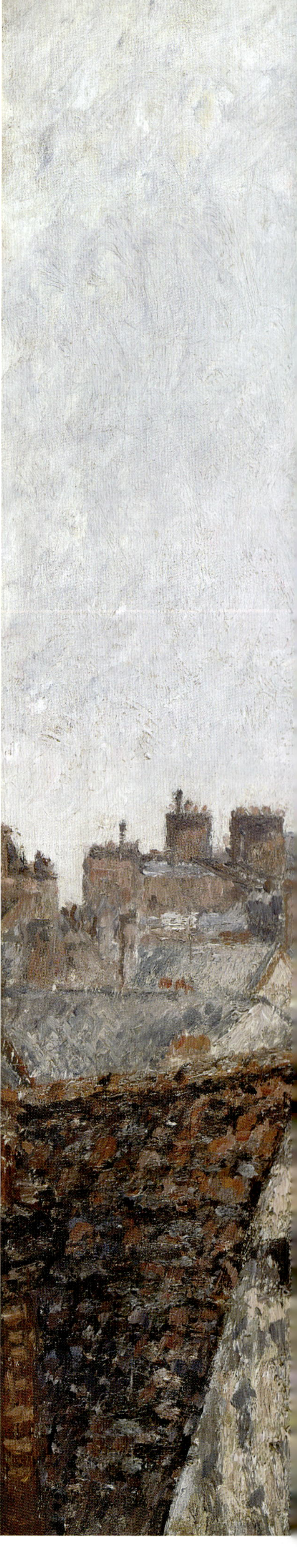

Camille Pissarro, The Roofs of Old Rouen, Gray Weather *(1896). Painted late in his life, Pissarro's view across the rooftops of Rouen synthesized aesthetic ideas that he had gathered through his long association with the Impressionist experiment. To capture the high panorama, he positioned his easel at the window in his hotel, recalling Monet's view in* Boulevard des Capucines *shown in the first exhibition (1874). His interest in Neo-Impressionism can be seen in the dabs of color on the roof, but his subtle evocation of the winter sky reveals his enduring belief in plein air painting.*

Toledo Museum of Art, Ohio. Oil on canvas (28½×36 inches).

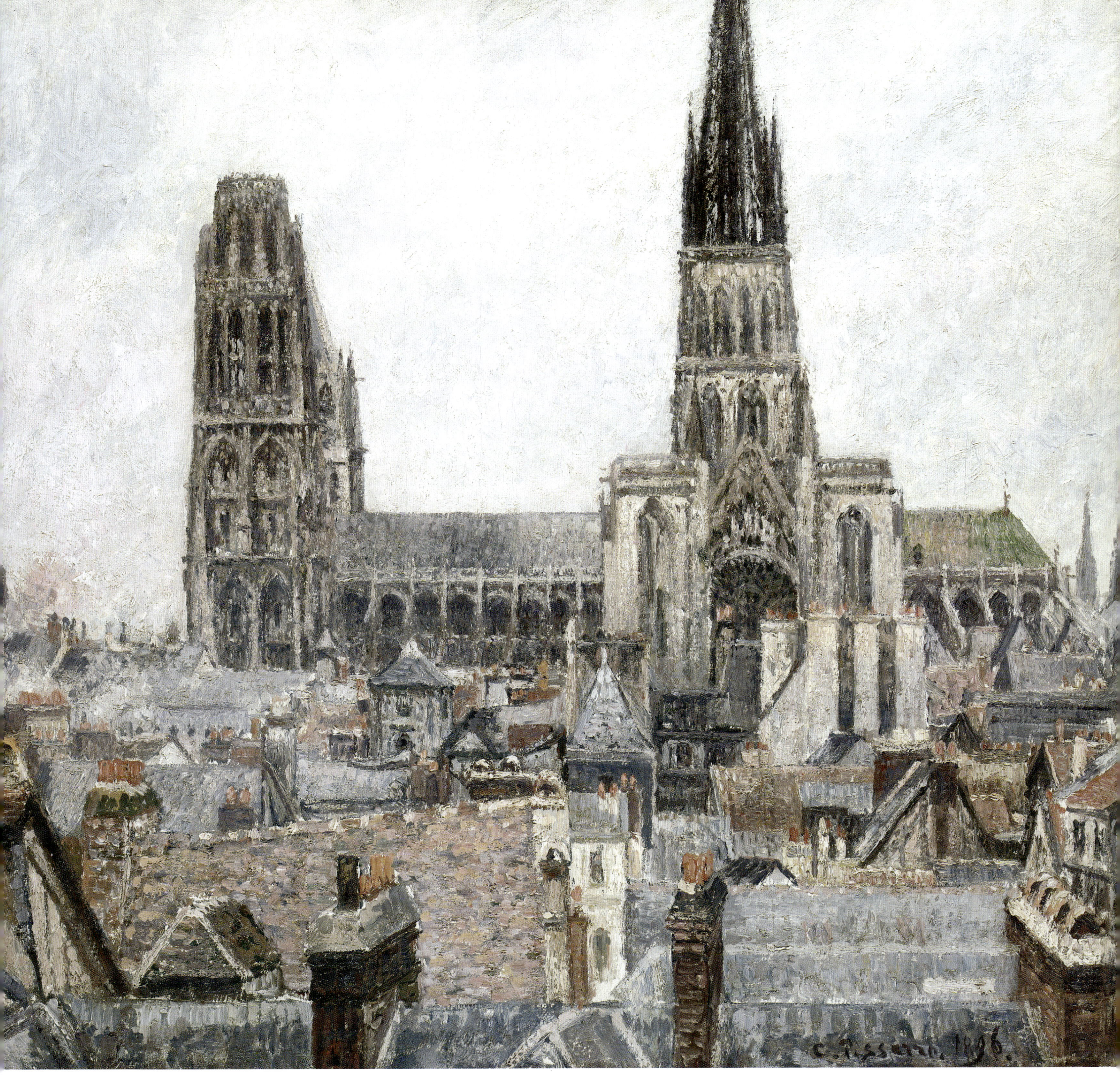
C. Pissarro. 1896.

Credits

Debra N. Mancoff, Ph.D., is an art historian and lecturer and the author of numerous books on nineteenth-century European and American painting, including Publication International, Ltd's, *Monet* and *Van Gogh.* Other titles include *Sunflowers, Monet's Garden in Art, Van Gogh: Fields and Flowers,* and *Mary Cassatt: Reflections of Women's Lives.* Ms. Mancoff is a scholar in residence at the Newberry Library and an adjunct associate professor and adjunct lecturer at The School of the Art Institute of Chicago.

Acknowledgments

Publications International, Ltd., has made every effort to locate the owners of all copyrighted material to obtain permission to use the selections that appear in this book. Any errors or omissions are unintentional; corrections, if necessary, will be made in future editions.

Translations of extracts on pages 7, 18, 52, 54, 55, 74, 76, 77, 92, 95, and 108 are from Charles S. Moffett et al. *The New Painting: Impressionism 1874–1886.* The Fine Arts Museums of San Francisco, 1986. All rights reserved.

Excerpts on the back cover and pages 6, 20, 23, 36, 38, and 54 from *Monet: A Retrospective* by Charles F. Stuckey. Copyright © 1985, Hugh Lauter Levin Associates, Inc.

Picture credits
Front cover: **Bridgeman Art Library, London/SuperStock**
Back cover: **Réunion des Musées Nationaux/Art Resource**

Art Resource: 119; Giraudon: 63; Erich Lessing: 31, 39, 61, 96; The New York Public Library: 106–107; Réunion des Musées Nationaux: 4–5, 6, 7, 8, 10, 11, 13, 18, 19 (top), 22, 26–27, 32–33, 34, 40–41, 45, 46, 48–49, 50, 56, 60, 65, 66–67, 73, 82–83, 88, 100, 102, 107, 108–109, 111, 114, 123, 126; Tate Gallery, London: 96–97; **© CORBIS:** Bettmann: 9; Burstein Collection: 52–53, 80; Christie's Images: 70–71, 82; Francis G. Mayer: 27, 44–45, 47, 81, 90, 101, 116, 117, 122; Philadelphia Museum: 47; **Image Select:** 16, 24; **SuperStock:** 15, 30, 68, 71, 75, 86, 89, 94, 103, 105, 115, 118–119, 124–125; Bridgeman Art Library, London: 14, 19 (bottom), 21, 23, 24–25, 28, 43, 57, 62, 64, 69, 87, 92–93, 98; Chateau de Malmaison, Paris, France/Lauros-Giraudon, Paris: 12, 34–35, 67, 78; Christie's Images: 85; Peter Harholdt: 124.

Page 17: Edgar Degas (French, 1834–1917), Visit to a Museum, about 1879–80, oil on canvas, 91.8368 cm (361⁄83263⁄4 in.). Museum of Fine Arts, Boston. Gift of Mr. and Mrs. John McAndrew; 69.49. ©2002 Museum of Fine Arts, Boston.

Page 28–29: Berthe Morisot, *The Harbor at Lorient,* Ailsa Mellon Bruce Collection, Photograph ©2002 Board of Trustees, National Gallery of Art, Washington, 1869, oil on canvas, 43.5×73 cm (17⅛×28¾ in.); framed: 64.7×95.2×7.6 cm (25½×37½×3 in.).

Page 37: Claude Monet, *Boulevard des Capucines,* 1873–1874, oil on canvas; 31⅝×23¾ inches (80.3×60.3 cm.) Collection of The Nelson-Atkins Museum of Art, Kansas City, Missouri (Purchase: the Kenneth A. and Helen F. Spencer Foundation Acquisition Fund) F72–35, Photograph by Robert Newcombe.

Page 42: Hilaire-Germain-Edgar Degas (French, 1834–1917), *The Dance Class,* probably 1874, oil on canvas; 32¾×30¼ in. (83.2×76.8 cm). The Metropolitan Museum of Art, Bequest of Mrs. Harry Payne Bingham, 1986 (1987.47.1) Photograph ©1987 The Metropolitan Museum of Art.

Page 51: Camille Pissarro, *Orchard in Bloom, Louveciennes,* Ailsa Mellon Bruce Collection, Photograph ©2002 Board of Trustees, National Gallery of Art, Washington, 1872, oil on canvas, 45.1×54.9 cm (17¾×21⅝ in.); framed: 70.8×80.6×5.7 cm (27⅞×31¾×2¼ in.).

Page 54: Gustave Caillebotte, *Boating on the Yerres (Perissoires sur l'Yerres),* 1877, oil on canvas, 40¾×61⅜ in. Milwaukee Art Museum, Gift of the Milwaukee Journal Company, in Honor of Miss Faye McBeath. M1965.25.

Page 55: Pierre-Auguste Renoir, French, 1841–1919, *The Garden in the rue Cortot, Montmartre,* 1876, oil on canvas, 59¾×38⅜ in. (151.8×97.5 cm). Carnegie Museum of Art, Pittsburgh; Acquired through the generosity of Mrs. Alan M. Scaife. 65.35. Photograph by Peter Harholdt.

Page 58: Claude Monet, *Woman with a Parasol—Madame Monet and Her Son,* Collection of Mr. and Mrs. Paul Mellon, Image ©2002 Board of Trustees, National Gallery of Art, Washington, 1875, oil on canvas, 100×81 cm (39⅜×31⅞ in.); framed: 119.4×99.7 cm (47×39¼ in.).

Page 59: Berthe Morisot, *Hanging the Laundry out to Dry,* Collection of Mr. and Mrs. Paul Mellon, Photograph ©2002 Board of Trustees, National Gallery of Art, Washington, 1875, oil on canvas, 33×40.6 cm (13×16 in.); framed: 52.4×60×5.7 cm (20⅝×23⅝×2¼ in.).

Page 72: Camille Pissarro, French, 1830–1903, *Edge of the Woods,* 1879, oil on canvas, 126×162 cm. ©The Cleveland Museum of Art, 2002. Gift of the Hanna Fund, 1951.356.

Page 76: Paul Gauguin, *The Market Gardens of Vaugirard,* 1879. Smith College Museum of Art, Northampton, Massachusetts.

Page 79: *Examen de Danse (Dance Examination),* 1880, Edgar Hilaire Degas. Denver Art Museum Collection: Anonymous Gift, 1941.6. ©Denver Art Museum 2003.

Page 84: Mary Cassatt (American, 1844–1926), *The Cup of Tea,* ca. 1879, oil on canvas; 36⅜×25¾ in. (92.4×65.4 cm). The Metropolitan Museum of Art, From the Collection of James Stillman, Gift of Dr. Ernest G. Stillman, 1922 (22.16.17). Photograph ©1998 The Metropolitan Museum of Art.

Page 91: Paul Gauguin, *The Little One is Dreaming, Etude,* 1881. Ordrupgaard, Copenhagen. Photograph by Pernille Klemp.

Page 98–99: Paul Signac, *Snow, Boulevard de Clichy, Paris,* 1886. The Minneapolis Institute of Arts.

Page 104–105: Paul Gauguin, *Paysage à Saint-Cloud,* 1885, oil on canvas, 22×39⅜ in. The Joan Whitney Payson Collection at the Portland Museum of Art, Maine. Promised gift of John Whitney Payson, 15.1991.4. Photo by Bernard C. Meyers.

Page 110: Paul Cézanne, French, 1839–1906, *Landscape near Aix, the Plain of the Arc River,* 1892–95, oil on canvas, 32¼×26 in. (81.9×66 cm). Carnegie Museum of Art, Pittsburgh; Acquired through the generosity of the Sarah Mellon Scaife family. 66.4.

Page 112: Claude Monet, French, 1840–1926, *Stacks of Wheat (End of Summer),* 1890/91, oil on canvas, 60×100 cm, Gift of Arthur M. Wood, Sr. in memory of Pauline Palmer Wood, 1985.1103. Photograph ©2001, The Art Institute of Chicago. All Rights Reserved.

Page 113: Claude Monet, *Water Lilies,* 1908, oil on canvas, 31½×39⅛ in. (80.01×99.38 cm). Dallas Museum of Art, gift of The Meadows Foundation, Inc.

Page 120: Paul Gauguin, French, 1848–1903, *Tehamana Has Many Ancestors (Merahi metua no Tehamana),* 1893, oil on canvas, 76.3×54.3 cm, Gift of Mr. and Mrs. Charles Deering McCormick, 1980.613. Photograph ©2001, The Art Institute of Chicago. All Rights Reserved.

Page 121: Mary Cassatt, American, 1844–1926, *The Child's Bath,* 1893, oil on canvas, 39½×26 in., Robert A. Waller Fund, 1910.2. Photograph ©2002, The Art Institute of Chicago. All Rights Reserved.

Page 126–127: Camille Pissarro (French, 1830–1903), *The Roofs of Old Rouen, Gray Weather,* 1896, oil on canvas, 28½×36 in. (72.3×91.4 cm), Toledo Museum of Art, Purchased with funds from the Libbey Endowment, Gift of Edward Drummond Libbey.

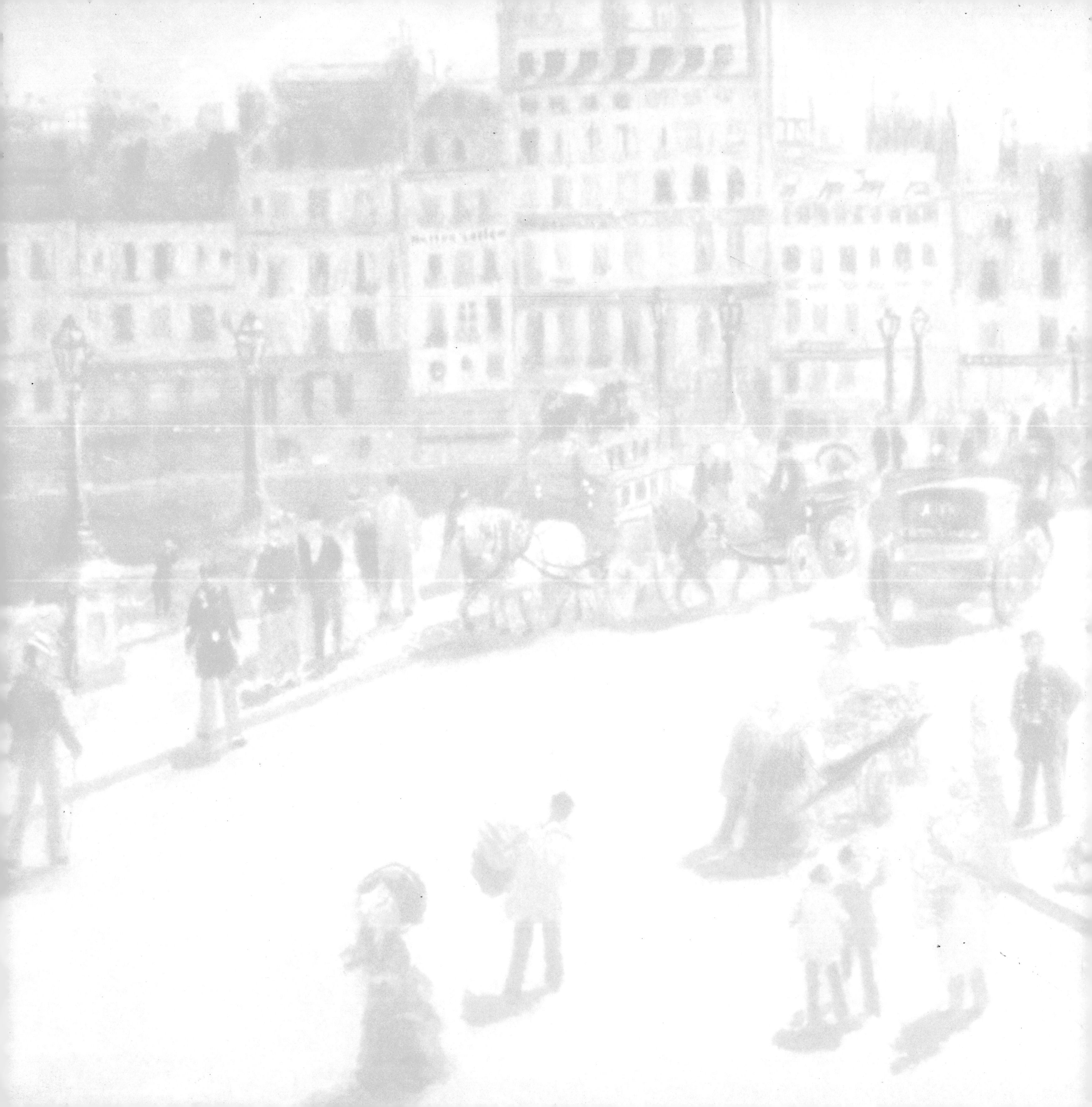